C000145436

Blackstone's
Police Q& A

Evidence and Procedure 2007

Blackstone's
Police Q&A

Evidence & Procedure 2007

Fifth edition

Huw Smart and John Watson

OXFORD
UNIVERSITY PRESS

OXFORD
UNIVERSITY PRESS

Great Clarendon Street, Oxford OX2 6DP

Oxford University Press is a department of the University of Oxford.
It furthers the University's objective of excellence in research, scholarship,
and education by publishing worldwide in

Oxford New York

Auckland Bangkok Buenos Aires Cape Town Chennai
Dar es Salaam Delhi Hong Kong Istanbul Karachi Kolkata
Kuala Lumpur Madrid Melbourne Mexico City Mumbai Nairobi
São Paulo Shanghai Taipei Tokyo Toronto

With offices in

Argentina Austria Brazil Chile Czech Republic France Greece
Guatemala Hungary Italy Japan Poland Portugal Singapore
South Korea Switzerland Thailand Turkey Ukraine Vietnam

Published in the United States
by Oxford University Press Inc., New York

British Library Cataloguing in Publication Data

Data available

Library of Congress Cataloging in Publication Data

Data available

Typeset by Laserwords Private Limited, Chennai, India
Printed in Great Britain
on acid-free paper by
Ashford Colour Press Limited, Gosport, Hampshire

ISBN 0-19-920334-2   978-0-19-920334-5

10 9 8 7 6 5 4 3 2 1

Contents

Contents

Introduction

Before you get into the detail of this book, there are two myths about multiple-choice questions (MCQs) that we need to get out of the way right at the start:

1. that they are easy to answer;
2. that they are easy to write.

Take one look at a professionally designed and properly developed exam paper such as those used by the Police Promotion Examinations Board or the National Board of Medical Examiners in the US and the first myth collapses straight away. Contrary to what some people believe, MCQs are not an easy solution for examiners and not a 'multiple-guess' soft option for examinees.

That is not to say that all MCQs are taxing, or even testing — in the psycho-metric sense. If MCQs are to have any real value at all, they need to be carefully designed and follow some agreed basic rules.

And this leads us to myth number 2.

It is widely assumed by many people and educational organisations that anyone with the knowledge of a subject can write MCQs. You need only look at how few MCQ writing courses are offered by training providers in the UK to see just how far this myth is believed. Similarly, you need only to have a go at a few badly designed MCQs to realise that it is a myth none the less. Writing bad MCQs is easy; writing good ones is no easier than answering them!

As with many things, the design of MCQs benefits considerably from time, training and experience. Many MCQ writers fall easily and often unwittingly into the trap of making their questions too hard, too easy or too obscure, or completely different from the type of question that you will eventually encounter in your own particular exam. Others seem to use the MCQ as a way to catch people out or to show how smart they, the authors, are (or think they are).

There are several purposes for which MCQs are very useful. The first is in producing a reliable, valid and fair test of knowledge and understanding across a wide range of subject matter. Another is an aid to study, preparation and revision for such examinations and tests. The differences in objective mean that there are slight differences in the rules that the MCQ writers follow. Whereas the design of fully validated MCQs to be used in high stakes examinations which will effectively determine who passes and who fails have very strict guidelines as to construction, content and style, less stringent rules apply to MCQs that are being used for teaching and revision. For that reason, there may be types of MCQ that are appropriate in the latter setting which would not be used in the former. However, in developing the MCQs for this book, the authors have tried to follow the fundamental rules of MCQ design but they would not claim to have replicated the level of psychometric rigour that is — and has to be — adopted by the type of examining bodies referred to above.

These MCQs are designed to reinforce your knowledge and understanding, to highlight any gaps or weaknesses in that knowledge and understanding and to help focus your revision of the relevant topics.

I hope that we have achieved that aim.

Good luck!

Blackstone's Police Q&As — Special Features

References to Blackstone's Police Manuals

Every answer is followed by a paragraph reference to Blackstone's Police Manuals. This means that once you have attempted a question and looked at an answer, the Manual can immediately be referred to for help and clarification.

Unique numbers for each question

Each question and answer has the same unique number. This should ensure that there is no confusion as to which question is linked to which answer. For example, Question 2.1 is linked to Answer 2.1.

Checklists

The checklists are designed to help you keep track of your progress when answering the multiple-choice questions. If you fill in the checklist after attempting a question, you will be able to check how many you got right on the first attempt and will know immediately which questions need to be revisited a second time. Please visit www.blackstonespolicemanuals.com and click through to the Blackstone's Police Q&As 2007 page. You will then find electronic versions of the checklists to download and print out. Email any queries or comments on the book to: police.uk@oup.com

Acknowledgements

This book has been written as an accompaniment to *Blackstone's Police Manuals*, and will test the knowledge you have accrued through reading that series. It is of the essence that full study of the relevant chapters in each *Police Manual* is completed prior to attempting the Questions and Answers. As qualified police trainers we recognise that students tend to answer questions incorrectly either because they don't read the question properly, or because one of the 'distracters' has done its work. The distracter is one of the three incorrect answers in an MCQ, and is designed to distract you from the correct answer, and in this way discriminate between candidates: the better-prepared candidate not being 'distracted'.

So particular attention should be paid to the *Answers* sections and students should ask themselves, 'Why did I get that question wrong?' and, just as importantly, 'Why did I get that question right?' Combining the information gained in the *Answers* section together with re-reading the chapter in the *Police Manuals* should lead to a greater understanding of the subject matter.

The authors wish to thank Katie at Oxford University Press for her support, patience and cajoling skills! Thanks also to Geraldine Mangley at OUP for her invaluable assistance. We would also like to show appreciation to Alistair MacQueen for his vision and support, without which this project would never have been started.

Huw would like to thank both Julie and their beautiful baby Hâf, for their constant strength and support during long evenings and weekends of writing, when he could have been having fun with the family.

John would like to thank Sue for her support; also David, Catherine and Andrew for not too many, 'Dad, can I have the computer please!!. . .'.

1 | Sources of Law and the Courts

STUDY PREPARATION

This chapter, which combines the first two chapters from the *Blackstone's Manuals*, examines what could be best described as the building blocks of criminal law, the body of laws; common, statutory and delegated legislation. This chapter also examines what are known as 'precedents' or the details of cases that have been 'decided' in the higher courts and the impact these have on current and future cases. Students should recognise that what they have erroneously called 'stated cases' for years are probably not 'stated'. But more importantly, they should recognise the importance of these authorities, not just in their working lives as police officers, but as students of the law in any capacity; particularly candidates for promotion. The chapter also deals with how the courts fit into the judicial picture, and how the 'building blocks' are built upon.

QUESTIONS

Question 1.1

The sources of criminal law are found partly in common law and partly in statute law.

Which of the following best describes 'common law'?

A Law that has existed for so long that it now has a statutory footing.

B Law that judges have decided should be part of English law.

C Law that High Court judges have decided is authoritative.

D Law that is part of the customs and traditions of this country.

Question 1.2

OLIVER has been summonsed to magistrates' court for a speeding offence. He is aware that at the magistrates' court in the neighbouring police area a person was found not guilty due to an administrative error by the police. OLIVER's case is very similar and he hopes to use the other case as a 'precedent' to secure his acquittal.

Which of the following is true?

A OLIVER can be acquitted, but only if the error is exactly the same in his case.

B OLIVER should be acquitted; the error is very similar to his case.

C OLIVER cannot use the other case as a 'precedent' as it was not the same magistrates' court.

D The decision of the other court is not binding in OLIVER's case; he may still be convicted.

Question 1.3

Cases in relation to the protection of human rights can be heard in the European Court of Human Rights.

In relation to the decisions of this court (Strasbourg case law) what is the obligation on UK courts?

A Their decisions should be considered and are binding on all UK courts.

B Their decisions should be considered and are binding only in inferior courts.

C Their decisions have no value to UK courts.

D They should be considered, but not necessarily applied.

Question 1.4

MALHIDE is appearing before the magistrates' court for an either-way offence. He wishes the matter to be dealt with by the magistrates, as he fears a substantial prison sentence at Crown Court. The magistrates, however, feel the matter should be committed due to the serious nature of the offence.

Which of the following is correct?

A The matter must be committed to Crown Court in these circumstances.

B The matter must be dealt with fully in the magistrates' court as the defendant wishes summary trial.

C The matter can be committed to Crown Court, but only if the defendant agrees.

D The matter can only be committed to Crown Court for sentencing as the defendant wishes summary trial.

Question 1.5

In considering points of law the courts must consider judicial precedents and consider whether they are bound by those judicial precedents.

Which of the following is correct in relation to being bound by other courts decisions?

A A judge in the Divisional Court is not bound by decisions made in the Court of Appeal.

B A magistrates' court is not always bound by the decisions of a Crown Court.

C An opinion about a point of law expressed by a High Court judge is always binding on inferior courts.

D A dissenting judgment given by a Law Lord holds no bearing on future cases heard in the lower courts.

Question 1.6

ROWAN has been summonsed for the offence of carrying an insecure load, contrary to reg. 100(2) of the Road Vehicles (Construction and Use) Regulations 1986 and s. 42 of the Road Traffic Act 1988. He has received a computer-generated summons.

The date of the alleged offence was 16 June. The information date printed at the head of the summons was 10 December; that is six days before the effluxion of the six months' limitation period. The summons, which was dated 9 January, included a statement of facts. It also bore the date when the information was printed, 20 December; that is four days outside the limit.

Bearing in mind this discrepancy in 'information' dates in the summons which of the following is correct as to whether the information was laid in time?

A The date at the top should be accepted as correct, as it was computer-generated information.

B It is for the defence to prove, on the balance of probabilities that it was *not* laid on time.

C It is for the magistrates to decide if it was laid on time, applying the criminal standard of proof.

D It is for the Clerk of the Court to decide if it was laid in time, on the balance of probabilities.

Question 1.7

Andrew is 17 years of age and appearing in youth court on a single charge of robbery. He has no previous convictions and a custodial sentence is unlikely.

As this is an indictable offence, what are the options for dealing with the matter?

A As it is an indictable offence it must be committed to Crown Court.

B The matter has to be dealt with by the youth court: it cannot be committed to Crown Court.

C Andrew will make the choice. He can elect trial by jury.

D The justices may commit to Crown Court if they feel the case is serious enough.

Question 1.8

MURPHY is a long-distance lorry driver, and on 21 January at 3 pm he committed a tachograph offence. This offence was not discovered until 28 January at 10 am during a police check on the company premises.

Given the limitations on proceedings for this offence, when should such proceedings be instituted by?

A 3 pm on 21 July.

B 10 am on 28 July.

C Midnight on 21 July.

D Midnight on 28 July.

Question 1.9

KNIGHT is appearing at magistrates' court at a mode of trial hearing. She wishes to know what sentence she might receive if she pleads guilty, and how much higher the plea would be should she plead not guilty and be convicted.

A The court can give an indication as to the likely sentence in both cases, but the magistrates have a broad discretion as to whether or not to provide such an indication.

B The court can give an indication as to the likely sentence but only where the accused indicates that they will plead guilty at the first opportunity to claim credit for a guilty plea.

C The court can give an indication and they are bound by this indication when sentencing is considered either after a guilty plea or on conviction.

D The court can give an indication for a guilty plea and are then only bound by this indication where the accused enters a guilty plea.

Question 1.10

BREWSTER was convicted at the Crown Court for an offence of theft. He wishes to appeal against his conviction, as he believes that the actions he took were not 'dishonest' as per s. 2 of the Theft Act 1968.

Does he require leave to appeal?

A Yes, as this is a mixed question of fact and law.

B Yes, as this is a question of law.

C No, as this is a question of law.

D No, as this is a mixed question of fact and law.

Question 1.11

HOUSE was convicted at Crown Court of an offence of burglary. At the *voir dire* during this trial, the defence sought to have a vital piece of evidence excluded, as they believed it had been obtained unlawfully. The trial judge refused their application, the evidence was adduced and the jury convicted HOUSE. He appealed, and the Court of Appeal decided that the judge's adverse ruling amounted to a wrong decision on a question of law and the evidence should have been excluded.

Which of the following is true?

A The Court of Appeal must direct that HOUSE is 'not guilty' and quash the conviction.

B The Court of Appeal must direct that HOUSE's conviction is unsafe and quash it.

C The Court of Appeal can, even in these circumstances, refuse to overturn the conviction.

D The Court of Appeal should refer the case to the House of Lords as it is on a point of law of general public importance.

Question 1.12

BUCKLEY was acquitted at Crown Court on an indictment for murder. The trial judge made a ruling in law relating to police surveillance that meant vital evidence was excluded. This ruling could impact on other cases involving such surveillance.

Which of the following is true in relation to what action the Attorney General can take?

A The Attorney General cannot refer this matter to the Court of Appeal as it does not relate to an unduly lenient sentence.

B The Attorney General can refer this matter to the Court of Appeal, and the Court of Appeal can order a re-trial.
C The Attorney General can refer this matter to the Court of Appeal, however, BUCKLEY will remain acquitted.
D The Attorney General cannot refer this matter to the Court of Appeal as the Crown Court judges ruling is not binding.

Question 1.13

Constable WYATT is seeking to challenge his Chief Constable's ruling that all officers may not transfer to other forces for the next 12 months due to staff shortages.

Can this matter be taken to judicial revue?
A No, as judicial revue relates only to matters arising in the courts.
B Only if the force's grievance procedures have been tried and failed to resolve the issue.
C Yes, however, the High Court cannot direct the Chief Constable to change the ruling.
D Yes, and the High Court can direct that the Chief Constable not have this ruling.

Question 1.14

HUGHES has been convicted at magistrates' court of an offence of burglary following a not guilty plea. The magistrates are now considering whether they can commit him to Crown Court for sentencing.

In relation to this which of the following is correct?
A They may now immediately commit HUGHES to Crown Court for sentencing.
B They may commit HUGHES to Crown Court for sentencing, but only where they assess their powers of punishment are insufficient.
C They may not commit HUGHES to Crown Court for sentencing as he pleaded not guilty and they accepted jurisdiction.
D They may not commit HUGHES to Crown Court for sentencing as they accepted jurisdiction.

Question 1.15

The Court of Appeal may make an order to quash the person's acquittal on a charge and order a retrial in line with the Criminal Justice Act 2003.

In which of the following cases would this be likely?

A Where certain evidence was not allowed in the original trial and that evidence would be compelling if allowed.

B Where new evidence becomes available, and it is in the interests of justice that this evidence be adduced.

C Where evidence not used at the previous trial becomes available and it is compelling evidence.

D Where the person has been convicted of a similar charge since the acquittal and it is in the interests of justice for a retrial to be held.

ANSWERS

Answer 1.1

Answer **C** — Common law is judge-made law. Law that exists and applies to a group based on historical legal precedents developed over hundreds of years. For example, murder is a common law offence. Because it is not written by elected politicians but, rather, by judges, it is also referred to as 'unwritten' law. Judges seek out these principles when trying a case and apply the precedents to the facts to come up with a judgment. Common law has been referred to as the 'common sense of the community, crystallised and formulated by our ancestors'. It should be noted that the common law can only be declared authoritatively by the judge(s) of the superior courts (i.e. from the High Court) and then only to the extent that it is necessary to do so for the purpose of deciding a particular case. For this reason, the development of the common law has always been dependent upon the incidence of cases arising for decision, and the particular facts of those cases. It has no statutory footing, therefore answer A is incorrect, and as not all judges can endorse common law as authoritative, answer B is incorrect. Although common law originated from the customs of the early communities, its sources lie in the principles of the law declared by the judges; therefore answer D is incorrect.

Evidence and Procedure, para. 2.1.2

Answer 1.2

Answer **D** — The system of courts in England and Wales is a hierarchy; the various courts being related to one another as superior and inferior. An inferior court is generally bound by the decision and directions of a superior court. For example, judges of the Divisional Court and Crown Courts are bound by the decisions of the Court of Appeal. Crown Court judges' rulings on points of law are persuasive authority (unless made by judges of the High Court sitting in the Crown Court), and are not binding precedents. There is no obligation on the part of other Crown Court judges to follow them.

County courts and magistrates' courts decisions are not binding. They are rarely important in law and are not usually reported in the law reports. If OLIVER was convicted and appealed and this appeal was heard in a superior court then the judgement of that court could be binding on the inferior courts. So OLIVER cannot be acquitted on 'precedent' in this case (therefore, answers A and B are incorrect) and whatever the locality of the magistrates' court is their decisions are not binding, and answer C is incorrect.

Evidence and Procedure, para. 2.1.4.1

Answer 1.3

Answer **D** — Human Rights Act 1998, s. 2 states:

(1) A court or tribunal determining a question which has arisen in connection with a Convention right must take into account any —
  (a) judgment, decision, declaration or advisory opinion of the European Court of Human Rights...

This means that where a court (from magistrates' courts upwards) or a tribunal is called upon to determine a question in connection with a Convention right, s. 2 requires it to take into account any judgment, decision, declaration or opinion of the Strasbourg court, which it considers to be relevant to that question. Such Strasbourg case law has not, however, been given binding effect by the 1998 Act; answers A and B are therefore incorrect. In *R* v *Davis* [2001] 1 Cr App R 115, it was confirmed that the obligation to take Strasbourg jurisprudence into account might be something less than an obligation to adopt or apply it, however, it must still be considered and is of value to UK courts; answer C is therefore incorrect. In *Tyrer* v *United Kingdom* (1978) 2 EHRR 1 it was recognised that the Convention was a 'living instrument which must be interpreted in the light of present day conditions'. It may well be that the decision of an earlier case may not be relevant where factors have changed over time, and for this reason the decisions are not binding.

Evidence and Procedure, para. 2.1.4.2

Answer 1.4

Answer **A** — This is known as a mode of trial hearing, the power to conduct a mode of trial hearing arises whenever an adult appears or is brought before a magistrates' court charged with an offence triable either way. The object of this hearing is to determine whether the case should be dealt with by a magistrates' court or by the Crown Court. The magistrates decide initially whether or not to deal with the case, basing their decision mainly on the seriousness of the offence and whether their powers of punishment are adequate; their decision is not affected by the conformity of the defendant, therefore, answer C is incorrect.

They will hear representations from both the prosecution and the defence. If they decide not to deal with the case it will be committed to the Crown Court. Where the magistrates accept jurisdiction, the defendant has the right to choose/elect between being dealt within the magistrates' court or the Crown Court. Note, this choice only arises when the justices agree to hear the case. Answers B and D are therefore incorrect.

A magistrates' court dealing with the trial of an either-way offence may, on conviction of the defendant, commit them to the Crown Court for sentencing in certain circumstances. These circumstances are usually linked to the seriousness of the offence and/or the seriousness of the defendant's previous convictions, which the magistrates will not usually be aware of until the end of the trial.

Evidence and Procedure, para. 2.2.2.5

Answer 1.5

Answer **B** — The system of courts in England and Wales is a hierarchy, the various courts being related to one another as superior and inferior. The directions of a superior court generally bind an inferior court. For example, judges of the Divisional Court and Crown Courts are bound by the decisions of the Court of Appeal. The Appeal Court is in turn bound by the decisions of the House of Lords, which is also bound — to an extent — by decisions of the European Court of Justice; answer A is therefore incorrect. Note that the enactment of the Constitutional Reform Act 2005 will see the introduction of a Supreme Court for England, Wales, Scotland and Northern Ireland that will replace the House of Lords as the highest appeal court.

Although the Crown Court is superior to a magistrates' court and enjoys wider powers it is still a 'lower' court and its decisions are not generally binding on other courts.

A judge, or court as a whole, may sometimes go beyond the facts of a particular case and give an opinion on some connected matter, which is intended to be of guidance in future cases. Such an opinion is known as an *obiter dictum*, and may be persuasive, but not binding, on other courts in a future case. Such *obiter dicta* are often made where an important point has arisen from the arguments in an appeal case but that point has not been directly raised by either party to the case, and even when made by a High Court judge they remain only persuasive; answer C is therefore incorrect.

Of course not all judges share the same legal opinion on a point of law as others they sit in judgment with. Such noncompliant views are known as 'dissenting judgment' and are more common amongst law lords. These judgments can also be very instructive and it is not uncommon for them to become law through Acts of Parliament at a later date (Lord Mustill's speech in the 'Spanner trial' involving sado-masochism (*R* v *Brown* [1993] 2 All ER 75, at 101); answer D is therefore incorrect.

Evidence and Procedure, para. 2.1.4.1

Answer 1.6

Answer **C** — A magistrates' court may not try a defendant for a summary offence unless the information was laid within six months of the time when the offence was allegedly committed (Magistrates' Courts Act 1980, s. 127(1), as qualified by s. 127(2)(a)); this is subject to any enactment which expressly permits a longer period.

In *Atkinson* v *DPP* [2004] 3 All ER 971 (Admin) it was held that, where there is uncertainty as to whether an information has been laid in time, the question should be determined according to the criminal standard of proof and the magistrates should decline to hear the matter unless satisfied so that they are sure that the information was laid in time. The ratio of the decision is that if, on evidence of whatever nature before the court, magistrates doubt the date of the information, such that it could have been laid outside the time limit, they are entitled to, and should, decline jurisdiction. It is a matter of fact for their determination in accordance with the ordinary criminal burden and standard of proof; therefore answers A, B and D are incorrect.

Evidence and Procedure, para. 2.2.4.1

Answer 1.7

Answer **B** — The Magistrates' Courts Act 1980, s. 24 states:

(1) Where a person under the age of 18 appears or is brought before a magistrates' court on an information charging him with an indictable offence other than homicide, he shall be tried summarily unless —

(a) the offence is such as is mentioned in subsection (1) or (2) of section 91 of the Powers of Criminal Courts (Sentencing) Act 2000 (under which young persons convicted on indictment of certain grave crimes may be sentenced to be detained for long periods) and the court considers that if he is found guilty of the offence it ought to be possible to sentence him in pursuance of subsection (3) of that section; or

(b) he is charged jointly with a person who has attained the age of 18 and the court considers it necessary in the interests of justice to commit them both for trial; and accordingly in a case falling within paragraph (a) or (b) of this subsection the court shall commit the accused for trial if either it is of opinion that there is sufficient evidence to put him on trial or it has power under section 6(2) above so to commit him without consideration of the evidence.

Generally, offences committed by juveniles are dealt with in the youth court, which is part of the magistrates' court. A juvenile is any person under the age of 18 years. Apart from homicide and a few specific exceptions outlined above, no other charge against such a person can be heard anywhere other than at a youth court. The general principle is that juveniles should be tried in the youth court, and as a result they are not given the option of electing trial by jury — answer C is therefore incorrect. Although this is a case of robbery, there is little chance of a custodial sentence. In deciding whether to commit to Crown Court or not, the current position is that the gravity of the offence, the young offender's previous convictions and the likely sentence on conviction should be considered by the youth court. Jurisdiction should be declined by that court only where the offence and circumstances surrounding it are such as to make it more than a vague possibility that a sentence of detention for a long period may be passed *D v Manchester City Youth Court* [2002] 1 Cr App R (S) 573. Andrew's case can only be heard in youth court, so answers A and D are incorrect.

Evidence and Procedure, para. 2.2.3

Answer 1.8

Answer **C** — A magistrates' court shall not try an information or hear a complaint unless the information was laid, or the complaint made, within six months from the time when the offence was committed, or the matter of complaint arose. The time runs from the commission of the offence, not from the date of its discovery.

A 'month' means a calendar month, and a month ends at midnight on the day of the next month, which has the same number as the day on which the offence was committed. For example, X commits a driving-licence offence at 10 am on 24 September; the information should be laid before midnight on 24 March the following year, i.e. within six months. So this makes the correct answer, midnight on 21 July, six months after the offence was committed. Answers A, B and D are therefore incorrect.

Evidence and Procedure, para. 2.2.4.1

Answer 1.9

Answer **D** — The Criminal Justice Act 2003 makes a number of significant changes to the plea before venue and mode of trial procedures. Paragraph 6 of sch. 3 substitutes an amended version of the Magistrates' Court Act 1980, s. 20. Under the new procedure, the accused is given the opportunity to request an indication from the magistrates of whether, if he were to be tried summarily and were to plead guilty at that stage, the sentence would be custodial or not (s. 20(3)) but not what the sentence might be on conviction; answer A is therefore incorrect. The magistrates are given a broad discretion whether or not to give such an indication (s. 20(4)).

This inquiry by the accused is not subject to an indicated guilty plea, but is there to assist the accused decide whether to plead guilty or not, and if the courts give an indication the accused may still plead not guilty; answer B is therefore incorrect

Where an indication is sought and given the court is only bound by this indication where the accused has entered a guilty plea; answer C is therefore incorrect.

Evidence and Procedure, para. 2.2.2.5

Answer 1.10

Answer **A** — Appeals from the Crown Court to the Court of Appeal (Criminal Division) normally require leave to be heard unless it is purely an appeal on a point of law. So is BREWSTER'S claim purely a point or question of law? If it was a point of law, the question would be: does the Theft Act cover 'dishonesty'? What is being asked is a mixed question (answer B is therefore incorrect): was what BREWSTER did dishonest as covered by the definition of dishonesty as per the Theft Act? This requires leave to be heard, and answers C and D are therefore incorrect. In the vast majority of cases leave to appeal is needed, before an appeal can be launched.

Evidence and Procedure, para. 2.2.5.5

Answer 1.11

Answer **C** — Whether an appeal, against conviction, to the Court of Appeal will be successful is governed by s. 2 of the Criminal Appeal Act 1968, as amended by the Criminal Appeal Act 1995, which states:

(1) Subject to the provisions of this Act, the Court of Appeal —
   (a) shall allow an appeal against conviction if they think that the conviction is unsafe; and
   (b) shall dismiss such an appeal in any other case.

This does not mean that every time a mistake has been made during a trial that a conviction must be overturned. The ultimate question is whether the conviction is unsafe (*Stafford* v *DPP* [1974] AC 878)? If the court takes the view that it is, and that there has been a 'miscarriage of justice', the conviction will not stand. The effect of this approach is that, on occasions, even if it concludes that certain evidence was admitted wrongly or that a judge failed to do something relevant to the defendant's trial, the Court of Appeal may still refuse to overturn the conviction — answer B is therefore incorrect. Allowing an appeal is not a verdict of 'not guilty' as the question for the Appeal Court's consideration is whether the conviction was safe and not whether the accused was guilty, therefore answer A is incorrect. The Court of Appeal does not refer matters to the House of Lords, although the defendant can have leave to appeal the Court of Appeal's decision to the House of Lords provided it is on a point of law of general public importance — answer D is therefore incorrect. In addition to allowing or dismissing an appeal where a defendant is found guilty by a jury, the Court of Appeal may substitute a conviction of an alternative offence on the same facts. Note that when the Constitutional Reform Act 2005 is enacted a Supreme Court for England, Wales, Scotland and Northern Ireland will replace the House of Lords as the highest appeal court.

Evidence and Procedure, para. 2.2.5.2

Answer 1.12

Answer **C** — Section 36 of the Criminal Justice Act 1972 provides that where a person has been tried on indictment and acquitted (whether on the whole indictment or some counts only) the Attorney General may refer to the Court of Appeal for its opinion on any point of law that arose in the case. However, the person's acquittal is not put in peril by the proceedings; therefore answer B is incorrect. Whatever the opinion expressed by the Court of Appeal — even if it decides that the trial judge was wrong and the facts of the case were such that the accused clearly ought to have been convicted — the acquittal is unaffected (s. 36(7)). By making a reference, the Attorney General may obtain a ruling that will assist the prosecution in future cases, but he cannot ask the court to set aside the acquittal of the party. In *Attorney General's Ref (No. 1 of 1975)* [1975] QB 773, Lord Widgery CJ stated that references by the Attorney General should not be confined to cases where 'very heavy questions of law arise', but should also be made when 'short but important points require a quick ruling of [the Court of Appeal] before a potentially false decision of law has too wide a circulation in the courts'. So although the ruling is not binding, a referral can be made to ensure that a potentially false decision of law does not affect future decisions of other courts — answer D is therefore incorrect. Although the Attorney General can refer cases that have unduly lenient sentences, this is not the only prerogative of this office, and answer A is therefore incorrect.

Evidence and Procedure, para. 2.2.5.6

Answer 1.13

Answer **D** — Judicial review is a method of challenging decisions made by administrative bodies and office holders such as the police service, not just the courts, therefore answer A is incorrect. Cases can range from policy decisions made by the organisation — such as the decision not to prosecute someone — to decisions made by individual supervisors (e.g. the cautioning of a juvenile). The circumstances under which a matter can go before the High Court for judicial review are quite limited. Generally, applications for judicial review can only proceed if there is no other method by which to appeal the decision, although this does not mean that any other internal fairness procedure has to have been tried — answer B is therefore incorrect. An application for judicial review must be made as soon as reasonably practicable and generally within three months of the decision. In reviewing the decision, the High Court can look at whether the administrative body or individual was acting within the law when making that decision; it will also consider whether the decision was a reasonable one, applying the *Wednesbury* principles (from the case of *Associated Provincial PictureHouses Ltd* v *Wednesbury Corporation* [1948] 1 KB 223), and whether the common law rules of natural justice were applied. If the High Court considers that a decision is unreasonable or unlawful it can make a declaration to that effect. This can include declaring a prohibiting order directing the administrative body (here the Chief Constable) not to perform an act which the court has found to be unlawful or outside the body's power (*Practice Direction (Administrative Court: Establishment)* [2000] 1 WLR 1654); answer C is therefore incorrect.

Evidence and Procedure, para. 2.2.5.7

Answer 1.14

Answer **D** — Where the defendant indicates a not guilty plea the magistrates will initially determine the mode of trial, by considering the seriousness of the offence, the defendant's previous convictions, and assessing whether their powers of punishment are sufficient (Magistrates' Courts Act 1980 s. 17A(4)).

Where the magistrates' court determine to hear the case summarily, even where the accused has pleaded not guilty or not entered any plea at the plea before venue hearing, and they find the accused guilty they cannot commit him/her for sentence to the Crown Court (Powers of Criminal Courts (Sentencing) Act 2000, s. 3). However in cases where the accused is charged with a specified violent or sexual offence (Criminal Justice Act 2003 s. 224) the magistrates may still hear the case summarily, with the accused's consent, but if convicted may commit him/her for sentence to the Crown Court (Magistrates' Courts Act 1980 s. 20(2)(c)).

In this case it is not a violent or sexual offence, the magistrates cannot commit the case to Crown Court for sentencing as they accepted jurisdiction; answers A, B and C are therefore incorrect.

Evidence and Procedure, para. 2.2.6.5

Answer 1.15

Answer **C** — The Criminal Justice Act 2003 has introduced a major statutory exception to the rule against double jeopardy.

Schedule 5 to the 2003 Act lists a series of 'qualifying offences' to which these provisions apply. They are all serious offences, which in the main carry a maximum sentence of life imprisonment.

Section 76 allows a prosecutor to apply to the Court of Appeal for an order to quash the person's acquittal for a qualifying offence or a lesser qualifying offence of which he could have been convicted at that time.

The application to the Court of Appeal to quash the acquittal requires the personal written consent of the DPP (s. 77(3)).

The Court of Appeal must order a retrial if:

(a) there is new and compelling evidence in the case; and
(b) it is in the interests of justice for an order to be made.

This then cannot relate to evidence presented at the previous trial, or simply the fact that they have offended again in similar circumstances. It is not about a 'second bite at the cherry' where the prosecution feel that the person should have been convicted and they feel that another jury may convict only on the original evidence. Answers A and D are therefore incorrect. Note that it is in the interests of justice that a retrial be ordered, not that any new evidence should or must be heard. Provided this new evidence is compelling AND it is in the interests of justice to so do, an order for a retrial must be made. Answer B is therefore incorrect.

Evidence and Procedure, para. 2.2.5.6

2 | Summonses and Warrants

STUDY PREPARATION

This chapter looks at the way in which prosecutions are started. Laying informations and securing the attendance of witnesses, defendants and evidence are
basic mechanics of the criminal justice procedure. As with other areas of practical relevance, this means that they will be of interest to trainers and examiners.

QUESTIONS

Question 2.1

In order to secure the attendance of parties to criminal and civil cases, courts and
tribunals may issue summonses and warrants to bring people and evidence before
then.

In relation to the issuing of a summons and a warrant to commit to prison, which
of the following is true?

A A justices' clerk can issue either the warrant or the summons.

B A justices' clerk can issue the summons only.

C A justices' clerk can issue the warrant only.

D A justices' clerk cannot issue either the warrant or the summons.

Question 2.2

O'KELLY wishes to take action to have a dangerous dog destroyed by attending
at the local magistrates' court and obtaining a destruction order under s. 2 of the
Dogs Act 1871.

How should O'KELLY proceed in this matter?

A By laying an information for the issue of a summons for the dog's owner to attend.
B By laying an information for the issue of a warrant for the dog's owner to attend.
C By laying a written complaint before the magistrate.
D By laying a verbal complaint before the magistrate.

Question 2.3

The Criminal Procedure Rules 2005 make provision for the laying of an information.

In relation to laying an information with regard to obtaining a summons for an offence of dangerous driving, which of the following is correct?

A The information must be laid in writing.
B The information must be laid orally at magistrates' court.
C The information can be made orally or in writing and must be made by the prosecutor in person.
D The information can be made orally or in writing and can be made by the prosecutor or an authorised person.

Question 2.4

RUBIN has been caught speeding by a mobile speed enforcement camera. His speed was more than twice the legal limit and the police force in whose area the speeding offence was committed wishes to issue a summons against him.

Is it in order for the force to lay an information to obtain a summons?

A Yes, provided the name of the actual force concerned is on the information.
B Yes, as a 'person' includes 'a body of persons corporate or unincorporate'.
C No, as it must be a named, actual person who lays the information.
D No, as it is the prosecutor or his counsel only who lays the information.

Question 2.5

Constable DURKIN has stopped a serving officer of the British Army for failing to comply with a red traffic signal. The Army officer was driving a vehicle that belongs to the British Army and has Army index plates. Constable DURKIN is unsure as to whether she can proceed by way of summons.

In relation to a member of the armed forces, which of the following is generally true?

A Being served on the individual officer concerned, a summons is effected.

B Being served on the individual officer concerned, as well as his or her commanding officer, a summons is effected.

C Being served on the individual officer's commanding officer, a summons is effected.

D A summons cannot be served on a serving officer of the British Army, whilst driving an army vehicle.

Question 2.6

WONG was reported by a police officer for careless driving. The prosecutor conceded that the evidence was weak and took time to consider the facts. Having not reached a firm decision on whether to take proceedings, the prosecutor laid the information before the court, simply to keep his options open. The information was laid one day within a six-month period since the incident. However, two months elapsed, due to further delays in making a decision, before the summons was actually served on WONG. The offence carries a statute bar of six months.

Should the magistrates allow the case to go ahead?

A Yes, the information was laid within the six-month period.

B Yes, the summons was served within six months of the information being laid.

C No, as the summons was not issued within the six-month period.

D No, owing to an abuse of the process of the court.

Question 2.7

WILKINSON is a civilian enforcement officer who is executing a warrant of arrest. The male who is the subject of the warrant demands that WILKINSON gives him his name.

Which of the following is correct in relation to what information WILKINSON is required to show in relation to executing the warrant

A WILKINSON must provide documentary evidence of his name.

B WILKINSON must provide his name, but this can be done verbally.

C WILKINSON need only give documentary evidence showing the authority by which he is employed.

D WILKINSON need only give documentary evidence showing that he is authorised to execute warrants.

Question 2.8

Constable McGEE is a serving officer in a Welsh police force, but Scottish in origin. Before going on leave he reads a Police National Computer (PNC) broadcast about an arrest warrant for an offence issued in Glasgow, which concerns a student he was at University with whom he knows well. Whilst on holiday on the south coast of England, he sees his friend against whom the warrant was issued.

Can he arrest his friend by executing the warrant?

A Yes, a warrant issued in Scotland can be executed in England or Wales by any constable.

B Yes, but only if the Scottish offence corresponds with an English law offence.

C No, the warrant would have to be in his possession to arrest in England.

D No, because he is not acting within his own force area.

Question 2.9

DICKERSON is a civilian enforcement officer employed by the local court and authorised in the prescribed manner. DICKERSON is executing a distress warrant at an address when he notices RYAN, for whom he knows an arrest warrant has been issued. DICKERSON does not have this warrant in his possession.

Can DICKERSON execute the warrant for arrest?

A Yes, a civilian enforcement officer can execute any warrant.

B Yes, an arrest warrant is one that can be executed by a civilian enforcement officer.

C No, a civilian enforcement officer must have possession of an arrest warrant.

D No, a civilian enforcement officer cannot execute an arrest warrant.

Question 2.10

Constable DICKINS, from the Metropolitan Police, carried out a check on the police national computer (PNC) on an Irish male. The check showed that a warrant was outstanding against the male, and that it had been issued in the Republic of Ireland.

Which of the following is correct in relation to the officer executing the warrant.

A The warrant can be executed provided the offence to which it relates corresponds to an offence in England and Wales.

B The warrant can be executed provided the offence to which it relates corresponds to an offence in England and Wales and has been issued for the purposes of arrest and prosecution.

C The warrant can be executed provided the person is accused of the commission of a specified offence and that the warrant has been issued for the purposes of arrest and prosecution.

D The warrant cannot be executed under in any circumstances in England and Wales.

Question 2.11

Constable SCRIVENS is an officer in an English police force. She has been given a summons, which was issued in Northern Ireland. She has been asked to serve the summons on behalf of the Police Service of Northern Ireland.

In relation to the serving of this summons, which of the following is correct?

A The summons must be served in person by the officer.

B The officer can post the summons, provided it is recorded delivery.

C The officer can post the summons, provided it is sent first class.

D The officer can post the summons to the person's last known or usual place of abode.

Question 2.12

Proceedings may be instigated against a person suspected of a criminal offence.

In relation to these proceedings, which of the following options is available for a public prosecutor under the Criminal Justice Act 2003?

A A public prosecutor must lay information before a justice for a summons to be issued.

B A public prosecutor can issue a 'written charge' charging the person to appear before the magistrates' court.

C The public prosecutor must lay written signed information before a justice for a summons to be issued.

D The public prosecutor must substantiate the information on oath before a justice for a summons to be issued.

ANSWERS

Answer 2.1

Answer **B** — A summons means a written order issued by a magistrate, or a magistrates' (justices') clerk on behalf of the magistrate. This means a justices' clerk can issue a summons and therefore answer D is incorrect, as is answer C. Unlike the issue of a summons, the justices' clerk is not allowed to issue any type of warrant; the information has to be made to a justice, and answer A is therefore incorrect.

Evidence and Procedure, para. 2.4.1.2

Answer 2.2

Answer **D** — A complaint is a verbal allegation made before a magistrate to the effect that a person has committed a breach of the law not being a criminal offence, and answer C is therefore incorrect. Acts of Parliament sometimes provide that proceedings are to be taken by way of complaint, and s. 2 of the Dogs Act 1871 is such an enactment, i.e. where proceedings instituted by 'information' are invalid, and answers A and B are therefore incorrect.

Evidence and Procedure, para. 2.4.1.3

Answer 2.3

Answer **D** — Rule 7.1 of the Criminal Procedure Rules 2005 provides that an information (i.e. an allegation that a person has committed an offence), may be laid orally *or* in writing. Answers A and B are therefore incorrect.

It may be laid either by the prosecutor in person, or by counsel or a solicitor on his/her behalf, *or* by any other authorised person. Answer C is therefore incorrect.

Under s. 1(1) of the Magistrates' Courts Act 1980, on an information being laid before him/her, a magistrate may issue either:

- a summons requiring the person named in the information to appear before a magistrates' court to answer thereto; or
- a warrant to arrest that person and bring him/her before a magistrates' court.

Evidence and Procedure, para. 2.4.3

Answer 2.4

Answer **C** — Rule 7.1(1) of the Criminal Procedure Rules 2005 states, 'An inform-ation may be laid ... by the prosecutor ... or by his counsel or solicitor or other person authorised in that behalf', and answer D is therefore incorrect. However, an information may not be laid on behalf of an unincorporated association, such as a police force — answer A is therefore incorrect. Also, since the definition of 'person' in the Interpretation Act 1978 as including a 'body of persons corporate or unin-corporate' was not intended to apply to the laying of informations (*Rubin* v *DPP* [1990] 2 QB 80), answer B is incorrect. It follows that an information must be laid by a named, actual person and must disclose the identity of that person. This could be met by laying informations in the name of the Chief Constable (who *is* a body corporate).

Evidence and Procedure, para. 2.4.3

Answer 2.5

Answer **B** — Generally, the service of a summons on a member of the armed forces is effected by its being served on the individual officer concerned, as well as on his or her commanding officer in the case of the army and RAF personnel, and answers A, C and D are therefore incorrect. If the person concerned serves in the Royal Navy or the Royal Marines, the commanding officer of a ship or other establishment is the other relevant person for the summons to be served on.

Evidence and Procedure, para. 2.4.5.2

Answer 2.6

Answer **D** — Deliberate delay of laying an information to obtain a summons has been considered by the courts. The leading authority on this is *R* v *Brentford Justices, ex parte Wong* [1981] QB 445. An information against Wong for careless driving was laid one day within the six-month period permitted by s. 127 of the Magistrates' Courts Act 1980. The prosecutor conceded that he had not then reached a firm de-cision on whether to take proceedings, but had laid the information simply to keep his options open. Having obtained a summons, there was a further delay, and it was several months before the summons was actually served. The magistrates indicated sympathy with the defence argument that the prosecution delay was improper but continued with the case. The Divisional Court, in considering the facts, held that the magistrates did have discretion to decline hearing the case if there had been an abuse of process, and what happened in this case could, and should, be regarded as an abuse of process and proceedings should have been stayed. Consequently, answers A, B and C are incorrect.

Evidence and Procedure, para. 2.4.5.2

Answer 2.7

Answer **A** — Rule 18.3(4) of the Criminal Procedure Rules 2005 provides that where a constable executes a warrant of arrest, commitment or detention they must, when arresting the relevant person:

- show the warrant (if they have it with them) to the relevant person; or
- tell the relevant person where the warrant is and what arrangements can be made to let that person inspect it;
- explain, in ordinary language, the charge and the reason for the arrest; and
- (unless a constable in uniform) show documentary proof of their identity.

If the person executing the warrant is one of the persons referred to in rule 18.3(b) or (c) (civilian enforcement officers or approved enforcement agencies), they must also show the relevant person a written statement under s. 125A(4) or s. 125B(4) of the Magistrates' Courts Act 1980, as appropriate. The written statement must include: the officer's name; the authority by which they are employed; and the fact they are authorised to execute warrants.

All of this must be shown by WILKINSON, not just the authority by which he is employed and the fact he is authorised to execute warrants; answers C and D are therefore incorrect. The proof must be documentary and not just provided orally; answer B is therefore incorrect.

Evidence and Procedure, para. 2.4.7.1

Answer 2.8

Answer **D** — Section 136(2) of the Criminal Justice and Public Order Act 1994 states:

A warrant issued in —
(a) Scotland; or
(b) Northern Ireland,

for the arrest of a person charged with an offence may (without any endorsement) be executed in England and Wales by any constable of any police force of the country of issue or of the country of execution, or by a constable appointed under section 53 of the British Transport Commission Act 1949, as well as by any other persons within the directions of the warrant.

There is no requirement that the offence the warrant relates to has a corresponding offence; answer B is therefore incorrect. The officer making the arrest also need not be in possession of the warrant at the time of the arrest; answer C is therefore incorrect.

However rule 18.3(3) of the Criminal Procedure Rules 2005 states:

A warrant of arrest, commitment or detention may be executed by —
  (a) the persons to whom it is directed; or
  (b) by any of the following persons, whether or not it was directed to them —
    (i) a constable for any police area in England and Wales, acting in his own police area...

In this scenario the officer is not within their own force area; answer A is therefore incorrect.

Evidence and Procedure, paras 2.4.7, 2.4.7.3

Answer 2.9

Answer **B** — Section 125A of the Magistrates' Court Act 1980 enables certain warrants to be executed in England and Wales by a civilian enforcement officer, provided he or she has been authorised in the prescribed manner, and answer D is therefore incorrect. However, this does not extend to all warrants, and answer A is therefore incorrect. An arrest warrant is one of those that can be executed by a civilian enforcement officer, but it does not stipulate that the warrant has to be in the officer's possession, and answer C is therefore incorrect.

Evidence and Procedure, para. 2.4.7.2

Answer 2.10

Answer **C** — The execution of warrants from other countries is dealt with by the Extradition Act 2003. This provides a fast-track extradition arrangement with Member States of the European Union and Gibraltar. Such warrants must state that the person in question is accused in the territory issuing the warrant of the commission of a specified offence and that the warrant has been issued for the purposes of arrest and prosecution.

There are therefore two factors, both of which must be present, prior to the warrant being lawfully executed:

- The person in question is accused in the territory issuing the warrant of the commission of a specified offence.
- The warrant has been issued for the purposes of arrest and prosecution.

This is answer C; answers A, B and D are therefore incorrect.

Evidence and Procedure, para. 2.4.7.3

Answer 2.11

Answer **A** — Postal service for summonses issued in England and Wales is permitted throughout Great Britain. However, postal service of a summons is not acceptable by the courts in Northern Ireland, therefore service of all Northern Ireland summonses in England and Wales must be made in person (answers B, C and D are therefore incorrect). Note that the service of a Scottish citation (their version of a summons) in England and Wales by post is permitted.

Evidence and Procedure, para. 2.4.5.3

Answer 2.12

Answer **B** — Section 29 of the Criminal Justice Act 2003 changes the way proceedings can be instituted in the magistrates' court. The section removes the power to lay an information for the purpose of obtaining the issue of a summons under s. 1 of the Magistrates' Courts Act 1980 (note, this does not apply to warrants), therefore answers A, C and D are incorrect. The purpose of this is to reduce the work of the magistrates' court, and it allows the 'public prosecutor' (which includes a police force in its definition) a new method of instituting proceedings.

Section 29 states:

(1) A public prosecutor may institute criminal proceedings against a person by issuing a document (a 'written charge') which charges the person with an offence.

(2) Where a public prosecutor issues a written charge, it must at the same time issue a document (a 'requisition') which requires the person to appear before a magistrates' court to answer the written charge.

Also of note is the Courts Act 2003, which at s. 42 allows for an information to be laid before a justice of the peace (except by a public prosecutor) that a person has, or is suspected of having, committed an offence. The justice may issue (s. 42(1)):

- a summons directed to that person requiring him to appear before a magistrates' court to answer the information; *or*
- a warrant to arrest that person and bring him before a magistrates' court.

Evidence and Procedure, para. 2.4.2

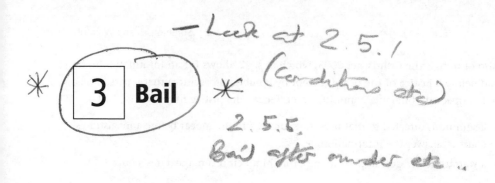

*   *— Look at 2.5.1*
    (conditions etc)
    2.5.5.
    Bail after murder etc..

3 Bail

STUDY PREPARATION

In terms of constitutional powers, the granting — and more importantly the denial — of bail is an area of fundamental importance. While there are lots of areas where tenuous human rights arguments have been raised since the 1998 Act was introduced, this one is for real. This area raises lots of questions about an individual's human rights — and therefore potentially lots of questions in exam papers.

For sergeants and inspectors, it is vital to know the extent of powers that exist to restrict or deny a person's bail. Practically this area is sometimes misunderstood, with many police officers (and lawyers) confusing the areas which will permit the police and courts to restrict a person's bail or to deny it all together.

QUESTIONS

Question 3.1

Officers have arrested McLAREN for an offence of theft and place him before the custody officer. The custody officer decides that, although further enquiries are necessary, there is currently insufficient evidence to charge and that there are no grounds to detain McLAREN.

In relation to releasing McLAREN, what can the custody officer do?

A She can release McLAREN on bail, which must be unconditional.

B She can release McLAREN on bail, which can have conditions.

C She cannot release McLAREN on bail in cases where there is insufficient evidence to charge.

D She cannot release McLAREN on bail where there are no grounds for detention.

Question 3.2

When a person is charged at a police station, the custody officer must make a decision about bail.

In relation to this decision and any representations made, which of the following is true?

A Only the person charged is allowed to make representations prior to the decision being made.

B If the person is legally represented, only the solicitor is allowed to make representations prior to the decision being made.

C Either the person charged or a solicitor is allowed to make representations prior to the decision being made.

D The custody officer does not need to listen to representations from anyone prior to the decision being made.

Question 3.3

CABALLERO was tried and convicted for an offence of manslaughter 10 years ago, for which he was *not* given a prison sentence due to the circumstances of the case. CABALLERO has recently been arrested for murder. However, CABALLERO has been charged with manslaughter again. The custody officer is considering bail.

Which of the following is true?

A CABALLERO cannot be given bail, unless he shows exceptional circumstances to justify it.

B CABALLERO cannot be given bail in any circumstances, as he has previously been convicted of a manslaughter offence.

C CABALLERO should be bailed, unless one of the grounds under s. 38(1) of the Police and Criminal Evidence Act 1984 applies.

D CABALLERO should be granted bail only if there are exceptional circumstances justifying it.

Question 3.4

The custody officer is considering whether SHILLITOE, having been charged with an offence of burglary, should be granted bail. The investigating officer believes that bail should be refused, as she suspects that SHILLITOE will commit further offences. The investigating officer believes this because SHILLITOE has previously offended whilst on bail.

Is the previous offending on bail relevant to the custody officer's decision?

A No, any reasonable grounds for refusing bail cannot be gained from previous incidents.

B No, 'commission of further offences' relates to non-imprisonable offences only.

C Yes, provided those offences committed on bail were burglary offences.

D Yes, provided it is considered with other factors, e.g. the strength of the evidence.

Question 3.5

MILLIGAN is appearing in court on a charge of murder, and the court is going to grant bail. There have been no formal reports on MILLIGAN's mental condition, and the prosecution have asked that, as a condition of the bail, the magistrates direct that MILLIGAN undergo an examination for the purpose of obtaining such a report.

Which of the following statements is true?

A The prosecution's application must be granted.

B The prosecution's application can be granted if the court considers it an appropriate condition.

C The prosecution's application cannot be granted as this is not a condition of bail.

D The prosecution's application cannot be granted as medical reports can be sought only after conviction.

Question 3.6

YOUSEL has been released from police custody on bail, with conditions to report to the police station every Wednesday at 9 pm and not to interfere with prosecution witnesses. YOUSEL wishes to have the conditions varied so he does not have to report to the police station.

Which of the following statements is true?

A YOUSEL must speak to the actual custody officer who bailed him.

B YOUSEL can speak to any custody officer at any station.

C YOUSEL risks having his conditions made more onerous by such a request.

D YOUSEL must be accompanied by his solicitor in making such a request.

Question 3.7

When granting bail, a custody officer can impose certain conditions of that bail.

Can a custody officer demand the surrender of the accused's passport?

A Yes, provided the custody officer thinks this to be an appropriate condition in the circumstances.

B Yes, provided there is a real and substantive risk that the accused will abscond.

C No, the European courts have ruled that this infringes a person's human rights.

D No, such a condition can be imposed only by a magistrate or judge.

Question 3.8

An accused has provided a surety to secure her surrender to custody, and then has failed to appear at court.

What must the securety prove in order to not forfeit his recognisance?

A That he took all possible steps to ensure that the accused attended court.

B That he informed the police, verbally, that the accused was likely not to turn up.

C That he took reasonable steps to ensure that the accused attended court.

D That he had not been involved in the accused's non-appearance.

Question 3.9

SULLY is an 11-year-old boy charged with burglary. There are clear grounds for the custody officer to refuse bail to prevent further offending. There is no secure local authority accommodation available, and the local authority can only provide accommodation from which it would be easy to escape.

In relation to detaining SULLY at the police station, which of the following is true?

A SULLY can be detained as no secure accommodation is available.

B SULLY can be detained provided there would be a risk to the public by placing him in the insecure accommodation.

C SULLY can be detained provided the custody officer certifies that it would have been impractical to find local authority accommodation.

D SULLY can be detained provided the custody officer certifies that it would have been impractical for him to be taken into local authority care.

Question 3.10

SHERGILL had been charged with assault causing actual bodily harm and had been granted conditional bail pending his trial in the Crown Court but was subsequently arrested for a breach of his bail conditions. He unsuccessfully applied in the Crown Court for a grant of bail. No record of the judge's reasons was made of the reasons to refuse bail, only a standard court form indicated that the reasons for the refusal of bail were SHERGILL's breach of his bail conditions.

Can SHERGILL now apply to the High Court for a judicial review of the refusal by the Crown Court to grant bail?

A Yes SHERGILL has an automatic right to have the refusal sent to the High Court for judicial review.

B Yes SHERGILL has a right to have the refusal sent to the High Court for judicial revue, but this would have to be an exceptional case for this to happen.

C No, there is no right for judicial review from the Crown Court's decision to refuse bail.

D No, the High Court does not consider any applications for bail, either directly or from judicial review.

Question 3.11

BREEZE was on unconditional bail on a charge of assault. The magistrates' court granted bail for a period of four weeks. BREEZE failed to appear and a warrant was issued. He was arrested three weeks later and taken before the court. When he gave evidence relating to a charge of absconding, BREEZE stated he had been in hospital at the time of the court date and left hospital a week later. He also stated he had not been given a copy of the court record of the date of his next appearance.

In relation to BREEZE's potential offence of absconding, which of the following is true?

A BREEZE did not commit the offence as he had reasonable cause not to surrender.

B BREEZE did not commit the offence because he did not receive a copy of the court record.

C BREEZE still committed the offence even though he had reasonable cause.

D BREEZE committed the offence simply by failing to appear in the first place.

Question 3.12

OLIVER, aged 19 years, has been charged with an offence of theft and is appearing before the magistrates' court where bail is being considered. The prosecution apply for bail to be denied asserting that OLIVER is a habitual drug user and likely to commit further offences whilst on bail. The prosecutor also maintains that bail should be refused as OLIVER was shown to have a Class A drug present in his body and has refused to undergo an assessment as to his dependence or propensity to misuse any specified Class A drug.

A As OLIVER has refused to undergo an assessment as to his dependence or propensity to misuse any specified Class A drug bail must be denied.

B Bail can be granted but only where OLIVER agrees to an assessment (or follow-up assessment) and it will be a condition of bail that it is undertaken.

C OLIVER can be granted bail in these circumstances but only where the court is satisfied that there is no significant risk of his committing an offence while on bail.

D OLIVER must be granted bail, as the prosecutor has not shown the use of a Class A drug contributed to the offence.

Question 3.13

BALDWIN was on bail to attend at a magistrates' court at a date in the future. Constable NEWELL received firm evidence that BALDWIN was not going to surrender but was certain to abscond. Constable NEWELL arrested BALDWIN at 11.20 am, on Monday, under s. 7(3) of the Bail Act 1976, and detention was authorised at 11.50 am. BALDWIN was taken to court at 10 am on Tuesday and appeared before a justice of the peace at 12 noon. The justice is of the opinion that BALDWIN will fail to surrender in the future.

In relation to what the justice may do next, which of the following is true?

A He may remand BALDWIN in custody as he was brought to court within 24 hours of detention being authorised.

B He may remand BALDWIN in custody as he was brought to court within 24 hours of the time he was arrested.

C He may *not* remand BALDWIN in custody as he was not put before a justice within 24 hours of detention being authorised.

D He may *not* remand BALDWIN in custody as he was not put before a justice within 24 hours of the time he was arrested.

Question 3.14

SILLITO was required to surrender her passport and not to leave the country as part of her bail conditions set by the Crown Court. She was to attend at the Court that afternoon and surrender her passport; however, she failed to do so and travelled that evening to Spain. On the day of her trial SILLITO returned and appeared at Court on time.

In relation to SILLITO's actions which of the following is correct?

A SILLITO has committed an offence of breaching her bail conditions and can be arrested for so doing.

B SILLITO has committed an offence of breaching her bail conditions and can be dealt with by the Crown Court there and then.

C SILLITO has committed no offences.

D SILLITO has committed an offence of contempt of court by not complying with her bail conditions.

Question 3.15

WHITE has been charged with several serious offences. The custody officer is deciding whether to grant bail or not, and needs to be aware of and give consideration to the rights and freedoms guaranteed under the European Convention on Human Rights when reaching that decision. There is, however, no evidence that WHITE has previously interfered with the course of justice while on bail.

In relation to the grounds on which to refuse bail, which of the following is true?

A The fact that the person had *not* previously 'interfered with the course of justice' whilst on bail would make refusing bail difficult to justify.

B The serious nature of the offences charged alone will be sufficient reason when considering 'fear of absconding' to justify remanding him in custody.

C Any previous offences need not be comparable with the offence charged when considering the prevention of crime to justify remanding him in custody.

D The fact there may be a public reaction that threatens 'the preservation of public order' to a release on bail would not help to justify remanding him in custody.

Question 3.16

MULLINGER was remanded in custody by the magistrates' court for an offence of robbery. He applied to the Crown Court for bail, and was granted conditional bail to report daily to his nearest police station. Two days later he failed to report and was arrested under s. 7 of the Bail Act 1976.

What action should the custody officer take?

A The custody officer should place him before the next available magistrates' court sitting.

B The custody officer should place him before the judge who granted him conditional bail.

C The custody officer should place him before the local Crown Court within 24 hours of his arrest.

D The custody officer should place him before the local magistrates' court within 24 hours of his arrest.

Question 3.17

Constable HASSELL attends a local major retail shop to deal with GREAVES, aged 17, for shoplifting. The officer listens to the store detective's evidence in the presence and hearing of GREAVES. Constable HASSELL detains the suspect and cautions her. Constable HASSELL then satisfies herself regarding the identity of GREAVES (who is a first-time offender) and considers how best to deal with this offence.

Which of the following is true?

A The officer cannot 'street bail' GREAVES as she is a youth offender.

B The officer can 'street bail' GREAVES, but this must be to the local police station.

C The officer can 'street bail' GREAVES to a police station, and this can be to any designated police station.

D The officer can 'street bail' GREAVES to the local Youth Offending Team office, which is in a non-designated police station.

Question 3.18

Sergeant MANN is giving SAUNDERS 'street bail' to attend at the police station at 3 pm next Tuesday.

What other conditions can the sergeant impose on this bail?

A As he is a sergeant he can grant bail with any condition available to a custody officer.

B As he is a sergeant he can impose conditions, but only relating to living and sleeping at a specified address.

C He can impose no more conditions than a constable, and they relate to notifying a change of address.

D He can impose no more conditions than the date, time and place SAUNDERS should surrender to custody.

Question 3.19

DRAKE has had his case adjourned by the magistrates' court for summary trial. The prosecution successfully applied for a condition of bail, in that DRAKE was required to surrender his passport. DRAKE wishes to appeal to the Crown Court against this condition.

Which of the following is true?

A DRAKE cannot appeal to the Crown Court about this condition of bail.

B DRAKE cannot appeal to the Crown Court about this or any other condition of bail.

C DRAKE can appeal to the Crown Court about any condition of bail imposed by the magistrates' court.

D DRAKE can appeal to the Crown Court provided he gives 7 days' warning to the prosecutor.

ANSWERS

Answer 3.1

Answer **A** — The meaning of 'bail in criminal proceedings' is contained in s. 1 of the Bail Act 1976 which states:

(1) In this Act 'bail in criminal proceedings' means —
   (a) bail grantable in or in connection with proceedings for an offence to a person who is accused or convicted of the offence, or
   (b) bail grantable in connection with an offence to a person who is under arrest for the offence or for whose arrest for the offence a warrant (endorsed for bail) is being issued.

This is further endorsed by by s. 1(6) which states:

Bail in criminal proceedings shall be granted (and in particular shall be granted unconditionally or conditionally) in accordance with this Act.

As the person, although not charged, has clearly been released 'in criminal proceedings', bail can be granted and answers C and D are therefore incorrect. Although it can be granted conditionally, answer B is incorrect because s. 47(1A) of the Police and Criminal Evidence Act 1984 states that where a person is bailed without being charged the custody officer cannot impose conditions on that bail.

Evidence and Procedure, para. 2.5.1

Answer 3.2

Answer **C** — This is a review of the person's detention. Therefore, to comply with the Police and Criminal Evidence Act 1984, the person, or his or her legal representative, should be given an opportunity to make representations to the custody officer prior to that officer's decision whether or not to grant bail. The review should be conducted with regard to PACE Code C, paras 15.1 to 15.7. Note that if the detained person was a juvenile, the opportunity to make representations should be extended to the 'appropriate adult'. This can also be extended, by the new Code of Practice, para. 15.3A, at the discretion of the person carrying out the review. This allows for representations from other people who have an interest in the detainee's welfare.

As it is either the person or his or her solicitor who can make representations, answers A and B are therefore incorrect. Also, the custody officer has to allow opportunities for representations to be made and answer D is therefore incorrect.

Evidence and Procedure, para. 2.5.4

37

Answer 3.3

Answer **C** — Section 25 of the Criminal Justice and Public Order Act 1994 deals with the issue of bail for those charged with certain offences such as manslaughter. In *R(O)* v *Harrow Crown Court* [2003] 1 WLR 2756, it was held that this section is compatible with Article 5 of the European Convention. Generally speaking, a person charged with manslaughter should not be given bail if he or she has a previous conviction for that offence, unless there are exceptional circumstances for granting bail, and answer B is therefore incorrect. Note that there is, however, a caveat where the previous conviction is manslaughter, as it says in s. 25(3), 'in the case of a previous conviction for manslaughter or of culpable homicide, if he was then sentenced to imprisonment'. As this was not the case, the 'exceptional circumstances' do not apply, and CABALLERO must be granted bail unless one of the grounds under s. 38(1) of the Police and Criminal Evidence Act 1984 apply; and answers A and D are therefore incorrect.

Evidence and Procedure, para. 2.5.5

Answer 3.4

Answer **D** — Section 38(1) of the Police and Criminal Evidence Act 1984 provides that a custody officer need not grant bail if there are reasonable grounds for believing that bail should be refused to prevent the accused, among other things, committing other offence(s). The custody officer should give due weight to whether the accused had committed offences when previously on bail (therefore answer A is incorrect) and also other factors. These factors are:

- the nature and seriousness of the offence and the probable method of dealing with the offender for it;
- the character, antecedents, associations and community ties of the accused;
- the accused's 'record' for having answered bail in the past;
- the strength of the evidence against the accused.

Although there are grounds for refusing bail that relate to non-imprisonable offences only, the one relating to 'commission of further offences' relates to imprisonable offences only (i.e. burglary), and therefore answer B is incorrect. The previous offending is not specific to the offence currently charged, and would therefore relate to any offence, and therefore answer C is incorrect — it is information which should be taken as a factor by the custody officer.

Evidence and Procedure, para. 2.5.6

Answer 3.5

Answer **A** — The general provisions as to bail are contained in s. 3 of the Bail Act 1976. Section 3(6A) deals with the court granting bail to a person accused of murder and states:

> In the case of a person accused of murder the court granting bail shall, unless it considers that satisfactory reports on his mental condition have already been obtained, impose as conditions of bail —
> (a) a requirement that the accused shall undergo examination by two medical practitioners for the purpose of enabling such reports to be prepared; and
> (b) a requirement that he shall for that purpose attend such an institution or place as the court directs and comply with any other directions which may be given to him for that purpose by either of those practitioners.

As can be seen, if bail is to be granted, the court is under a statutory obligation to impose such a condition and not only if it is appropriate, and therefore answer B is incorrect. As it is the law, it is a condition of bail, and therefore answer C is incorrect. Although requests for medical reports can be sought following conviction, they *must* be requested where the person is bailed; and as no such report has already been obtained, answer D is therefore incorrect.

Evidence and Procedure, para. 2.5.7.1

Answer 3.6

Answer **C** — Section 3A of the Bail Act 1976 applies to bail granted by a custody officer.

In relation to varying imposed bail conditions, s. 5A(2) states:

> Where a custody officer has granted bail in criminal proceedings he or another custody officer serving at the same police station may, at the request of the person to whom it was granted, vary the conditions of bail; and in doing so he may impose conditions or more onerous conditions.

YOUSEL must visit the police station where the original conditions were imposed, and therefore answer B is incorrect. However, any custody officer can be consulted, and therefore answer A is incorrect. Section 3A does not obligate the presence of a legal representative, therefore answer D is incorrect. The legislation allows YOUSEL the opportunity to have the bail conditions varied, but in doing so he risks the imposition of more onerous conditions (s. 5A(2) of the Bail Act 1976).

Evidence and Procedure, para. 2.5.7.4

Answer 3.7

Answer **B** — Under s. 3A of the Bail Act 1976, conditions can be imposed where it is necessary to do so for the purpose of preventing a person from:

- failing to surrender to custody; *or*
- committing an offence while on bail; *or*
- interfering with witnesses or otherwise obstructing the course of justice, whether in relation to himself or any other person.

One of those conditions is that of the accused having to surrender his passport, and this is available to both the court and the custody officer, and therefore answer D is incorrect. In making such a decision, the custody officer has to take into account the punitive nature of any conditions imposed and can only place conditions where there is a 'real' risk of the accused absconding. It would not be sufficient merely to think it was appropriate, and must be based on 'a real and not a fanciful risk' (*R* v *Mansfield Justices, ex parte Sharkey* [1985] QB 613), and therefore answer A is incorrect. Any imposition of bail, with or without conditions, amounts to an interference with a person's rights under the European Convention on Human Rights, and the European Court and Commission have examined the question of bail. Their approach generally is that an accused person should be released unconditionally unless factors that would otherwise lead to a refusal of bail can be met by imposing bail conditions. Against this background, the European Court has accepted that the surrender of a passport is a legitimate condition (*Schmid* v *Austria* (1985) 44 DR 195), and therefore answer C is incorrect.

Evidence and Procedure, para. 2.5.7.3

Answer 3.8

Answer **C** — Rule 21 of the Crown Court Rules 1982 empowers the court to forfeit a surety's recognisance if there has been default in performing the obligations imposed. However, in *R* v *Warwick Crown Court, ex parte Smalley* [1987] 1 WLR 237, it was held there is no requirement of proof that any blame is attached to the surety for the accused's non-appearance, and therefore answer D is incorrect. It is also not necessary for the surety to show that he took all possible steps to ensure the appearance of the accused, and therefore answer A is incorrect. If the surety had taken all *reasonable* steps to ensure attendance, but the accused nevertheless let him down, the recognisance ought not to be forfeited (*R* v *York Crown Court, ex parte Coleman* (1987) 86 Cr App R 151). Part of those reasonable steps might well be notifying the police that the accused is unlikely to surrender to custody. However, such notification must be in writing, and therefore answer B is incorrect.

Evidence and Procedure, para. 2.5.7.5

Answer 3.9

Answer **D** — A custody officer who authorises an arrested juvenile to be kept in police custody must secure that the arrested juvenile is moved to local authority accommodation unless he or she certifies that, by reason of such circumstances as are specified in the certificate, it is impracticable to do so, or that, in the case of a juvenile who has attained the age of 12, no secure accommodation is available *and* that keeping him in other local authority accommodation would not be adequate to protect the public from serious harm from him (s. 38(6) of the Police and Criminal Evidence Act 1984). PACE Code C, Note 16D clearly states:

> The availability of secure accommodation is only a factor in relation to a juvenile aged 12 or over when the local authority accommodation would not be adequate to protect the public from serious harm from the juvenile.

As SULLY is only 11 years of age, answers A and B are incorrect. Note 16D also states, 'the lack of secure local authority accommodation shall not make it impracticable for the custody officer to transfer him'. This means that, unless the exception applies, the custody officer must physically hand him over to the care of the local authority. However, this does not apply to SULLY who is only 11 years old, and therefore answer C is incorrect.

Evidence and Procedure, para. 2.5.9

Answer 3.10

Answer **B** — The Criminal Justice Act 1967, s. 22 states:

> (1) Where (a) a magistrates' court withholds bail in criminal proceedings or imposes conditions in granting bail in criminal proceedings, and (b) it does so where an application to the court to state a case for the opinion of the High Court is made, the High Court may grant bail or vary the conditions.

Thus, the High Court can entertain an application for bail (or to vary the conditions) under s. 22 only if the accused is appealing by way of case stated against conviction (or sentence, although such appeals are rarely appropriate) and the magistrates have withheld bail or granted only conditional bail; answer D is therefore incorrect.

There is also the possibility of judicial review. In *R (M)* v *Isleworth Crown Court* [2005] EWHC 363, it was held that, although the High Court has jurisdiction to judicially review a refusal of bail, that jurisdiction should be exercised sparingly; answer C is therefore incorrect. This decision was followed in *R (Shergill)* v *Harrow Crown Court* [2005] EWHC 648, confirming that s. 29(3) of the Supreme Court Act 1981 does not preclude the Divisional Court from considering applications for judicial review of a decision to refuse bail, but that it was only in exceptional cases that the Court would consider it right to review the decision of a Crown Court judge in whom the relevant powers had been vested; answer A is therefore incorrect.

Evidence and Procedure, para. 2.5.12.5

Answer 3.11

Answer **C** — Section 6 of the Bail Act 1976 creates the offence of absconding. By s. 6(1), if a person released on bail fails without reasonable cause to surrender to custody, he is guilty of an offence. The burden of showing reasonable cause is on the accused (s. 6(3)). Moreover, a person who had reasonable cause for failing to surrender on the appointed day nevertheless commits an offence if he fails to surrender *as soon after the appointed time as is reasonably practicable* (s. 6(2)). The fact that BREEZE did not surrender to the court until being arrested means that, although he had reasonable cause, he failed to surrender and therefore still commits the offence (answer A is incorrect). The offence is not absolute and is not committed simply by failing to surrender to custody, and therefore answer D is incorrect. Section 6(4) of the 1976 Act states:

> A failure to give a person granted bail in criminal proceedings a copy of the record of the decision shall not constitute a reasonable cause for that person's failure to surrender to custody.

Therefore answer B is incorrect.

Evidence and Procedure, para. 2.5.11

Answer 3.12

Answer **C** — Section 19(4) of the Criminal Justice Act 2003 adds paras. 6A to 6C to the Bail Act 1976, sch. 1, part I. These provide that an accused aged 18 or over who has been charged with an imprisonable offence will not be granted bail where the three conditions set out in para. 6B apply, namely:

(1) there is drug test evidence that the person has a specified Class A drug in his body (by way of a lawful test obtained under the PACE 1984, s. 63B or the Criminal Justice Act 2003, s. 161);

(2) either he is charged with an offence under the Misuse of Drugs Act 1971, s. 5(2) or (3), and the offence relates to a specified Class A drug, or the court is satisfied that there are substantial grounds for believing that the misuse of a specified Class A drug caused or contributed to the offence with which he is charged, or that offence was motivated wholly or partly by his intended misuse of a specified Class A drug; and

(3) the person does not agree to undergo an assessment (carried out by a suitably qualified person) of whether he is dependent upon or has a propensity to misuse any specified Class A drugs, or he has undergone such an assessment but does not agree to participate in any relevant follow-up which has been offered.

All three conditions must apply, and as the scenario gives no evidence that the use of a Class A drug contributed to the offence answer A is therefore incorrect. In this scenario this particular grounds for denying bail is not met, however the court is under no obligation to grant bail where it believes the person may commit offences whilst on bail; answer D is therefore incorrect.

However, even where all three elements are present, the court may still grant bail if it is satisfied that there is no significant risk of his/her committing an offence whilst on bail; answer A is therefore incorrect.

Although bail can be granted if an assessment or follow-up is proposed and agreed to this is not conditional on bail being granted, the court can grant bail if it is satisfied that there is no significant risk of his/her committing an offence whilst on bail; answer B is therefore incorrect. Where a defendant agrees to an assessment (or follow-up assessment) it will be a condition of bail that it is undertaken (Bail Act 1976, s. 3(6D)).

Evidence and Procedure, para. 2.5.13.1

Answer 3.13

Answer **D** — Section 7(3) of the Bail Act 1976 states:

A person who has been released on bail in criminal proceedings and is under a duty to surrender into the custody of a court may be arrested without warrant by a constable —
(a) if the constable has reasonable grounds for believing that that person is not likely to surrender to custody ...

Following arrest under s. 7(3), the person arrested must be brought before a magistrate as soon as practicable, and in any event within 24 hours (s. 7(4)). Note that the section clearly states that the person must be brought before a magistrate (justice) and *not* brought merely to the court precincts, and therefore answers A and B are incorrect. This requirement is absolute, and since the justice's jurisdiction under s. 7(5) to remand a detainee in custody only arises once s. 7(4) has been complied with, a detainee who is brought before the justice out of time cannot be remanded in custody (*R* v *Governor of Glen Parva Young Offenders Institution, ex parte G (a minor)* [1998] QB 887). The 24 hours is calculated from the time of arrest and not the time detention was authorised and therefore answer C is incorrect.

Evidence and Procedure, para. 2.5.11.2

Answer 3.14

Answer **C** — The Divisional Court has held that the purpose of placing restrictions on an individual's movement under the Bail Act 1976 is to ensure that they attend the trial. If the conduct breaching bail is known about at the time, that bail could be revoked, and s. 7 of the Bail Act 1976 provides a power of arrest without warrant if the constable:

- has reasonable grounds for believing that the person is not likely to surrender to custody;
- has reasonable grounds for believing that the person is likely to break, or reasonable grounds for suspecting that the person has broken, any conditions of bail.

However, s. 7 does not itself create any offence. Answer A and B are therefore incorrect.

In *R* v *Ashley* [2004] 1 WLR 2057, the accused was convicted of contempt of court, arising out of breaches of bail conditions. He had been released on bail subject to conditions that required him to surrender his passport and not to leave the country. He broke both conditions but returned to face trial on the appointed day. Although the defendant had breached bail conditions by leaving the country, he did return for his trial. It followed that the judge did not have power to deal with him by way of contempt of court. Answer D is therefore incorrect.

Evidence and Procedure, para. 2.5.11

Answer 3.15

Answer **A** — The European Court and Commission have identified four grounds where the refusal of bail may be justified under the European Convention on Human Rights:

- fear of absconding;
- interference with the course of justice;
- the prevention of crime;
- the preservation of public order.

In relation to fear of absconding, the seriousness of the offence alone has been deemed not to be a sufficient reason to suppose a person will necessarily abscond (*Yagci and Sargin* v *Turkey* (1995) 20 EHRR 505), and answer B is therefore incorrect. In considering the prevention of crime, the European Court has held that, where the offender's previous convictions were not comparable either in nature or seriousness with the offence(s) charged, their use as grounds for refusing bail would not be acceptable for the purposes of Article 5 of the Convention (*Clooth* v *Belgium* (1991) 14 EHRR 717), and answer C is therefore incorrect. The temporary detention of a person where the particular gravity of the offence(s) and the likely public reaction mean that the release may give rise to public disorder was considered in *Letellier* v *France* (1991) 14 EHRR 83 in relation to the preservation of public order. This was held to be a sound reason for remanding in custody, and answer D is therefore incorrect. In *Ringeisen* v *Austria* (1971) 1 EHRR 455, interference with the course of justice was considered. If the detained person has previously been bailed and there was no evidence of interference with the course of justice, remanding in custody to prevent interference with the course of justice would be very difficult to justify.

Evidence and Procedure, para. 2.5.16

Answer 3.16

Answer **D** — Section 7 of the Bail Act applies whether either the magistrates or the Crown Court give the person bail. This includes what is referred to as 'judge in chambers' applications for review of a decision by the lower court to remand in custody. The detainee must be brought before a magistrate; answers B and C are therefore incorrect.

Where a defendant is brought before a justice under s. 7(4) for breach of bail conditions, the justice must deal with him in accordance with s. 7(5) and decide whether to grant or refuse bail. Note that the detainee must be taken to court within 24 hours of his arrest and not the next available session, therefore answer A is incorrect (*R* v *Teesside Magistrates' Court, ex p Ellison* [2001] EWCA Admin 11).

Evidence and Procedure, paras 2.5.11.2, 2.5.12.4

Answer 3.17

Answer **D** — The Criminal Justice Act 2003 allows an officer to 'street bail' an offender as an alternative to arresting him or her and taking him or her straight to the police station, as was required by s. 30 of PACE prior to being amended by the 2003 Act. Section 30A of PACE now states:

(1) A constable may release on bail a person who is arrested or taken into custody in the circumstances mentioned in section 30(1).

(2) A person may be released on bail under subsection (1) at any time before he arrives at a police station.

(3) A person released on bail under subsection (1) must be required to attend a police station.

(4) No other requirement may be imposed on the person as a condition of bail.

(5) The police station which the person is required to attend may be any police station.

As can be seen in s. 30A(5) above, the person can be bailed to any police station, including non-designated ones; answers B and C are incorrect. There is nothing in the 2003 Act that restricts street bail to adult offenders, and therefore answer A is incorrect. It is perfectly acceptable, and some might add inherently sensible, to 'street bail' a youth offender straight to the Youth Offending Team office. The only consideration outlined in the 2003 Act in relation to bail to non-designated stations is contained in s. 30C(2) of the 1984 Act:

(2) If a person is required to attend a police station which is not a designated police station he must be —
(a) released, or
(b) taken to a designated police station,
not more than six hours after his arrival.

Evidence and Procedure, paras 2.5.2.2, 2.5.2.4

Answer 3.18

Answer **D** — The fact the officer is a sergeant, and eligible to be a custody officer, is irrelevant; the power to grant 'street bail' is given to a constable. Although under the Bail Act 1976 conditions can be imposed on an accused (and the ones mentioned in answers B and C are some of these conditions), these do not extend to 'street bail', therefore answers A, B and C are incorrect. Section 30A(4) of the Police and Criminal Evidence Act 1984 states: '(4) No other requirement may be imposed on the person as a condition of bail.' This is other than the requirement to surrender to bail at a specified date and time at a police station.

Evidence and Procedure, para. 2.5.2.2

Answer 3.19

Answer **A** — Section 16 of the Criminal Justice Act 2003 allows a person granted bail by the magistrates' court to appeal to the Crown Court against particular conditions of bail (answer B is therefore incorrect). This section applies where a magistrates' court grants bail to a person in a case relating to:

- adjournment for trial;
- intention as to plea adjournment;
- initial procedure on information against an adult for offence triable either way;
- intention as to plea by child or young person adjournment;
- a preliminary hearing;
- remand for medical examination.

However, the conditions of bail that can be appealed against are limited:

(2) Subject to the following provisions of this section, the person concerned may appeal to the Crown Court against any condition of bail falling within subsection (3).

(3) A condition of bail falls within this subsection if it is a requirement —
   (a) that the person concerned resides away from a particular place or area,
   (b) that the person concerned resides at a particular place other than a bail hostel,
   (c) for the provision of a surety or sureties or the giving of a security,
   (d) that the person concerned remains indoors between certain hours,
   (e) imposed under section 3(6ZAA) of the 1976 Act (requirements with respect to electronic monitoring), or
   (f) that the person concerned makes no contact with another person.

Passport seizure is not on the list; answer C is therefore incorrect.

On an appeal under this section the Crown Court may vary the conditions of bail. There is no time limit, or advance notification required to the prosecutor; answer D is therefore incorrect.

Evidence and Procedure, para. 2.5.12.3

4 | Court Procedure and Witnesses

STUDY PREPARATION

This is what the whole process is all about. Although, logically, this chapter should appear at the end of the book, it makes practical sense to consider its contents here. The mechanics of getting evidence before a court largely come from statute and, as you would expect, contain a fair amount of detail.

It is important to understand who can give what evidence and under what circumstances; it is also important to know some of the more general restrictions that are placed on witnesses' evidence-in-chief and cross-examination.

QUESTIONS

Question 4.1

MUIRHEAD was due to stand trial at the Crown Court, charged with an offence of armed robbery, and failed to appear. There had been numerous remands based on medical certificates supplied by the defendant, and a full medical report had been asked for by the Crown Court. This had not been supplied and there was no indication why MUIRHEAD was absent.

Can the trial proceed in his absence?

A No, only at magistrates' courts can a trial take place in the defendant's absence.

B No, as the offence is a serious one the trial must take place in his presence.

C Yes, the trial can go ahead with or without legal representation.

D Yes, the trial can go ahead, but it is desirable that counsel represents MUIRHEAD.

Question 4.2

Children below a certain age are not permitted to be present in court during another person's trial unless they are witnesses.

At what age does this restriction end?

A 14 years of age.
B 15 years of age.
C 16 years of age.
D 17 years of age.

Question 4.3

DAWLISH has been convicted of an offence of assault at magistrates' court. The District Judge is going to pass a community sentence on DAWLISH and is considering whether he needs to give reasons for, and explain the effects of, the sentence passed under s. 174 of the Criminal Justice Act 2003.

Does the District Judge have to give reasons as to why a community sentence has been passed?

A No, s. 174 of the Criminal Justice Act 2003 only applies to a judge handing down a sentence at Crown Court.
B No, s. 174 of the Criminal Justice Act 2003 only applies where a custodial sentence is imposed.
C Yes, and the District Judge must mention any important aggravating factors.
D Yes, and the District Judge must mention any important aggravating or mitigating factors.

Question 4.4

YAU has been jointly charged with BELTON with an offence of blackmail and both face trial as co-accused. The prosecution wish to use YAU as a witness against BELTON, as YAU has indicated that BELTON was the main protagonist. This is supported by independent evidence.

In what circumstances can YAU give evidence against BELTON?

A Only if YAU promises to plead guilty to the offence at a later date, after BELTON's trial.
B If YAU pleads guilty on the day of the trial.
C YAU can give evidence with no restrictions.
D If the prosecutor tells YAU he will not be prosecuted.

Question 4.5

PROUD has been charged with an offence of theft, and her husband is a potential witness to the incident. PROUD's solicitor wishes to call PROUD's husband to give evidence on her behalf.

In relation to PROUD's husband, which of the following is true?

A He is a competent witness but not compellable.
B He is a competent witness and is compellable.
C He is not a competent witness and is not compellable.
D He is not a competent witness but is compellable.

Question 4.6

BURGIN is appearing in court on a charge of sexual activity with a child under 13. The victim has been called to give evidence and the defence question whether she is the age that she claims to be.

What evidence can be given to show the girl's age?

A Evidence of her parent that she is that age.
B Evidence of her birth certificate will suffice.
C Evidence of her birth certificate, supported by proof of identity.
D Any evidence of identity will suffice.

Question 4.7

ELDER is 17 years old and a witness to an offence of kidnapping. She is to be called to the Crown Court to give evidence for the prosecution, but ELDER has been receiving threats from the accused's family who have yet to be dealt with for this intimidation. To avoid the accused's family attending and intimidating the witness, the prosecution seek 'a special measures direction' to have ELDER's evidence given in private.

Who, if anyone, can the court exclude under this 'special measures direction'?

A Any person, including the accused, but not his or her legal representatives.
B Any person except the accused and his or her legal representatives.
C The public only; the press would be allowed to stay, as would the accused and his or her legal representatives.
D In this case the special measures direction may not be given as it is not a sexual offence.

Question 4.8

Constable WHALE and Constable CREASEY are witnesses in a case of theft. Both officers made pocket notebook entries regarding the incident, and have refreshed their memory from those notebooks prior to giving evidence. Constable WHALE is now giving her evidence-in-chief and wishes to consult her pocket notebook.

In relation to refreshing memory, which of the following is true?

A She cannot refer to her pocket notebook as she made the notes in consultation.

B She cannot refer to her pocket notebook as she refreshed her memory prior to giving evidence.

C She can refer to her pocket notebook, but only for exact details, i.e. index numbers.

D She can refer to her pocket notebook, provided she states that it records her recollection of the case.

Question 4.9

BLEWITT and GIBBONS are jointly charged with robbery. BLEWITT goes into the witness box and gives an account of events, but GIBBONS does not give sworn testimony. Counsel for GIBBONS asks no questions of BLEWITT in cross-examination. Counsel for GIBBONS suggests to the jury in her closing speech that the co-accused and a prosecution witness had committed the offence charged, and not her client.

Which of the following is correct?

A Counsel for GIBBONS can make this suggestion as it relates to the co-accused.

B Counsel for GIBBONS can make this suggestion as she is not prosecuting counsel.

C Counsel for GIBBONS cannot make this suggestion as it was not put to him in cross-examination.

D Counsel for GIBBONS cannot make this suggestion as her client did not give evidence.

Question 4.10

ZAGERAKAS refused to attend court as a witness and was summonsed by the court to attend to give evidence as a witness. ZAGERAKAS gives evidence but refuses to answer any questions put to him by the defence.

Which of the following is true in relation to contempt of court?

A ZAGERAKAS is in contempt of court, but cannot be imprisoned for this.

B ZAGERAKAS is in contempt of court and can be imprisoned for this.

C ZAGERAKAS is not in contempt of court, as he gave evidence.

D ZAGERAKAS is not in contempt of court; although he can be summonsed to attend court, he is not obliged to give evidence nor to answer any questions.

Question 4.11

SOUTHWELL is standing trial at Crown Court for an offence of rape. His defence is based on consent and SOUTHWELL wishes to cross-examine the victim on her previous sexual behaviour, with the leave of the court.

In relation to this, which of the following statements is correct?

A Neither SOUTHWELL nor his legal representative can ask questions about the victim's previous sexual behaviour.

B SOUTHWELL can ask such questions, provided they relate to behaviour at or about the same time as the incident charged.

C SOUTHWELL's legal representative can ask questions about the victim's previous sexual behaviour.

D SOUTHWELL's legal representative can ask such questions provided they relate to sexual behaviour at or about the same time as the incident in question.

Question 4.12

MILLIKEN is standing trial on a charge of violent disorder, which occurred during a large-scale public disorder situation. The prosecution relied heavily on the evidence of several police officers, some of whom gave evidence that they had seen the accused committing the offence. The officers were cross-examined only in relation to the evidence they had given. MILLIKEN, whilst giving evidence, accused certain police officers of a conspiracy to fabricate the evidence against him. This was the first time the prosecution had been made aware of the defence's intention to raise this as an issue. The prosecutor wishes to recall the officers to rebut the accusation.

At this stage in the trial, having closed their case, will the prosecution be allowed to call evidence?

A Yes, but only if the defence accepts that there was a misunderstanding between counsel.

B Yes, as they could not reasonably have anticipated this defence.

C No, because this issue was not raised in cross-examination.

D No, because the prosecution must call the whole of their defence before closing their case — no exceptions.

Question 4.13

LOCKE is a 14-year-old girl who was sexually assaulted. The defendant in the case is about to be tried in the Crown Court and LOCKE will have to give evidence in court. She stated that she is likely to be embarrassed about giving evidence in open court, but she is not afraid to give evidence nor is she refusing to give evidence. The prosecution are seeking a 'special measures' direction for the visually-recorded interview the police conducted to be admitted as her evidence-in-chief.

In relation to this application, which of the following is true?

A It **must** be granted as the child is under 17 years of age.

B It may be granted unless the court believes it would not be in the interest of justice to do so.

C It will not be granted as the child is not in fear of giving evidence.

D It will not be granted as the child has not refused to give evidence in open court.

Question 4.14

HEYES is appearing at Crown Court charged with stealing a bicycle and is representing himself. The jury are sworn and during the opening of the case by the prosecution HEYES states that he wishes to be represented by counsel. The trial takes place and the jury has retired to consider their verdict. HEYES decides to change his plea to guilty.

What should the judge direct following this requested change of plea?

A The jury should be dismissed and the judge should record a guilty plea entered.

B The jury should be dismissed and the judge should record a verdict of guilty.

C The jury should be directed by the judge to return a formal verdict of guilty.

D The jury should be allowed to carry on their deliberations; a change of plea is acceptable only up until the jury retire to consider their verdict.

Question 4.15

STRACHAN was an 81-year-old woman who was allegedly raped by HILL. STRACHAN also suffered from Alzheimer's disease. A videotape of the complainant's police interview was made. Although her answers were confused, she stated that a man had had sexual intercourse with her against her wishes. Expert evidence indicated that at the time of her interview she was not fit to give evidence in court owing to her dementia.

Which of the following is true in relation to the videotaped evidence?

A Her evidence cannot be admitted as she has impaired intellect and is not a competent witness.

B Her evidence cannot be admitted; she cannot be a competent witness as she is not available to attend court due to dementia.

C Her evidence can be admitted, however the jury must be warned about the reliability of her evidence.

D Her evidence can be admitted, if the court decide her evidence ought to be admitted in the interests of fairness.

Question 4.16

Annabelle is a $3^{1}/_{2}$-year-old child who was sexually assaulted and the prosecution wish to use her as a witness.

Which of the following is correct as to whether Annabelle will be a competent witness or not?

A She will competent witness without any restrictions.

B She is a competent witness provided she displays such competence throughout the whole of her evidence.

C She is not a competent witness as she is under 4 years of age.

D She is not a competent witness as she is unlikely to be able to give intelligible evidence.

ANSWERS

Answer 4.1

Answer **D** — This area has been tested by appeal to the House of Lords, particularly in relation to Article 6 of the European Convention on Human Rights. Their Lordships affirmed that the Crown Court could conduct a trial in the absence of the defendant (*R* v *Jones* [2003] 1 AC 1); therefore, answer A is incorrect. This was a serious step and could take place only in exceptional circumstances.

In *Jones*, Lord Bingham did not consider that the seriousness of the offence was a relevant consideration in deciding whether the trial should go ahead; therefore, answer B is incorrect. The overriding concern was that the trial, if conducted in the defendant's absence, was as fair as the circumstances could permit and led to a just outcome. Those objects were equally important whether the offence was serious or relatively minor. Secondly, it was generally desirable that a defendant be represented even if he had voluntarily absconded, therefore answer C is incorrect.

Evidence and Procedure, para. 2.6.6

Answer 4.2

Answer **A** — There is extremely limited power at common law for a court to sit *in camera* (where the public are excluded), but this is supplemented by certain statutory provisions. One of these is that no child (i.e. a person *under* the age of 14) is permitted to be in court while criminal proceedings are in progress against a person other than the child himself, except where the child's presence is required as a witness or 'otherwise for the purposes of justice' (s. 36 of the Children and Young Persons Act 1933). The restriction will be lifted when the child turns 14 years of age. Therefore, answers B, C and D are incorrect.

Evidence and Procedure, para. 2.6.10.2

Answer 4.3

Answer **D** — Section 174 of the Criminal Justice Act 2003 imposes a general statutory duty on the courts to give reasons for, and explain the effects of, the sentence passed.

The court must explain in non-technical terms its reasons for deciding on the sentence passed, the structure of the sentence, what it requires the offender to do, what will happen if it is not done, and any power which exists to vary or review the sentence (s. 174(1)). In addition, certain specific matters must be dealt with (s. 174(2)). If a custodial or community sentence is being passed, the court must explain why the offence is sufficiently serious to warrant such a sentence. Any reduction for a guilty plea must be mentioned in the reasons, together with any aggravating or mitigating factors which the court regarded as being of particular importance.

This applies to all courts, including magistrates' courts, and includes community sentences; answers A and B are therefore incorrect. The person imposing the sentence must mention any aggravating or mitigating factors that were considered, not just those aggravating factors that may have meant such a sentence was warranted; answer C is therefore incorrect.

Evidence and Procedure, para. 2.6.4

Answer 4.4

Answer **B** — A co-accused may give evidence for the prosecution only if he or she has ceased to be a co-accused, and answer C is therefore incorrect. A person would cease to be a co-accused when:

- the person pleads guilty, either on arraignment or during the course of the trial;
- the person is tried separately and convicted (although not mentioned in the *Evidence & Procedure Manual*, this would include when he or she was acquitted (*R v Rowland* (1826) Ry & M 401));
- the prosecution enter a *nolle prosequi*, putting to an end the proceedings against the person.

In all of these cases, a former co-accused becomes both competent and compellable for the prosecution.

So the accused must have pleaded guilty either before or during the trial, and answer A is therefore incorrect. Although a *nolle prosequi* is a 'promise not to prosecute', it must have been entered as such in the court records and it would not suffice that the accused had been promised he would not be prosecuted. Therefore, answer D is incorrect, although there would almost certainly be a breach of process here.

Evidence and Procedure, para. 2.6.12.5

Answer 4.5

Answer **B** — As far as competence and compellability are concerned, the law distinguishes between witnesses for the prosecution and witnesses for the defence. Here, the witness is one for the defence, and the law says that the spouses and civil partners of the accused are competent to give evidence for the accused (s. 80(1)(b) of the Police and Criminal Evidence Act 1984). This remains the case even if they are jointly charged with an offence. Subject to one exception only, the spouse or civil partner is also compellable to give evidence for the accused (s. 80(2)). The exception is where the spouses are jointly charged with an offence (s. 80(4)). Consequently, when giving evidence on behalf of the defence, a spouse or civil partner will always be competent. Answers C and D are therefore incorrect. In this scenario the husband is also compellable, as he is not jointly charged with the offence, and answer A is therefore incorrect. The Civil Patnership Act 2004 made ss. 80 and 80A of PACE 1984 applicable to 'civil partners' as well and wives and husbands. Legal civil partners are same- sex couples who have registered their partnership in accordance with the 2004 Act.

Evidence and Procedure, para. 2.6.12.6

Answer 4.6

Answer **C** — Issues surrounding age are dealt with by s. 9 of the Family Law Reform Act 1969, which states:

> The time at which a person attains a particular age expressed in years shall be the commencement of the relevant anniversary of the date of his birth.

This requires proof of date of birth (not just identity), and answer D is therefore incorrect. A birth certificate is usually accepted as evidence of age; but if a certificate of birth is produced to prove age, evidence must also be adduced positively to identify the person as the person named in the certificate (*R* v *Rogers* (1914) 10 Cr App R 276) and answer B is therefore incorrect. The oral testimony of a member of the family will not suffice, although if the parent was present at the birth, that evidence together with the certificate of birth may suffice — answer A is therefore incorrect.

Evidence and Procedure, para. 2.6.12.8

Answer 4.7

Answer **B** — Section 25(1) of the Youth Justice and Criminal Evidence Act 1999 states that 'a special measures direction' may provide for the exclusion of *any* persons from the court whilst the witness is giving evidence, and answer C is therefore incorrect. This does not include the exclusion of the accused, legal representatives and any interpreter acting for the witness (s. 25(2)), and answer A is therefore incorrect. This direction may be used only where the proceedings relate to a sexual offence, *or* there are reasonable grounds to believe that the witness has been or will be intimidated by any person other than the accused — answer D is therefore incorrect.

Evidence and Procedure, para. 2.6.14.3

Answer 4.8

Answer **D** — The Criminal Justice Act 2003 provides statutory rules that enable witnesses to refer to a document to refresh their memories. This replaces the many authorities and judicial discretion that existed prior to the 2003 Act being enacted. Section 139 of the 2003 Act states:

(1) A person giving oral evidence in criminal proceedings about any matter may, at any stage in the course of doing so, refresh his memory of it from a document made or verified by him at an earlier time if —

 (a) he states in his oral evidence that the document records his recollection of the matter at that earlier time, and

 (b) his recollection of the matter is likely to have been significantly better at that time than it is at the time of his oral evidence.

So the officer can refer to her notebook, irrespective of any factors under which such notes were made, if she states it is her recollection, and such recollection is likely to be significantly better than it is now whilst giving evidence-in chief. Answers A, B and C are therefore incorrect. However the Court of Appeal has made it clear that training or coaching witnesses in relation to a forthcoming criminal trial is prohibited (*R* v *Momodou: R* v *Limani* [2005] EWCA Crim 177).

Evidence and Procedure, para. 2.6.15

Answer 4.9

Answer **C** — A party who fails to cross-examine a witness upon a particular matter in respect of which it is proposed to contradict, tacitly accepts the truth of the witness's evidence-in-chief on that matter; this includes the prosecuting counsel and any counsel for co-accused, so answer B is therefore incorrect. They will not thereafter be entitled to invite the jury to disbelieve the witness in that regard.

Answer A is incorrect as the fact that the person is alleged to have committed the offence is of no consequence. The proper course is to challenge the witness while he is in the witness box, or at any rate to make it plain to him at that stage that his evidence is not accepted. In *R v Bircham* [1972] Crim LR 430, counsel for the accused was not permitted to suggest to the jury in his closing speech that the co-accused and a prosecution witness had committed the offence charged, where the allegation had not been put to either in cross-examination. In *R v Bingham* [1999] 1 WLR 598, it was held that a defendant who goes into a witness box exposes himself to cross-examination by the prosecution or any co-accused. This is true even if no evidence-in-chief is offered, or questions asked by defence counsel.

Evidence and Procedure, para. 2.6.20

Answer 4.10

Answer **B** — The prosecution or defence can apply for a summons requiring a witness to attend a magistrates' court (Magistrates' Courts Act 1980, s. 97) or the Crown Court (Criminal Procedure (Attendance of Witnesses) Act 1965, s. 2). Where appropriate, such an application can be used as a pre-emptive measure to secure the attendance of witnesses.

There are two conditions that must be satisfied before a court issues a summons:

- that the person is likely to be able to give evidence likely to be material evidence, or produce any document or thing likely to be material evidence for the purpose of any criminal proceedings, and
- that it is in the interests of justice.

Where a witness is summonsed but refuses to give evidence or to answer some question asked of them, they may be dealt with for contempt of court; answers C and D are therefore incorrect. The court has a range of powers to deal with contempt and these include imprisonment (*R v Haselden* [2000] All ER (D) 56); answer A is therefore incorrect.

Evidence and Procedure, para. 2.6.12.2

Answer 4.11

Answer **D** — Section 34 of the Youth Justice and Criminal Evidence Act 1999 states:

No person charged with a sexual offence may in any criminal proceedings crossexamine in person a witness who is the complainant ...

This means that SOUTHWELL himself cannot cross-examine the victim about any matters, and answer B is therefore incorrect. Should SOUTHWELL wish the complainant to be cross-examined, he must, or the court may, appoint a legal representative. Even when this is the case, there are restrictions on questions that can be asked of the victim. Section 41(1) states:

> If at a trial a person is charged with a sexual offence, then, except with the leave of the court —
> (a) no evidence may be adduced, and
> (b) no question may be asked in cross-examination, by or on behalf of the accused at the trial, about any sexual behaviour of the complainant.

'On behalf of' would include a legal representative, but there are exceptions, with leave of the court. Section 41(2) of the 1999 Act states:

> The court may give leave only in relation to any evidence or question only on an application made by or on behalf of an accused, and may not give such leave unless it is satisfied — ...

Section 41(3) states that:

> This subsection applies if the evidence or question relates to a relevant issue in the case and either —
> (a) that the issue is not an issue of consent; or
> (b) it is an issue of consent and the sexual behaviour of the complainant to which the evidence or question relates is alleged to have taken place at or about the same time as the event which is the subject matter of the charge against the accused ...

So in the facts of the question, consent is in issue and counsel could ask questions, with leave of the court; therefore, answer A is incorrect. The House of Lords have considered the very restrictive phraseology of s. 41(3) of the 1999 Act and a person's right to a fair trial. The overriding theme is that the test of admissibility was whether the evidence, and questioning relating to it, was nevertheless so relevant to the issue of consent that to exclude it would endanger the fairness of the trial under Article 6 of the European Convention on Human Rights. If that test were satisfied, the evidence should not be excluded (*R v A (No. 2)* [2001] UKHL 25, [2001] 3 All ER), but still must be recent; answer C is therefore incorrect.

Evidence and Procedure, paras 2.6.20.2, 2.6.20.4

Answer 4.12

Answer **B** — It is a general rule that all of the evidence on which the prosecution intend to rely should be called before the closure of their case (*R* v *Francis* [1991] 1 All ER 225). There are, however, some exceptions to this general rule, and answer D is incorrect. The three recognised exceptions are:

- evidence not previously available;
- failure to call evidence by reason of inadvertence or oversight; *and*
- evidence in rebuttal of matters arising *ex improviso* (evidence which becomes relevant in circumstances which the prosecution could not have foreseen at the time when they presented their case).

In the facts outlined in the question, only the third exception arises. The principle of *ex improviso* deals with instances where during the case for the defence issues are raised that the prosecution could not have reasonably anticipated when they presented their case. In such instances the judge can allow the prosecution to call evidence in rebuttal of the defence put forward (*R* v *Pilcher* (1974) 60 Cr App R 1). This is true whether the issue is raised during cross-examination or in evidencein-chief given by a defence witness, and answer C is therefore incorrect. The judge also has discretion to admit evidence of a formal, technical or uncontentious nature, which, by reason of inadvertence or oversight, has not been adduced by the prosecution before the close of their case. In *R* v *Francis* , the prosecution called an identification witness to give evidence that at a group identification he had identified the man standing in position number 20, but failed to call any evidence to prove that the man standing at that position was the appellant. The failure was due to a simple misunderstanding between counsel. The discretion of the judge to admit evidence after the close of the prosecution case is not limited to cases where an issue has arisen *ex improviso*, or where what has been omitted is a mere formality, and *Francis* was one of those rare cases falling outside the two established exceptions. Evidence can be adduced in circumstances where the defence do not accept there was a misunderstanding, and answer A is therefore incorrect.

Evidence and Procedure, para. 2.6.22

Answer 4.13

Answer **B** — The Youth Justice and Criminal Evidence Act 1999, s. 27 states:

(1) A special measures direction may provide for a video recording of an interview of the witness to be admitted as evidence in chief of the witness.

(2) A special measures direction may, however, not provide for a video recording, or a part of such a recording, to be admitted under this section if the court is of the opinion, having regard to all the circumstances of the case, that in the interests of justice the recording, or that part of it, should not be so admitted.

This section replaces the Criminal Justice Act 1988, s. 32A, and clearly outlines that it is not a matter of course that the court makes this direction, therefore answer A is incorrect. It is a matter for the court to decide in the light of all the available circumstances. As s. 27(2) clearly states, the direction may be given unless the court believes it would not be in the interests of justice to do so. In R (DPP) v Redbridge Youth Court [2001] 4 All ER 411, it was held that an accused could successfully oppose this order if it was established that the quality of the witness's evidence would not be affected by their appearance in court. This is the test, and not just fear or refusal to testify; therefore, answers C and D are incorrect.

Evidence and Procedure, para. 2.6.14.5

Answer 4.14

Answer **C** — The judge may allow the accused to change his plea from not guilty to guilty at any stage prior to the jury returning their verdict; answer D is therefore incorrect.

The procedure is that the defence ask for the indictment to be put again; the accused then pleads guilty, and the jury empanelled as a result of the original not guilty plea formally return a verdict. Assuming the change of plea comes after the accused has been put in the charge of a jury, the jury should be directed to return a formal verdict of guilty.

In *R* v *Heyes* [1951] 1 KB 29, the accused pleaded not guilty to charges of stealing and receiving certain property. During the opening of the prosecution case and after advice from counsel who had at that stage been allotted to him, he changed his plea to guilty of receiving. Consequently, where a jury had heard that a prisoner wishes to withdraw his plea of not guilty and admit his guilt, the proper proceeding is to direct it to return a verdict. The judge should not make any announcement of guilt, but direct the jury to return such a formal verdict; answers A and B are therefore incorrect.

Evidence and Procedure, para. 2.6.5

Answer 4.15

Answer **D** — In considering whether a witness is able to give 'intelligible testimony' the Youth Justice and Criminal Evidence Act 1999, s. 55(8) defines this as testimony where the witness is able to:

- understand questions put to him as a witness; and
- give answers to them which can be understood.

Clearly, there is no inherent reason why a person suffering from a mental condition would not make a reliable witness. In *R v Barratt* [1996] Crim LR 495, a witness was suffering from a psychiatric condition and the court considered that her evidence was as reliable as that of any other witness save for certain aspects affected by her condition. Answer A is therefore incorrect.

Witnesses suffering from a mental disorder, mental impairment or a learning disability might be allowed 'special measures' to help them with giving evidence in criminal proceedings (s. 16(2) of the 1999 Act). By s. 31 a statement made in a document (including a videotape) was admissible as evidence of any fact of which direct oral evidence by the maker would be admissible if, by reason of his bodily or mental condition, he was unfit to attend as a witness. Answer B is therefore incorrect.

Section 27 of the 1999 Act provided that the statement was not admissible without leave, which the court could not grant unless satisfied that it ought to be admitted in the interests of justice.

However, if the court does admit that evidence the jury will *not* be warned about that witness's reliability, this would be wholly inappropriate. Answer C is therefore incorrect.

Evidence and Procedure, para. 2.6.12.9

Answer 4.16

Answer **B** — Dealing first with the competence of witnesses in general the Youth Justice and Criminal Evidence Act 1999, s. 53 makes clear that the age of a witness does not determine whether he or she is competent to give evidence. It cannot therefore be said that below a particular age a witness is too young to give evidence. Rather, the test is as set out in s. 53(3) whether the witness is able:

(a) to understand the questions put to him or her; and
(b) to give answers that can be understood.

It is for the court to make a judgment on this, and age and expectations as to whether a child will be able to give intelligible evidence are not automatic disbars for a child being a competent witness; answers C and D are therefore incorrect. In *G v DPP* [1997] 2 All ER 755, 'intelligible testimony' was defined as evidence which is capable of being understood.

A child under the age of 4 years could still be a competent witness as long as they display such competency throughout the whole of their evidence (*R v P* [2006] EWCA Crim 3). In *P* the child was very young, just 3½, but the court held that was not in itself necessarily an insurmountable obstacle for the prosecution, but competency to give evidence relates to the whole of a witness's evidence and not just to part of it; answer A is therefore incorrect.

Evidence and Procedure, para. 2.6.12.7

Youth Justice and Youth Crime and Disorder

STUDY PREPARATION

Of all the areas covered by this subject, this one has probably seen the most changes over recent years. Youth justice is a central focus of the Government's overall crime and disorder strategy, and it is therefore a very important area for study.

The overall aims of the Crime and Disorder Act 1998 should be understood, along with the framework for youth justice that it introduced. Reprimands and warnings are important, as are parenting, child safety and curfew orders.

QUESTIONS

Question 5.1

The youth justice scheme is referred to under s. 37 of the Crime and Disorder Act 1998.

What is its principal aim?

A To prevent offending by children and young persons.
B To prevent disorder by children and young persons.
C To establish a separate judicial process for children and young persons.
D To establish a local strategy to support children and young persons who are offenders.

Question 5.2

The Youth Court has made an anti-social behaviour order against Patrick who is 14 years old. The court is also considering whether it should also make a parenting order under s. 9 of the Crime and Disorder Act 1998.

In relation to such a parenting order which of the following is correct?

A The court is statutorily bound to make a parenting order in these circumstances.

B The court must make a parenting order if it is satisfied that the relevant condition is fulfilled.

C The court must make a parenting order if it is satisfied that the relevant condition is fulfilled and must state in open court why it is necessary.

D The court may only make a parenting order where a person under the age of 16 is convicted of an offence by the court.

Question 5.3

LEAHY, who is a youth, pleaded guilty at Youth Court to a minor case of criminal damage. The court made a referral order to the youth offending team. A youth offender panel was formed and they are now considering making LEAHY pay for the cost of repair to the item he damaged.

Can the youth offender panel take this action?

A Yes, and this can be done without LEAHY's consent.

B Yes, provided LEAHY agrees to the proposed programme.

C No, a financial reparation cannot be ordered, but unpaid work can be considered.

D No, the only programme that can be considered is that of mediation.

Question 5.4

A magistrates' court has issued a child safety order under s. 11 of the Crime and Disorder Act 1998 against a 9-year-old child and the child's parents wish to appeal against this decision.

To where, if anywhere, can the parents appeal against the making of this child safety order?

A The Crown Court.

B The High Court.

C The Queens Bench Divisional Court.

D There is no right of appeal against the making of this child safety order.

Question 5.5

Reprimands and warnings are provided for by s. 65 of the Crime and Disorder Act 1998.

In relation to these, which of the following statements is correct?
A The victim must consent before a reprimand or warning can be given.
B A reprimand can be given provided there is evidence to support a charge.
C A warning can be given where any previous warning was more than 2 years ago.
D Where the accused is 17 years of age, the reprimand/warning must be given in the presence of an appropriate adult.

Question 5.6

A parenting order can be imposed by a court for compliance by the parent.

What is the maximum period of time for which an order can be imposed?
A 6 months.
B 12 months.
C 18 months.
D 24 months.

Question 5.7

A parenting order is being considered by the court in relation to BRIAN, who is 10 years of age and has been convicted of a theft, which took place on a Saturday. Part of this order would involve counselling sessions, and the child being escorted to school.

In relation to the proposed parenting order, which of the following statements is true?
A It cannot be made as such orders apply to a child under the age of 10 years only.
B It cannot include the child being escorted to school, as his offence was not committed on a school day.
C The magistrate should specify the amount of counselling needed.
D A member of the youth offending team should specify the amount of counselling needed.

Question 5.8

SHEILA is a particularly unruly 15-year-old, in relation to whom the courts are considering a parenting order. Owing to her misbehaviour at home, SHEILA's uncle and aunt are currently looking after her, but they have no legal guardianship.

Can a parenting order be imposed on SHEILA's uncle and aunt?

A Yes, for the time being, they are caring for SHEILA.

B Yes, provided the court's opinion is that they are caring for SHEILA.

C No, the order can be imposed on the biological parents only.

D No, as they do not have legal guardianship.

Question 5.9

ANDREW is 13 years old, and has been convicted of an offence at court. The court, however, is not satisfied that the making of a parenting order would be desirable in the interests of preventing the commission of any further offence by ANDREW.

In relation to the options the court may take regarding the parenting order, which of the following statements is true?

A The court must impose the order as ANDREW is under 16 (a young person) and has been convicted of an offence.

B The court must impose the order as ANDREW is under 14 (a child) and has been convicted of an offence.

C The court need not impose the order, but must say in open court why it is not desirable.

D The court need not impose the order as it retains a discretion not to impose an order.

Question 5.10

The Serious Organised Crime and Police Act 2005, sch. 10, inserted a new section into the Crime and Disorder Act 1998 (s.13A) for the provision of parental compensation orders where parents are ordered to pay compensation for their children's behaviour.

Which of the following is correct in relation to parental compensation orders?

A An order may be made where the child caused damage in excess of £2,500.

B An order may be made where the child caused any damage and the maximum amount of compensation is £2,500.

E   An order may be made where the child caused damage in excess of £5,000.
D   An order may be made where the child caused any damage and the maximum amount of compensation is £5,000.

Question 5.11

A child can be placed under supervision for a permitted maximum period by the imposition of a child safety order.

How long is that maximum period?
A   3 months.
B   6 months.
C   12 months.
D   15 months.

Question 5.12

The Government has introduced child curfew schemes to tackle the problem of un-supervised young children (under 10) committing crime, anti-social activities, and causing harm and misery to local communities.

If such a scheme is imposed, during what specified times must the curfew take effect?
A   9 pm to 6 am.
B   9.30 am to 6.30 pm.
C   9 pm to 7 am.
D   10 pm to 7 am.

Question 5.13

Constable MAKINS is on patrol at 11.30 pm when she finds RICHARD, who is 9 years old, in a public place. RICHARD is in breach of a child curfew scheme that has been imposed.

Which of the following statements is true in relation to Constable MAKINS?
A   She must take the child to his home and should consider informing the local authority.
B   She must take the child to his home and must inform the court which ordered the curfew.
C   She may take the child to his home and must inform the local authority.

D She may take the child to his home and must inform the court which ordered the curfew.

Question 5.14

An anti-social behaviour order can be applied for in relation to youth justice and youth offending.

At what age must a person be before such an order can be sought against them?
A 10 years of age.
B 11 years of age.
C 14 years of age.
D 17 years of age.

Question 5.15

Truants may be removed to designated premises.

Which rank of police officer is responsible for instigating this power?
A At least the rank of inspector.
B At least the rank of chief inspector.
C At least the rank of superintendent.
D At least the rank of inspector, provided they are responsible for crime and disorder.

Question 5.16

An authority to remove truants to designated premises is in effect and Constable JONES found TREGERT, who is of compulsory school age, absent from school with no lawful authority.

What should Constable JONES do?
A TREGERT must be returned to his own school.
B TREGERT must be returned to any school in the local education authority.
C TREGERT can be returned to any place the local authority has nominated.
D TREGERT can be returned to any place the local education authority has nominated.

ANSWERS

Answer 5.1

Answer **A** — One of the functions of the Crime and Disorder Act 1998 is the prevention of disorder by all manner of people, not just children and young persons. There are specific sections which deal with disorder by children and young persons, but s. 37 is not one of those, and answer B is therefore incorrect. Section 37(1) of the Crime and Disorder Act 1998 states:

> It shall be the principal aim of the youth justice system to prevent offending by children and young persons.

Answers C and D are therefore incorrect.

Evidence and Procedure, para. 2.7.2

Answer 5.2

Answer **B** — Parenting orders are about influencing parental responsibility and control. The orders were introduced to give parents more help and support to change the criminal and/or anti-social behaviour of their children in providing a framework where parents participate in their child's supervision. The strategy here is one of prevention in attempting to dissuade a recurrence of criminality or truancy.

Section 9(1) of the Crime and Disorder Act 1998 provides a statutory requirement in favour of making an order where the relevant condition relates to where a child or young person (under 16) is convicted of an offence, a similar duty, and similar exception, applies where the offender has been made subject to an anti-social behaviour order (s. 9(1B)); answer D is therefore incorrect.

There is no statutory binding on the court to make an order, only where the relevant conditions apply can an order be made; answer A is therefore incorrect.

If the court is not so satisfied that an order should be made, it shall state in open court that it is not and why not. This exception is where the court does not consider a parenting order necessary, not where it does deem such an order appropriate; answer C is therefore incorrect.

Evidence and Procedure, para. 2.8.2.4

Answer 5.3

Answer **B** — Sections 23 to 27 of the Powers of Criminal Courts (Sentencing) Act 2000 deal with youth offender contracts. This is a programme of behaviour to prevent re-offending, but it has to be agreed between the offender and the panel (s. 23(5)), and therefore answer A is incorrect. The terms of the programme may include a number of provisions; attendance at mediation sessions is one of them, but is by no means exclusive, and answer D is therefore incorrect. The measures can include unpaid work or service, in addition to financial or other reparation to the victim, and therefore answer C is incorrect.

Evidence and Procedure, para. 2.7.3.1

Answer 5.4

Answer **B** — There is an appeal process for when a child safety order is imposed; answer D is therefore incorrect. The right of appeal is to the High Court against a magistrates' court making a child safety order (s. 13(1) of the Crime and Disorder Act 1998); answers A and C are therefore incorrect.

Evidence and Procedure, para. 2.8.3

Answer 5.5

Answer **C** — Although a reprimand or warning under s. 65 of the Crime and Disorder Act 1998 requires the consent of the offender (s. 65(1)(c)), it does not require the consent of the victim. The victim effectively has no say in the course of action the police take, and answer A is therefore incorrect (a decision not to prosecute is susceptible to judicial review however).

The evidence available must do more than support a charge and must be at a level where there is a reasonable prospect of the child or young person being convicted of the offence, and therefore answer B is incorrect. The presence of an appropriate adult is necessary only where the offender is *under* the age of 17, and answer D is therefore incorrect. Note that a second warning is available only after a 2-year gap. A second warning is available only once; if, after another 2-year gap, the offender committed another offence, he or she would not qualify for a warning.

Evidence and Procedure, para. 2.7.6.3

Answer 5.6

Answer **B** — Under s. 8 of the Crime and Disorder Act 1998, a parenting order lasts for a period not exceeding 12 months, and answers A, C and D are therefore incorrect.

Evidence and Procedure, para. 2.8.2

Answer 5.7

Answer **D** — A parenting order can be imposed on a child or young person. For the purposes of the Crime and Disorder Act 1998, 'child' is someone under the age of 14 and 'young person' is someone of 14 years or over but under 18 (s. 117), and answer A is therefore incorrect. A parenting order is defined by s. 8(4)(a) as an order which requires the parent 'to comply, for a period not exceeding twelve months, with such requirements as are specified in the order'. The requirements provided by s. 8(4)(a) above are not specified, but in drafting the legislation certain examples were given. These included a parent escorting their child to school and a child being supervised by a responsible adult during the evenings (answer B is therefore incorrect). The counselling is defined in s. 8(4)(b) as 'to attend for a concurrent period not exceeding three months and not more than once in any week, such counselling and guidance sessions as may be specified in directions given by the responsible officer'. The responsible officer can be an officer of a local probation board, a social worker of a local authority social services department, a person nominated by a person appointed as chief education officer (under s. 532 of the Education Act 1996) and a member of a youth offending team; answer C is therefore incorrect.

Evidence and Procedure, para. 2.8.2

Answer 5.8

Answer **B** — Under s. 8(2) of the Crime and Disorder Act 1998, a parenting order may be made against:

- one or both biological parents (this could include an order against a father who may not be married to the mother);
- a person who is a guardian.

Therefore, answer C is incorrect.

A guardian is defined as any person who, in the opinion of the court, has for the time being the care of a child or young person (s. 117(1)). It is not a matter of 'legal' guardianship, as the court will decide who is *in fact* a 'guardian'; therefore, answer D is incorrect. For the same reason, answer A is also incorrect.

Evidence and Procedure, para. 2.8.2.3

Answer 5.9

Answer **C** — In relation to parenting orders, the court will be required to establish whether or not the making of such an order is 'desirable' in the circumstances of a particular case. This is seen as an entirely subjective test and the court generally retains discretion not to impose an order. Section 9(1)(a) of the Crime and Disorder Act 1998, however, provides a statutory requirement in favour of making an order (unless the court makes a referral order) where the relevant condition relates to where a child or young person (under 16) is convicted of an offence; therefore, answer D is incorrect. If, however, the court is not satisfied that the 'relevant condition' is fulfilled (i.e. that the making of a parenting order would be desirable in the interests of preventing the commission of any further offence by the child or young person under 16), the court must state in open court that it is not so satisfied, and why it is not. There is then some limited discretion where s. 9(1)(a) applies, and therefore answers A and B are incorrect.

Evidence and Procedure, paras 2.8.2.3, 2.8.2.4

Answer 5.10

Answer **D** — Section 13A of the Crime and Disorder Act 1998 Act states:

(1) A magistrates' court may make an order under this section (a "parental compensation order") if on the application of a local authority it is satisfied, on the civil standard of proof —

  (a) that the condition mentioned in subsection (2) below is fulfilled with respect to a child under the age of 10; and

  (b) that it would be desirable to make the order in the interests of preventing a repetition of the behaviour in question.

(2) The condition is that the child has taken, or caused loss of or damage to, property in the course of —

  (a) committing an act which, if he had been aged 10 or over, would have constituted an offence; or

  (b) acting in a manner that caused or was likely to cause harassment, alarm or distress to one or more persons not of the same household as himself.

So where a child under 10 years of age commits an offence which would in effect be an offence contrary to the Criminal Damage Act 1971, their parents could face paying compensation under the parental compensation scheme. There is no value on the amount of damage caused; answers A and C are therefore incorrect. The amount of compensation specified cannot exceed £5,000 in all (s. 13A(4)); answer B is therefore incorrect. Collection and enforcement conditions are the same as if the parent had been convicted of an offence (s. 13A(6)).

Note that this section, at the time of writing, is not yet in force.

Evidence and Procedure, para. 2.8.6

Answer 5.11

Answer **C** — The permitted maximum period of supervision of a child safety order is 12 months.(s. 11(4) of the Crime and Disorder Act 1998). Therefore answers B, C and D are incorrect.

Evidence and Procedure, para. 2.8.3.1

Answer 5.12

Answer **A** — Section 14(2)(a) of the Crime and Disorder Act 1998 states that a curfew will be 'during specified hours (between 9 pm and 6 am)'. Therefore, answers B, C and D are incorrect.

Evidence and Procedure, para. 2.8.5

Answer 5.13

Answer **C** — Section 14 of the Crime and Disorder Act 1998 states that it is a local authority, in liaison with the Secretary of State (who needs to confirm it), that makes a child curfew scheme. Therefore, as the courts do not impose a curfew, they do not need to be informed of a breach, and answers B and D are incorrect.

If there has been a contravention of a curfew notice, s. 15 of the 1998 Act states:

(2) The constable shall, as soon as practicable, inform the local authority for the area that the child has contravened the ban.

(3) The constable may remove the child to the child's place of residence unless he has reasonable cause to believe that the child would, if removed to that place, be likely to suffer significant harm.

Informing the local authority who imposed the scheme is mandatory; but taking the child home is not, and therefore answer A is incorrect.

Section 15(3) does not state what a constable should do with a child if he or she does not remove the child to its home. However, it would seem appropriate to use the power under s. 46 of the Children Act 1989 in removing the child to suitable accommodation, i.e. a police station or into the care of social services.

Evidence and Procedure, para. 2.8.5.1

Answer 5.14

Answer **A** — An anti-social behaviour order (ASBO) is defined by s. 1 of the Crime and Disorder Act 1998, and s. 1(1) outlines that:

(1) An application for an order under this section may be made by a relevant authority if it appears to the authority that the following conditions are fulfilled with respect to any person aged 10 or over ...

The person must, then, be 10 years of age; answers B, C and D are incorrect. Note that this age is consistent with the abolition of *doli incapax*, the rebuttable presumption of criminal law that a child aged 10 or over is incapable of committing an offence, as prescribed by s. 34 of the 1998 Act.

Evidence and Procedure, para. 2.8.4

Answer 5.15

Answer **C** — Section 16 of the Crime and Disorder Act 1998 provides that a police officer of or above the rank of superintendent may instigate the power conferred on a constable to remove the child or young person to designated premises. Answers A, B and D are therefore incorrect. Although it is increasingly common for officers to be responsible for crime and disorder issues in their locality, this has not reduced the authorising rank for this power.

Evidence and Procedure, para. 2.8.7

Answer 5.16

Answer **C** — A local authority is under an obligation by s. 16 of the Crime and Disorder Act 1998 to designate premises in a police area ('designated premises') as premises to which children and young persons of compulsory school age may be removed under this section, and they must notify the chief officer of police for that area of the designation. When an order to remove truants has been issued, if a constable has reasonable cause to believe that a child or young person found by him in a public place in a specified area during a specified period:

- is of compulsory school age; *and*
- is absent from a school without lawful authority,

the constable may remove the child or young person to designated premises, or to the school from which he is absent. He does not *have* to be returned to either his own school, or another school in the local education authority area, so answers A and B are therefore incorrect. Provided a particular place has been designated (or nominated) by the local authority, the child may be returned there. Note, it is the local authority who designates, not the local education authority; answer D is therefore incorrect.

Evidence and Procedure, paras 2.8.7, 2.8.7.1

6 | Sentencing

STUDY PREPARATION

Sentencing of offenders is a complicated business, and frequently subject to appeal and legal challenge. Aggravating factors and mitigating factors have to be considered. The Criminal Justice Act 2003 has introduced the concept of adult sentencing being set out in statute, namely: punishment, crime reduction, the reform and rehabilitation of offenders, public protection, and reparation. These purposes will not apply to offenders under 18 years of age, where the sentence is fixed by law, where offences require certain custodial sentences, and where provisions under the Mental Health Act 1983 apply. This chapter deals with only the parts of the corresponding chapter in the *Blackstone's Police Manual* that are included in the national examination syllabus.

QUESTIONS

Question 6.1

Short-term prisoners on home curfew are subject to a specific period of curfew.

In relation to that period, which of the following is true?

A The minimum period is nine hours and there is no maximum.

B The minimum period is nine hours and the maximum is 12 hours.

C The minimum period is 12 hours and there is no maximum.

D The minimum period is 10 hours and the maximum is 12 hours.

Question 6.2

GRIFFITHS pleaded guilty at magistrates' court in relation to possession of drugs. She had provided the prosecution with information that helped prosecute a drug supplier and is looking to have a reduction in sentence for her assistance in catching the drug supplier.

In relation to this which of the following is correct?

A A reduction in sentence will be given if there is a written agreement with a specified prosecutor.

B A reduction can be given, but GRIFFITHS will have to be sent to Crown Court for sentencing.

C A reduction cannot be given as the offence for which GRIFFITHS gave assistance is not connected to the offence she was charged with.

D A reduction cannot be given as this relates to where a defendant pleads guilty in the Crown Court.

Question 6.3

A compulsory referral order can be made in accordance with the Powers of Criminal Courts (Sentencing) Act 2000, s. 17(1).

In which of the following circumstances should such an order be made?

A Offender is charged with an imprisonable offence, pleads not guilty and is subsequently convicted.

B Offender is charged with a non-imprisonable offence, and pleads guilty to it.

C Offender is charged with an imprisonable offence and pleads guilty it.

D Offender is charged with a non-imprisonable offence, pleads not guilty and is subsequently convicted.

Question 6.4

Brian is 14 years old, and is appearing in youth court for an offence of theft. He has one previous conviction for criminal damage. The court is considering a referral order (the Powers of Criminal Courts (Sentencing) Act 2000).

Which of the following is true?

A A referral order can be made, and his parents can, if the court wishes, be required to attend meetings of the youth offender panel.

B A referral order can be made, although he has a previous conviction it is not a 'like' offence.

C A referral order can be made, and his parents can be ordered to attend meetings of the youth offender panel.

D A referral order cannot be made as Brian has a previous conviction.

Question 6.5

Community orders made under the Criminal Justice Act 2003, s. 177 can impose certain requirements on an offender.

In relation to alcohol treatment requirements, which of the following is correct?
A The offender must get treatment to reduce or eliminate their alcohol dependency for a period of at least six months.
B The offender must get treatment to reduce or eliminate their alcohol dependency for a period of at least 12 months.
C The offender must get treatment to reduce or eliminate their alcohol dependency for a period of at least six months, and the offender must be willing to submit to treatment.
D The offender must get treatment to reduce or eliminate their alcohol dependency for a period of at least 12 months, and the offender must be willing to submit to treatment.

Question 6.6

SMITHSON has been released from prison and is subject to a home-detention curfew. He is arrested for an offence of theft and is taken before the local custody officer.

What action should the custody officer now take?
A Inform HM Prison Service Parole Unit and ask them to attend and collect the prisoner.
B Inform HM Prison Service Parole Unit and seek their directions on SMITHSON's disposal.
C Inform HM Prison Service Parole Unit and deal with the prisoner as normal, but he is not entitled to bail.
D Inform HM Prison Service Parole Unit and deal with the prisoner as normal.

Question 6.7

GOLLINGS is on a home-detention curfew, and is seen by Constable ROBINS in the early hours in breach of his curfew.

What action should Constable ROBINS take?
A Arrest GOLLINS and take him to the nearest HM Prison.
B Arrest GOLLINS and take him to the custody officer.
C Follow local policy as there is no power to arrest GOLLINS.

D Request HM Prison Service Parole Unit to revoke GOLLINS's licence. There is no power of arrest.

Question 6.8

McDONAGH has been convicted at Crown Court for an offence of theft by shoplifting. The Court passes a community order which includes an exclusion order prohibiting McDONAGH from entering the city centre area on Saturdays between 8 am and 8 pm. A few weeks later McDONAGH is seen in the city centre at 2.30 pm by Constable DEW.

What action should the officer now take?

A The officer can only warn the offender that she has failed without reasonable excuse to comply with any of the requirements of the order and inform the offender that if there is a reoccurrence within the next 12 months she will be liable to be taken back before the court.

B The officer must tell the offender that she has failed without reasonable excuse to comply with any of the requirements of the order and take her immediately back before the court.

C The officer should direct McDONAGH to leave the area immediately and warn her that failure to do so is a specific offence.

D The officer should arrest the offender for failing to comply with the community order.

ANSWERS

Answer 6.1

Answer **A** — Release of short-term prisoners subject to home curfew is provided by s. 253 of the Criminal Justice Act 2003.

The home-detention curfew is set up for a prisoner to complete their sentence and runs for a minimum period of 14 days and a maximum period of 60 days. The prisoner is required to agree to the curfew conditions. The governor at the relevant prison determines the details of the curfew. This will normally be from 7 pm to 7 am and may be varied. The minimum period of curfew is nine hours but there is no maximum. This leaves option A as the correct answer; answers B, C and D are therefore incorrect.

Evidence and Procedure, para. 2.9.2.17

Answer 6.2

Answer **B** — The Serious Organised Crime and Police Act 2005 has introduced a statutory framework where some form of dispensation in relation to proceedings or sentencing may apply to those offenders who provide assistance in investigations and prosecutions. One of these is that when determining what sentence to pass on the defendant the court may take into account the extent and nature of the assistance given or offered.

However this only applies where a defendant pleads guilty in the Crown Court, or is sent to that Court for sentence (s. 73(1) and (2)). Although there has to be a written agreement with a specified prosecutor for the court to consider a reduction, it is not automatic that a reduction will be given; answer A is therefore incorrect.

The legislation does not specify that the assistance given relates to the charge the defendant actually faces before a reduction can be considered; answer C is therefore incorrect.

Evidence and Procedure, para. 2.9.2.18

Answer 6.3

Answer **C** — Referral orders were introduced to tackle offending behaviour and its causes. In certain circumstances, a youth court (and in exceptional circumstances an adult magistrates' court) is required to sentence a young offender by ordering them to be referred to a youth offender panel. Section 16 of the Powers of Criminal Courts (Sentencing) Act 2000 provides the circumstances which must exist before the court is required to make a referral order and states:

(1) This section applies where a youth court or other magistrates' court is dealing with a person aged under 18 for an offence and —
  (a) neither the offence nor any connected offence is one for which the sentence is fixed by law;
  (b) the court is not, in respect of the offence or any connected offence, proposing to impose a custodial sentence on the offender or make a hospital order (within the meaning of the Mental Health Act 1983) in his case; and
  (c) the court is not proposing to discharge him absolutely in respect of the offence.
(2) If —
  (a) the compulsory referral conditions are satisfied in accordance with section 17 below, and
  (b) referral is available to the court,
the court shall sentence the offender for the offence by ordering him to be referred to a youth offending panel.

Section 17 states:

(1) For the purposes of section 16(2) above the compulsory referral conditions are satisfied in relation to an offence if the offence is an offence punishable with imprisonment and the offender —
  (a) pleaded guilty to the offence and to any connected offence;
  (b) has never been convicted by or before a court in the United Kingdom of any offence other than the offence and any connected offence; and
  (c) has never been bound over in criminal proceedings in England and Wales or Northern Ireland to keep the peace or to be of good behaviour.

So compulsory referral orders can only be given in relation to imprisonable offences (Referral Orders (Amendment of Referral Conditions) Regulations 2003 (SI 2003/1605)), therefore answers B and D are incorrect, and the offender has to plead guilty to the offence, so answer A is also incorrect.

Evidence and Procedure, para. 2.9.4.5

Answer 6.4

Answer **D** — Referral orders are available for an offender under the age of 18 years but only on his/her first conviction, for any offence — therefore answer B is incorrect. A conditional discharge in relation to a previous offence does count as a conviction (s. 17(5)).

The referral order will specify the youth offending team responsible for implementing the order and the period during which the contract is to have effect. The minimum period of an order is three months and the maximum is 12 months (s. 18(1)).

Where an offender is being dealt with for associated offences, more than one referral order can be made and their compliance periods can run concurrently or consecutively, but must not exceed 12 months (s. 18(6)).

A court making a referral order may make an order requiring the attendance of parents or another appropriate person at meetings of the youth offender panel. Where the offender is under 16 years of age, the making of such an order is compulsory, not at the court's discretion. Answer A is therefore incorrect (s. 20(1) and (2)). However, as he has previous convictions this compulsory order is superfluous and a referral order cannot be made, therefore answer C is incorrect.

Evidence and Procedure, para. 2.9.4.5

Answer 6.5

Answer **C** — Community orders will be provided by s. 177 of the 2003 Act, which will allow the courts to sentence a person aged 16 years or over, where convicted of an offence, to a 'community order' and impose on them certain conditions. One of the listed conditions is an alcohol-treatment requirement. This means a requirement that the offender must submit, during a period specified in the order, to treatment by, or under the direction of, a specified person having the necessary qualifications or experience with a view to the reduction or elimination of the offender's dependency on alcohol. However, the offender must willingly submit to treatment and the period of treatment be not less than six months. So they must willingly attend for six months, and answers A, B and D are therefore incorrect.

Evidence and Procedure, para. 2.9.4.1

Answer 6.6

Answer **D** — The guidance provided to police forces in relation to persons who are subject to a home-detention curfew, and subsequently arrested for other offences is as follows:

Where arrested:
custody officer to notify the monitoring contractor immediately of:

- details of the prisoner,

- details of the offence,
- whether the prisoner is to be bailed or retained in custody,
- whether the prisoner continues to wear the electronic tag,
- custody officer to notify the monitoring contractor when the prisoner is released.

Where charged:

- custody officer to immediately inform HM Prison Service Parole Unit,
- custody officer to inform contractor if the prisoner is to be returned to prison,
- custody officer to remove and collect the monitoring unit.

Where a person is charged with an offence whilst subject to a home-detention curfew, the PACE Code C in relation to detention following charge continues to apply. The question of bail is not affected by their curfew breach, and answer C is therefore incorrect. The custody officer is responsible for their treatment and disposal, not the prison service, therefore answers A and B are incorrect. Note, this is an arrest for an offence, and is a separate issue from that of the enforcing of his home-detention curfew.

Evidence and Procedure, para. 2.9.2.17

Answer 6.7

Answer **C** — Any reports of a breach of curfew are to be made to HM Prison Service Parole Unit. This Unit may make a decision to revoke or vary the curfew order. The relevant prison governor may also make variations to the order. There is no power to arrest any person solely found breaching his/her curfew, as no actual offence has been committed and local policy should be followed, therefore answers A and B are incorrect. Where the police consider that a prisoner subject to a home-detention curfew represents a serious risk to the public, they may make a request for the curfew order to be revoked. Any such request should be authorised by an officer of the rank of superintendent or above and made to HM Prison Service Parole Unit at the Home Office. So the constable cannot seek revocation of the licence directly herself, and answer D is therefore incorrect.

Evidence and Procedure, para. 2.9.2.17

Answer 6.8

Answer **C** — The court can give an offender a community order as provided by the Criminal Justice Act 2003. There are various different formats that this order can take, and one of those is an Exclusion Requirement (s. 205) which is a provision prohibiting the offender from entering a place specified in the order for a specified period, this period being no more than two years. The order may specify different places for different periods or days.

Breaching an order is not a specific offence in itself, therefore even with the amended power of arrest given by s. 24 of the Police and Criminal Evidence Act 1984 the officer cannot arrest McDONAGH; answer D is therefore incorrect.

Initially the responsible officer is under a duty to warn the offender that he/she has failed without reasonable excuse to comply with any of the requirements of the order. They must describe the circumstances of the failure, state that it is unacceptable and inform the offender that if there is a reoccurrence within the next 12 months he/she will be liable to be taken back before the court (sch. 8, para. 5).Where the offender again breaches the order the responsible officer is required to lay an information before the issuing court. The court may then issue a summons or warrant to bring the offender back before the court to be dealt with (sch. 8, paras 6 and 7). There is no power for the officer to take McDONAGH back before the court on this occasion; answer B is therefore incorrect.

Although clearly the officer should warn McDONAGH answer A states that she can **only** give out this warning, and for this reason answer A is incorrect. The officer has power under s. 112 of the Serious Organised Crime and Police Act 2005 to direct a person to leave a place which they are prohibited from entering by virtue of the requirement (s. 112(1)). If a person contravenes such a direction they are guilty of an offence (s. 112(5)).

Evidence and Procedure, para. 2.9.4.1

7 | Evidence and Similar Fact Evidence

STUDY PREPARATION

The subject matter covered in this chapter is at the heart of the whole area of evidence and procedure. Most of this chapter is concerned with the fundamentals — what type of evidence can be given by whom to show what. There is a fair amount of complex law in this part, and unfortunately it has to be separated and assimilated.

It is critical to understand the issues of weight and admissibility. It is also critical to understand the different standards of proof, civil and criminal — the latter because it is the only way in which you can prove any criminal liability and the former because it is relevant to issues that the defendant may have to prove. The standard of proof is different from the burden of proof (although they are closely linked), and again it is important to know where the relevant burden lies.

Documentary evidence is increasingly relied upon in criminal trials and this area needs attention.

A further area of great practical importance is the legislation that sets out when adverse inferences can be drawn from silences or failure by the defendant to mention certain things. These are often confused, with some officers getting the various components mixed up; decided cases help to decipher when inferences may and may not be drawn.

QUESTIONS

Question 7.1

YEMAN was jointly charged with CUSACK with burglary. YEMAN has previously pleaded guilty and is about to give evidence for the prosecution at CUSACK's trial.

In relation to YEMAN's previous convictions at what point should they be disclosed to the jury?

A Prior to giving evidence, unless the defence objects.

B Prior to giving evidence, unless the prosecution objects.

C After giving evidence, unless the defence objects.

D After giving evidence, unless the prosecution objects.

Question 7.2

CAMPBELL was stopped by police officers and lawfully searched. The officers found 6.79g of heroin and £200 cash, and CAMPBELL was arrested for possession of a Class A drug with intent to supply. During his audio-recorded interview, and acting on his solicitor's advice, he made no comment to any of the questions asked. At the conclusion he gave the officers a prepared statement in which he accepted possession of the drugs for his own use, and stated the £200 was obtained by selling designer shirts. At his trial during his evidence in chief he stated the £200 was from the sale of designer sunglasses.

Will adverse inferences be drawn from his refusal to answer questions during the police interviews?

A No inferences can be drawn as he was acting on solicitor's advice.

B No inferences can be drawn as he gave evidence at court.

C Inferences can be drawn because he refused to answer questions and handed in a prepared statement.

D Inferences may be drawn because his evidence-in-chief was inconsistent with the statement.

Question 7.3

DE MARCO is on trial at Crown Court on a charge of theft. The prosecution are aware that she has previous convictions for perjury and perverting the course of justice; on both occasions she lied to the police and the courts.

In relation to this tendency to be untruthful, at what point may these previous convictions be brought to the jury's attention?

A Only where the prosecution believe her case is fictitious.

B Only where it would help explain to the jury that she is a dishonest person.

C Only where she tries to indicate that she has no previous convictions.

D Only where the defence suggests a prosecution witness is untruthful.

Question 7.4

Detective Constable GARDNER has been investigating a complicated fraud. A large amount of evidence has been obtained, all of which is admissible. Detective Constable GARDNER has, however, heard that the judge can exclude evidence, even though it is admissible.

In relation to this, which of the following statements is true?

A The trial judge always has the discretion to exclude any evidence tendered by the prosecution.

B The trial judge has discretion to exclude evidence, but only when so requested by the defence.

C The trial judge has discretion to exclude evidence only where s. 78 of the Police and Criminal Evidence Act 1984 has been clearly breached.

D The trial judge has no discretion to exclude legally admissible evidence.

Question 7.5

PREECE has been arrested for an offence of burglary and requests PARSONS, a solicitor, to advise him. PARSONS advises PREECE not to answer questions during the interview, and PREECE takes this advice. During PREECE's trial, the prosecution allege that the defence have manufactured a story that is not true since the interview, and ask for inferences to be drawn from the silence during the interview.

What evidence can PREECE adduce to counter this submission?

A He may call his solicitor to give evidence to rebut this allegation, and the solicitor must give evidence if so called.

B He may give evidence to rebut this allegation, but may not call his solicitor.

C He may not give evidence to rebut this allegation, but his solicitor can give such evidence if he or she agrees to do so.

D No evidence can be given to rebut this allegation as the advice is covered by legal privilege.

Question 7.6

ASQUITH is on trial for an offence of rape, and has been sworn to give evidence. Prosecuting counsel asks him, 'It is true, is it not, that you did have sexual intercourse with Miss DAVIES, and at that time you clearly knew that she did not consent?' ASQUITH remains silent, and refuses to answer the question.

Will the jury be entitled to draw any inferences from ASQUITH's refusal to answer this question?

A No, ASQUITH has a right not to incriminate himself and inferences may not be drawn.

B No, the prosecution have no right to ask such questions, and inferences may not be drawn.

C Yes, ASQUITH has refused without good cause to answer the question, and inferences may be drawn.

D Yes, and the inferences drawn from this refusal would be enough to convict.

Question 7.7

Constable NICHOLS is giving evidence at the trial of BRIDGES, who is charged with a drink driving offence. Constable NICHOLS has been asked to explain the workings of the breath test device, which she does. She is then asked to produce the device, as real evidence, to the court for inspection.

In relation to Constable NICHOLS, which of the following statements is correct?

A She must produce the actual device used to carry out the test or her oral evidence may be adversely affected.

B Failure to produce the actual device used will adversely affect the evidence obtained on the machine.

C She may produce a similar device, as there is no requirement to produce the actual device used.

D Failure to produce the actual or a similar device will have no adverse affect on her oral evidence.

Question 7.8

FLYNN was the driver of a vehicle involved in a fatal road traffic collision, he was also taken to hospital where he refused to carry out a hospital procedure as set out by s. 9 of the Road Traffic Act 1988 as he has a fear of needles. He was arrested for causing death by dangerous driving and interviewed when deemed fit. Acting on solicitor's advice he remained silent to the limited questions asked. Following extensive investigation where several witnesses claim FLYNN had drunk copious amounts of alcohol and was driving in excess of 90 mph at the time of the collision he was again interviewed three months after the collision. Again acting on solicitor's advice he remained silent. At his trial FLYNN gave evidence that he had drunk very little alcohol and was driving within the speed limit. His counsel argued that no inferences could be drawn on his silence at the first interview due to lack of evidence disclosed by the police to him and no inferences could be drawn on his silence on the second interview as it should not have been held as the police had at that time sufficient evidence to charge.

In relation to whether inferences could be drawn from his silence during his two interviews which of the following is correct?

A No inferences from first interview as the solicitor advised silence due to lack of disclosure of evidence by the police.

B No inferences from second interview only because the second interview should not have been held; he should have been charged.

C No inferences drawn from either due to lack of disclosure of evidence and that no second interview should have been held; he should have been charged.

D Inferences could be drawn from both interviews as they were both properly conducted.

Question 7.9

CALLARD has been summonsed for an offence of failing to conform to a red light at automatic traffic signals. Her defence is that the traffic signals were not working properly at the time she allegedly drove through the red light.

Which of the following statements is true?

A The prosecution must prove beyond all reasonable doubt that the lights were working correctly.

B The defence must prove beyond all reasonable doubt that the lights were *not* working correctly.

C The prosecution must prove on the balance of probabilities that the lights were working correctly.

D The defence must prove on the balance of probabilities that the lights were *not* working correctly.

Question 7.10

Doctor LANFORD has been charged with two, separate indecent assaults on female patients, where he touched their breasts in an indecent and unwanted manner. One patient was receiving a vaginal examination; the other had an in-growing toe-nail. Both women state that the doctor used unusual and offensive language during the assaults. The doctor admits he carried out the medical examinations, but denies indecently assaulting either patient.

Will the evidence of each patient be admitted to corroborate the allegation of the other?

A No, as neither patient witnessed the other's incident.

B No, as the reasons for their medical examinations differed.

C Yes, the evidence is likely to be admitted as similar fact evidence.

D Yes, it is not hearsay and any oral statement made by the accused is admissible as evidence.

Question 7.11

HYDE was the victim of a serious sexual assault and she is alleging that WILSON raped her. There are no witnesses to the incident and no physical evidence. There is, however, substantial circumstantial evidence. WILSON has denied being the perpetrator, but has been charged and will appear at the Crown Court.

In relation to corroboration, which of the following statements is true?

A In this case corroboration is required in law.

B Although corroboration is not required, the judge must give a corroboration warning to the jury.

C In this case corroboration is not required at all.

D Although corroboration is not required, the judge may choose to give a corroboration warning to the jury.

Question 7.12

PHILLIPS is a paedophile who commits homosexual acts with young boys. Following a complaint from one boy, PHILLIPS is arrested and charged. His *modus operandi* is to sit the boys on the floor and then dance around them wearing a doctor's white coat and carrying a stethoscope, prior to requiring the boys to perform oral sex on him. The investigation reveals that there are five other victims who were assaulted in this way, but no charges were made.

Can the five boys give evidence of what happened to them at the trial for the offence PHILLIPS is now charged with?

A No, it is evidence of bad character and would not be allowed.

B No, because PHILLIPS was never charged in relation to those boys.

C Yes, as the striking similarity rule applies.

D Yes, the evidence of the five boys is corroboration that the offence charged took place.

Question 7.13

BURNS is charged with an offence of murder. The circumstances are that he allowed a man, GREY, whom he had met in a nightclub, to stay at his house. At some point a fight took place and GREY was fatally stabbed by BURNS. In his defence, BURNS has given sworn evidence that he stabbed GREY as a last resort to fight off his continued sexual advances. BURNS adduces evidence that he finds homosexuality repugnant. To rebut this, the prosecution wish to introduce BURNS's previous convictions; one for buggery with a man, and two for gross indecency in men's public toilets (both offences pre-dating the Sexual Offences Act 2003).

Is the judge likely to allow this evidence to be adduced?

A No, the previous convictions have nothing in common with the offence charged.

B No, as homosexuality is not 'misconduct' and as such is not a propensity to commit misconduct.

C Yes, as this is a matter in issue between the defendant and the prosecution.

D Yes, this will allow the jury to have a clear picture of the defendant and help understand the case.

Question 7.14

CHILDS has been charged with conspiracy to defraud, and an investigation is in progress. The fraud squad has discovered that CHILDS used to send pager messages to a contact in Switzerland. This was done by contacting the pager company, who wrote down the message on a pad and then transmitted it electronically. Some of these messages show CHILDS was involved in fraud; however, the operator of the machine had no knowledge of whether the messages were true or not.

Is it likely that the written message pad could be tendered as evidence in a 'business document' under s. 117 of the Criminal Justice Act 2003?

A Yes, it fits the relevant criteria and would be admitted.

B No, the person who made the document has to know the truth of its contents.

C Yes, provided the witness was unavailable to attend court.

D No, as CHILDS is not the maker of the document it is inadmissible.

Question 7.15

Non-expert witnesses, in certain cases, can give evidence of opinion to the court.

In relation to this, which of the following statements is true?

A Only police officers may give evidence that in their opinion a person is drunk.

B Police officers may identify prohibited drugs only if they are specially trained to do so.

C Police officers can give their opinion as to the speed of a moving vehicle.

D Non-expert witnesses can give only the estimated price of an antique piece of furniture.

Question 7.16

TURNER has been charged with an offence of forgery. He intends to call a handwriting expert to rebut the prosecution evidence at his trial at the Crown Court.

Which of the following statements is true?

A The defence do not have to provide pre-trial disclosure to the prosecution on this matter.

B The defence must allow the prosecution to consider whether the witness is competent to give expert opinion.

C The defence must furnish the prosecution with a summary of the evidence the expert will give.

D The defence must furnish the prosecution with a statement, in writing, of the expert's finding.

Question 7.17

RIDLEY was a witness in a murder trial, and is well known to both co-accused. The defendants had, through an intermediary, arranged to 'warn off' RIDLEY's wife about giving evidence against them. RIDLEY fears for his wife's safety and refuses to attend court and give evidence in person. The prosecution wish to have RIDLEY's statement read out in court instead of him appearing personally.

In relation to this which of the following is correct?

A The statement cannot be read out as it is the defendant's right to examine witnesses against them under the Human Rights Act 1998, sch. 1 part I art. 6(3)(d).

B The statement cannot be read out, as the threat that caused the fear was not made to the witness directly.

C The statement can be read out and the evidence is treated as if it had been given in person.

D The statement can be read out, however the jury should be warned that it should exercise caution in accepting the hearsay evidence.

Question 7.18

HINDSON is suspected of being involved in the distribution of internet child pornography. During his police interviews he states that he is a lay preacher and could not be involved in child pornography. HINDSON is charged and is appearing at the Crown Court; he turns up in clerical collar and is sitting in the dock. The police are aware that he was not ordained as a priest, and is not a lay preacher. HINDMAN is not going to give evidence himself at the trial.

In relation to HINDSON portraying himself as a religious person, which of the following is correct?

A The jury can be made aware that the way he is dressed is giving a false impression.

B The jury can be made aware that the way he is dressed is giving a false impression *and* that he lied about it during interview.

C The jury can be made aware that he lied about being a lay preacher during interview.

D The jury cannot be made aware of this portrayal as he is not going to give evidence in court that he is a lay preacher.

Question 7.19

BUTLER stands charged with the rape of two women. In both cases, whilst being driven in BUTLER's car, the women were forced to take part in oral intercourse to the point of ejaculation. The women were then taken to a wooded area and raped. BUTLER's ex-girlfriend is willing to give evidence that, albeit by consent, she regularly performed oral intercourse in the car and then went to a wooded area and had sexual intercourse with him. BUTLER's defence is that of mistaken identity.

Is it likely that the ex-girlfriend will be allowed to give this evidence?

A No, as what took place with her was not an offence; it would not be allowed as similar fact evidence.

B No, this is evidence of bad character and would not be allowed even as similar fact evidence.

C Yes, this is *prima facie* circumstantial evidence tending to show guilt, and would be allowed.

D Yes, it is likely that this evidence will be allowed under the similar fact principle.

Question 7.20

DAWLISH has been accused of an assault by his neighbour, and has attended voluntarily at the police station. He is not arrested but is interviewed regarding the assault. During the interview, the police officer notices there are marks on DAWLISH's knuckles consistent with details of the assault allegation. The officer reasonably believes that the marks may be attributable to the accused's participation in the assault. The officer asks DAWLISH to account for the marks, and DAWLISH refuses to answer the question.

Can inferences be drawn from DAWLISH's refusal at court?
A Yes, provided the officer gave a 'special warning' before asking the question.
B Yes, he has failed to account for a mark which may be attributable to the crime charged.
C No, as he was not arrested for the offence.
D No, there is no evidence linking the mark to the assault.

Question 7.21

HUXTABLE is a barrister representing TOMKINS, who is charged with burglary. During her opening speech she tells the jury that TOMKINS will accept that he was in the area of the factory, but he will deny that he actually committed the burglary. TOMKINS is horrified, as he did not want his counsel to admit that he was near the factory.

In relation to this admission by counsel, which of the following is true?
A The admission may be admitted as counsel is the accused's agent.
B The admission may be admitted as it appears to be a confession (s. 76 of PACE).
C The admission is not admissible, counsel is not an agent for the accused.
D The admission is hearsay as it is not made by the accused, and is not admissible.

Question 7.22

SYMES was convicted of murder but on appeal his conviction was quashed due to the oppressive nature of the police interviews where confession evidence was obtained. He is now seeking civil damages against the police force. His case is that his confession was obtained by oppression by the officers who interviewed him, working under the directions of a detective superintendent. He wants to adduce evidence that the interviewing officer and the detective superintendent had a number of incidents of similar malpractice laid against them in previous cases, and that in all those cases the accused was acquitted or had his or her conviction overturned due to the officers' oppressive interview tactics.

In relation to similar fact evidence, in this civil case which of the following is true?

A Evidence of similar facts relate only to behaviour of the accused, not that of witnesses.

B Evidence of similar facts cannot be used in civil cases.

C Evidence of similar facts may be admitted in these circumstances.

D Evidence of similar facts will be admitted, as it is prejudicial to the officers.

Question 7.23

YAXLEY is appearing at Crown Court charged with assaulting an off-duty police officer who tried to intervene when YAXLEY was seen being violent towards his girlfriend in the street. YAXLEY has called his girlfriend as a defence witness to give evidence that the argument was a tiff, and that they were happily going home when the incident broke out, she claimed that she had been tipsy but had not taken any drugs. The prosecution wish to cross-examine the witness in relation to a previous caution for possession of cocaine.

Is it likely that this previous caution will be admissible under s. 100 of the Criminal Justice Act 2003?

A Yes, as this directly relates to her credibility as a witness and has substantial probative value.

B Yes, as she asserted in her own evidence that she had not taken drugs on that night.

C No, as the caution has no bearing on any issue in this case.

D No, as only evidence of a previous conviction would be admissible to impugn the credibility of the witness.

Question 7.24

SCHRAMM moved to the United Kingdom seven years ago. She had convictions in Holland for offences contrary to their criminal law. Four months ago she received a police caution in relation to a theft offence by shoplifting. She is now appearing in court on another theft offence and wishes to use the fact that she has no UK convictions, and adduce evidence of her good character.

Can she adduce evidence of good character?

A Yes, as she has no previous convictions in this country and cautions do not count as 'bad character'.

B Yes, as she has no previous convictions in this country and cautions are *not* convictions in this context.

C No, she is not entitled to adduce such evidence as she has a recent caution; the foreign convictions, however, are not relevant.

D No, she is not entitled to adduce such evidence as she has a recent caution and a foreign court conviction: both are relevant.

ANSWERS

Answer 7.1

Answer **B** — Where an accomplice is giving evidence for the Crown, their previous convictions should normally be disclosed by the prosecution to the jury at the outset of a trial unless counsel for the defence indicates otherwise (*R v Taylor* [1999] 2 Cr App R 163). Consequently answers A, C and D are incorrect.

Evidence and Procedure, para. 2.10.18.1

Answer 7.2

Answer **D** — There have been numerous domestic and European case decisions about failure to advance facts following legal advice to remain silent, and more recent cases have attempted to unravel the difficulties experienced in this area. These cases have accepted that a genuine reliance by a defendant on his/her solicitor's advice to remain silent is not in itself enough to preclude adverse comment; answer A is therefore incorrect. The real question to be answered is whether the defendant remained silent, not because of legal advice, but because there was no satisfactory explanation to give (*R v Beckles* [2005] 1 All ER 705 and *R v Bresa* [2005] EWCA Crim 1414).

Where an accused, following legal advice, fails to answer questions during interview but presents a prepared statement, no adverse inference can be drawn where the accused's defence does not rely on any facts not mentioned in the interview (*R v Campbell* [2005] EWCA Crim 1249); answer C is therefore incorrect. However, this would not be the case when evidence of facts relied on during the trial were not contained within the pre-prepared statement (*R v Turner* [2004] All ER 1025).

Prepared statements can be a dangerous device for an innocent accused who later discovers that something significant has been omitted. In *Turner* it was noted that, as inconsistencies between the prepared statement and the defence at trial do not necessarily amount to reliance on unmentioned facts, the judge must be particularly careful to pinpoint any fact that might properly be the subject of a s. 34 direction. Alternatively, the jury might more appropriately be directed to regard differences between the prepared statement and the accused's evidence as constituting a previous lie rather than as the foundation for a direction under s. 34.

What is important is that the inferences hinge on whether the evidence given in chief varies from that given in interview, and although evidence was given by the accused as to why he had that £200 it varied from the reason given in his prepared statement; answer B is therefore incorrect.

Evidence and Procedure, para. 2.10.6.1

Answer 7.3

Answer **A** — The admissibility of relevant evidence under the Criminal Justice Act 2003 is wide ranging, and convictions may become routinely admissible unless the courts make wide use of the exclusionary power.

The Government felt the rules of evidence had to be amended to reflect public concern that evidence relevant to the search for truth was being excluded. The approach preferred in the 2003 Act, s. 101(1)(d) is that where the accused's previous convictions or other misconduct (including a propensity to be untruthful) are relevant to an issue in the case then, unless the court considers they will have a disproportionate effect, the evidence should be admitted. This suggests the court should articulate the reason for excluding, rather than admitting, a particular conviction or other piece of evidence suggestive of misconduct.

Certainly a propensity to be 'untruthful' may well be relevant to help explain a 'dishonesty' offence. However there are some safeguards to the defendant, and the prosecution's case generally must raise some question as to the truthfulness of some important aspect of the accused's case. Where they don't have this belief the convictions cannot be adduced; but where they do, convictions will become routinely admissible unless the courts make wide use of the exclusionary power.

Answers B, C and D reflect other situations where bad character evidence can be admitted, but specifically to this question, evidence of previous untruthfulness will only be adduced where it is suggested the defendant's case is untruthful.

Evidence and Procedure, para. 2.10.18.2

Answer 7.4

Answer **A** — At common law, the trial judge has a discretion to exclude any evidence if it is felt that its prejudicial effect outweighs its probative value, and answer D is therefore incorrect. It is for the judge to ensure that the accused receives a fair trial (*R v Sang* [1980] AC 402). The judge can apply the discretion even where the defence make no formal submissions, and answer B is therefore incorrect. Although s. 78 of the Police and Criminal Evidence Act 1984 allows evidence to be excluded, the judge's common law discretion goes beyond that particular section (e.g. hearsay evidence) and therefore answer C is incorrect.

In deciding whether to admit the evidence or not, the judge will consider the relevance of the evidence to the issue at hand. In *Kuruma, Son of Kaniu* v *The Queen* [1955] AC 197, Lord Goddard CJ said (at p. 203):

> ... the test to be applied in considering whether evidence is admissible is whether it is relevant to the matters in issue. If it is, it is admissible and the court is not concerned with how the evidence was obtained. While this proposition may not have been stated in so many words in any English case there are decisions which support it, and in their lordships' opinion it is plainly right in principle.

In *Jeffrey* v *Black* [1978] QB 490, it was held that 'an irregularity in obtaining evidence does not render the evidence inadmissible'.

Evidence and Procedure, para. 2.10.2.2

Answer 7.5

Answer **A** — Where a defendant says that advice was received from his or her solicitor not to answer questions, he or she is entitled to give evidence of the conversation with the solicitor prior to interview to rebut any allegation of post-interview fabrication, and answer C is therefore incorrect. In *R* v *Daniel*, it was also held that the defendant is entitled to call the solicitor to give evidence of the advice given before interview (*R* v *Daniel* (1998) 162 JP 578), and answer B is therefore incorrect. The fact that the defendant calls the solicitor waives any legal privilege that may have existed, and answer D is therefore incorrect. Of course, having given evidence-in-chief, the prosecution will be entitled to cross-examine the solicitor on that pre-interview conversation.

Evidence and Procedure, para. 2.10.6.1

Answer 7.6

Answer **C** — A jury may draw inferences where a defendant refuses, without good cause, to answer a question properly put. The court must inform the accused that if he or she fails to give evidence, or, being sworn, refuses to answer questions without good cause, the jury may draw such inferences as appear proper from such a failure to give evidence or a refusal to answer any question (*Practice Direction (Criminal Proceedings: Consolidation)* [2002] 1 WLR 2870, para. 44, defendant's right not to give evidence). Once the defendant becomes a sworn witness, he or she loses the privilege against self-incrimination, and answer A is therefore incorrect. Also, the defendant may be asked questions that tend to incriminate him or her, and answer

B is therefore incorrect. So here inferences may be drawn. However, such inferences alone, without supporting evidence, would not be sufficient to convict, and answer D is therefore incorrect.

Evidence and Procedure, paras 2.10.6.5, 2.10.6.6

Answer 7.7

Answer **C** — Real evidence usually takes the form of a material object for inspection by the court. This evidence is either to prove that the material object in question exists, or to enable the court to draw an inference from its own observation as to the object's value and physical condition. It is normally accompanied by written testimony and identified by a witness. This testimony usually includes an explanation of the connection between the exhibit and the facts in issue, or the relevance to an issue. Little, if any, weight can attach to real evidence in the absence of accompanying testimony identifying the object and connecting it with the facts in issue. There is no rule of law that an object must be produced, or its nonproduction excused, before oral evidence may be given about it. For example, it is not necessary for the police to produce the very breath test device used by them on a particular occasion (see *Castle* v *Cross* [1984] 1 WLR 1372) and answers A and B are therefore incorrect. However, the weight of the oral evidence may be adversely affected by the non-production of the object in question (*Armory* v *Delamirie* (1722) 1 Str 505), i.e. where the officer fails to produce the actual or a similar device, and answer D is therefore incorrect.

Evidence and Procedure, para. 2.10.11

Answer 7.8

Answer **D** — This question really tests your knowledge of evidence, custody officers procedure and interviews; questions in the national examination also test wide ranging knowledge. So although this question could be in other chapters it is in this one as it mostly relates to s. 34 of the Criminal Justice and Public Order Act 1994, inferences from silence.

In relation to the first interview consider what evidence the police should have disclosed to the solicitor prior to this interview. There is obviously a statutory disclosure duty after charge, however, this is not necessarily the case at the interview stage of the investigation. There is no specific provision within the Police and Criminal Evidence Act 1984 for the disclosure of any information by the police at the police station, with the exception of the custody record and, in identification cases, the initial description given by the witnesses. Further, there is nothing within the Criminal Justice and Public Order Act 1994 that states that information must be disclosed before an inference from silence can be made. Indeed, in *R v Imran* [1997] Crim LR 754 the court held that it is totally wrong to submit that a defendant should be prevented from lying by being presented with the whole of the evidence against him/her prior to the interview.

In *R v Argent* [1997] Crim LR 346 the court dismissed the argument that an inference could not be drawn under s. 34 of the Criminal Justice and Public Order Act 1994 because there had not been full disclosure at the interview. However, the court did recognise that it may be a factor to take into account, but it would be for the jury to decide whether the failure to answer questions was reasonable. Consider this though, at this stage of the investigation, a few hours after the collision what actual evidence did the police have? Very little, if any, inferences could be drawn, therefore, provided the accused was given an opportunity to give his version of events; answers A and C are therefore incorrect.

In relation to the second interview Code C of the Police and Criminal Evidence Act 1984 codes of practice provides that as soon as a police officer believes that a prosecution should be brought against a suspect and there is sufficient evidence for it to succeed and that the person has said all that he wishes to say about the offence, he shall without delay bring him before the custody officer who is then responsible for considering whether or not he should be charged. Bearing in mind the accused has had no opportunity to comment on the evidence the police have gathered it would be unfair not to allow them the opportunity to say what they wish about the offence. In any case the phrase in Code C is 'sufficient evidence for it to succeed' not 'sufficient evidence to charge' and if the accused's answers led the police to believe that a prosecution is not likely to succeed then that accused must be given the opportunity to say what they wish; answers B and C are therefore incorrect.

In *R v Flynn, The Times*, 8 June 2001, the court held that the police are entitled to conduct a second interview with a suspect, having obtained evidence from their witnesses which was not available in the first interview, and adverse inference could be drawn from the suspect's silence.

Evidence and Procedure, para. 2.10.6.1

Answer 7.9

Answer **D** — There is a rule of law called presumption of regularity, which covers this point. This rule includes a presumption that mechanical and other instruments were in working order at the time of their use. For example, automatic traffic signals are presumed to be in proper working order unless the contrary is proved (*Tingle Jacobs & Co.* v *Kennedy* [1964] 1 WLR 638). This presumption assists the prosecution and answers A and C are therefore incorrect. As in all cases, the defence have to prove their point on the balance of probabilities only, and answer B is therefore incorrect. Note that there are no cases on this to date, but many defences now only require 'evidential' proof rather than proof on 'the balance of probabilities'.

Evidence and Procedure, para. 2.10.16.2

Answer 7.10

Answer **C** — Where an accused faces more than one charge of a similar nature, or where evidence of similar allegations is tendered in support of one charge, the evidence of one accuser may be admissible to support the evidence of another. The underlying principle is that the probative value (the usefulness of the evidence) of multiple accusations may depend in part on their similarity, but also on the unlikelihood that the same person would find himself or herself falsely accused on different occasions by different and independent individuals. There are cases in which evidence was admitted because features were identified which were so bizarre as to amount to striking similarity in the true sense. One of these cases is *Lanford* v *General Medical Council* [1990] 1 AC 13, which the outline of this question broadly follows. In that case, the evidence of each patient was rightly admitted to corroborate the allegation of the other, and therefore answers A and B are incorrect. Any comment made by the doctor would not normally be admissible, as it does not relate to the facts in issue, i.e. the assault, and answer D is therefore incorrect. For further reference, see *R* v *Tabassum* [2000] Crim LR 686.

Evidence and Procedure, para. 2.12.4.4

Answer 7.11

Answer **D** — Only treason, perjury and speeding require corroboration in law, and answer A is therefore incorrect. A corroboration warning is no longer a requirement in cases of complaints of sexual offences, and answer B is therefore incorrect. It is a matter of discretion for the judge whether such a warning should be given, and so answer C is therefore incorrect. In *R* v *Makanjuola* [1995] 1 WLR 1348, Lord Taylor LCJ gave guidelines in respect of the exercise of the discretion:

> It is a matter for the judge's discretion what, if any warning, he considers appropriate in respect of such a witness as indeed in respect of any other witness in whatever type

of case. Whether he chooses to give a warning and in what terms will depend on the circumstances of the case, the issues raised and the content and quality of the witness's evidence. In some cases, it may be appropriate for the judge to warn the jury to exercise caution before acting upon the unsupported evidence of a witness. This will not be so simply because the witness is a complainant of a sexual offence nor will it necessarily be so because a witness is alleged to be an accomplice. There will need to be an evidential basis for suggesting that the evidence of the witness may be unreliable. An evidential basis does not include mere suggestion by cross-examining counsel.

Evidence and Procedure, para. 2.10.20

Answer 7.12

Answer **C** — This is a good example of what strikingly similar evidence is about. Clearly evidence given by the boys about incidents not subject to the charge is evidence of bad character and therefore not generally admissible. However, it would be allowed where its probative value in deciding if PHILLIPS is guilty or not outweighs the prejudicial effect the evidence would have on the defendant; answer A is therefore incorrect. The example used in the question is an illustration adopted by Lord Hailsham in *DPP* v *Boardman* [1975] AC 421 (at p. 454) of the man who commits repeated homosexual offences and whose victims all state that he was attired in 'the ceremonial headdress of a Red Indian chief or other eccentric garb'. It should not be supposed that all similar fact evidence must reflect this degree of idiosyncrasy. Everything depends on the unlikelihood of repetition being attributable to mere coincidence. It is not necessary that the previous behaviour was subject to a formal charge — even non-criminal behaviour can be given as 'similar fact' — and answer B is therefore incorrect. As far as corroboration is concerned, the classic definition of corroboration is to be found in *R* v *Baskerville* [1916] 2 KB 658 (per Lord Reid):

> ... evidence in corroboration must be independent testimony which affects the accused by connecting or tending to connect him with the crime. In other words, it must be evidence which implicates him, that is, which confirms in some material particular not only the evidence that the crime has been committed, but also that the prisoner committed it.

The evidence of the boys is of similar fact, but would not extend to corroboration according to this definition, and answer D is therefore incorrect.

Evidence and Procedure, para. 2.12.4.1

Answer 7.13

Answer **D** — Evidence is likely to be admissible if it goes beyond mere evidence of a tendency to commit crime and has a crucial bearing upon the question whether the offence charged was committed by this particular defendant, even 'bad character evidence'.

Part of the definition of bad character in s. 98 of the Criminal Justice Act 2003 directs the court to consider whether the evidence shows a disposition 'towards misconduct', where misconduct means 'the commission of an offence or other reprehensible behaviour'. It would seem unlikely that a homosexual disposition is *per se* 'reprehensible' and therefore not misconduct. However the question is asking about the adducing of previous convictions, not a disposition; answer B is therefore incorrect.

However the question here is not about such propensity, but rather the previous convictions of the defendant. The second part of s. 98 has to do with the alleged facts of the offence with which the defendant is charged. Under s. 101, evidence of a defendant's bad character can be entered if it is 'a matter in issue between the defendant and the prosecution'; however s. 103(1)(a) defines this as

(a) the question whether the defendant has a propensity to commit offences of the kind with which he is charged, except where his having such a propensity makes it no more likely that he is guilty of the offence.

Here the convictions would not show a propensity to commit murder; therefore answer C is incorrect.

That said bad character evidence can be adduced as important explanatory evidence, or evidence to correct a false impression given by the defendant. In both these cases the evidence is likely to be adduced, evidence without which it would be 'impossible or difficult to understand other evidence in the case'. Answer A is therefore incorrect.

Evidence and Procedure, para. 2.10.18.2

Answer 7.14

Answer **A** — Amongst the criteria for admitting a business document under s. 117 of the Criminal Justice Act 2003 are:

- that the information was received in the course of business;
- that the information contained in the document was supplied by a person (whether or not the maker of the statement) who had, or who may reasonably be supposed to have had, personal knowledge of the matters dealt with.

Both these points are contained in the question (note the maker of the document only has to have knowledge of the matters dealt with on the document, not of whether the messages were true or not). Answer B is therefore incorrect. It is immaterial that the accused was not the maker of the document and answer D is therefore incorrect. Also, in relation to business documents, provided the criteria outlined above are fulfilled, it is immaterial whether the witness is able to attend court or not — the document will be admitted and answer C is therefore incorrect.

Evidence and Procedure, para. 2.10.14.9

Answer 7.15

Answer **C** — In relation to non-expert evidence, the courts have allowed the following non-expert opinion evidence from a witness:

- identification of a person or object;
- the speed of a moving vehicle;
- evidence as to temperature or time;
- the value of an item.

Note, however, that non-expert opinion evidence should not be received on the value of less commonplace objects or objects, such as antiques and works of art, the valuation of which calls for expertise; therefore, answer D is incorrect.

One example of non-expert evidence that is likely to be given by police officers is provided by the case of *R* v *Davies* [1962] 1 WLR 1111. In *Davies*, it was held that any competent witness may give evidence that in his or her opinion a person is drunk provided that he or she describes the facts on which his or her opinion is based; therefore, answer A is incorrect. As can be seen, this is not restricted just to police officers, but covers any competent witness.

Although scientific evidence (expert) is not always required to identify a prohibited drug, police officers' descriptions of a drug must be sufficient to justify the inference that it was the drug alleged (*R* v *Hill* (1993) 96 Cr App R 456). As such, they can give non-expert opinion, even though not specially trained; therefore, answer B is incorrect.

Evidence and Procedure, para. 2.10.19.1

Answer 7.16

Answer **D** — Expert evidence will be appropriate in handwriting cases, and evidence of an expert witness may be admitted. It is for the judge to decide whether a witness is competent to give expert opinion and answer B is therefore incorrect. The Criminal Procedure Rules 2005 provide for regulations to be made requiring pre-trial disclosure. These rules, contained within the Crown Court (Advance Notice of Expert Evidence) Rules 1987 (SI 1987/716) and the Magistrates' Courts (Advance Notice of Expert Evidence) Rules 1997 (SI 1997/705), require any party intending to produce expert evidence to furnish to the other parties in the proceedings a statement in writing of the expert finding. This allows the other parties to review the statement and, if necessary, call their own expert witness. (Note that this applies equally to the defence as it does to the prosecution, and answer A is therefore incorrect.) A summary will not suffice and answer C is also therefore incorrect.

Evidence and Procedure, para. 2.10.19.2

Answer 7.17

Answer **D** — One of the principles of the Criminal Justice Act 2003 is that in considering the fairness of a trial a balance must on occasions be struck between the interests of the public in enabling the prosecution case to be properly presented and the interest of a particular accused in not being put in a disadvantageous position, for example by the death or illness of a witness. To that end s. 116 allows in cases where a witness is unavailable for a statement not made in oral evidence in the proceedings to be made admissible as evidence. There are many factors named in s. 116 where a witness is not available; one of those is that where through fear the relevant person does not give (or does not continue to give) oral evidence in the proceedings either at all or in connection with the subject matter of the statement, and the court gives leave for the statement to be given in evidence (s. 116(2)(e))

In relation to s. 116(2)(e), 'fear' is to be widely construed and can include fear of the death or injury of another person or of financial loss (s. 116(3)); answer B is therefore incorrect.

The use of such hearsay evidence for the prosecution does not of itself contravene the 'fair trial' provisions of the European Convention on Human Rights, provided the court retains the power to assess the interests of justice by reference to the risk of unfairness to the accused As a rule, the accused should be given an adequate and proper opportunity to challenge and question a witness against him, either at the time the statement was made or at some later stage of proceedings

If the reason for the witness's failure to give evidence in person is that they were intimidated by or on behalf of the accused, who then contests the admissibility of the statement for the prosecution, the strong principle that the accused should not profit from their own wrong is likely to factor into the decision whether a statement should be read out without the witness giving evidence in chief.

In *R v Sellick and Sellick* [2005] EWCA Crim 651 the court felt the need to register an important point and took a strong line in respect of cases where intimidation is either clearly proved or highly probable. If an accused has been clearly shown to have kept a witness away by fear, they cannot complain that his Article 6(3)(d) right has been infringed, since he is the author of his inability to examine the witness at trial. Even in cases where intimidation is no more than a high probability, it cannot be right to have an absolute rule that, where the evidence adduced is the sole or decisive evidence, it cannot be read without infringing the accused's Article 6 rights. Such a rule would serve to ensure that the more subtle and less easily established forms of intimidation would provide defendants with the opportunity of excluding the most material evidence against them.

Where such evidence is allowed the court must take counterbalancing measures by exercising care to ensure that the quality of the evidence is compelling, taking steps to draw the jury's attention to aspects of the credibility of the witness and giving a clear direction to the jury to exercise caution ensuring fairness, and thus compliance with art. 6(1); answer C is therefore incorrect.

Evidence and Procedure, para. 2.10.14.7

Answer 7.18

Answer **A** — Section 105 of the Criminal Justice Act deals directly with 'evidence to correct a false impression' per s. 101(1)(f) of that Act.

(1) For the purposes of section 101(1)(f) —
   (a) the defendant gives a false impression if he is responsible for the making of an express or implied assertion which is apt to give the court or jury a false or misleading impression about the defendant...

These assertions can be made whilst being questioned under caution about the offence with which they are charged or on being charged with that offence or officially informed that he might be prosecuted for it. However, evidence of the assertion must also be given in the proceedings: as HINDMAN will not give any evidence then this section does not bite. Answers B and C are therefore incorrect.

The accused may be held to have given a false impression by means of conduct and this includes 'dress' (s. 105(4) and (5)). It is unclear how such a provision will operate in practice; however where someone dresses to give the jury a false impression then the prosecution can adduce evidence of bad character, but only going directly to the falsity of the impression. This is so even if the accused does not give evidence themselves, as the court will view the 'dress' itself as an assertion which is apt to give a false impression. Answer D is therefore incorrect.

Evidence and Procedure, para. 2.10.18.2

Answer 7.19

Answer **D** — Evidence is likely to be admissible at court if it goes beyond mere evidence of a propensity to commit crime and has a crucial bearing upon the question whether the offence charged was committed by this particular defendant. In these cases the evidence of previous offences or actions of the accused *may be* admissible because they *connect* the defendant with the offence charged. If so, the evidence that he or she has a disposition to commit that kind of offence or act in a particular way is relevant because it makes it more likely that he or she committed the offence charged. Therefore, the probative value of that evidence may outweigh any prejudicial effect it might have on the defendant's case. This is one of the basic principles relating to 'similar fact' evidence. Thus, evidence of non-criminal behaviour/bad character can be admitted as outlined in the Criminal Justice Act 2003, and answers A and B are therefore incorrect. It is not circumstantial evidence as it is not evidence of relevant facts from which the facts in issue (the rape charged) may be presumed with more or less certainty; therefore, answer C is incorrect. It is, however, 'similar fact' and is likely to be allowed. The facts of this case are similar to those of *R* v *Butler* (1986) 84 Cr App R 12, where such evidence was adduced.

Evidence and Procedure, para. 2.12.4.2

Answer 7.20

Answer **C** — Section 36 of the Criminal Justice and Public Order Act 1994 provides that inferences can be drawn from an accused's failure to give evidence, or a refusal to answer any question about any object, substance or mark which may be attributable to the accused in the commission of an offence. An inference may be drawn only where four conditions are satisfied:

- the accused has been arrested;
- a constable reasonably believes that the object, substance or mark (or the presence of the accused (s. 37)) may be attributable to the accused's participation in a crime (s. 36 (an offence 'specified by the constable') or s. 37 (the offence for which he or she was arrested));

- the constable informs the accused of his or her belief and requests an explanation;
- the constable tells the suspect (in ordinary language) the effect of a failure or refusal to comply with the request.

The interviewing officer is required to give the accused a 'special warning' for an inference to be drawn from a suspect's failure or refusal to answer a question about one of these matters or to answer it satisfactorily. However, as one of the four factors has not been met this becomes irrelevant, and answer A is therefore incorrect. For similar reasons, answer B is also incorrect. There does not have to be evidence linking the mark to the crime; simply that it may be attributable to the accused in the commission of an offence. Answer D is therefore incorrect.

Evidence and Procedure, para. 2.10.6.4

Answer 7.21

Answer **A** — An admission made by the agent of an accused person, such as his legal adviser, may be admissible against him (*R* v *Turner* (1975) 61 Cr App R 67); therefore answer C is incorrect. Although at first sight such an admission may appear to be a confession, and thus to be governed by the rules of admissibility in the Police and Criminal Evidence Act 1984, s. 76, this, in fact, is not the case, for the section applies only to a confession made 'by an accused person' and, by s. 82(1) of the 1984 Act, 'confession' includes any statement adverse to 'the person who made it'; answer B is therefore incorrect.

Who is an agent of the accused may be inferred from the circumstances in *Turner*, where it was held that it is permissible to infer from the fact that a barrister makes an admission in court on behalf of and in the presence of his client, that he was authorised to make it. This is hearsay evidence, but is admissible as such and is governed by the relevant sections of the Criminal Justice Act 2003, which place hearsay evidence on a more statutory footing.

Evidence and Procedure, para. 2.10.14.5

Answer 7.22

Answer **C** — In *R* v *Z* [2000] 2 AC 483, Lord Hobhouse gave the reasons why similar fact evidence may be admitted. He said (at p. 508):

> Similar facts are admissible because they are relevant to the proof of the defendant's guilt. The evidence relating to one incident taken in isolation may be unconvincing. It may depend upon a straight conflict of evidence between two people. It may leave open

seemingly plausible explanations. The guilt of the defendant may not be proved beyond reasonable doubt. But, when evidence is given of a number of similar incidents, the position may be changed. The evidence of the defendant's guilt may become overwhelming. The fact that a number of witnesses come forward and without collusion give a similar account of the defendant's behaviour may give credit to the evidence of each of them and discredit the denials of the defendant. Evidence of system may negative a defence of accident. This is the simple truth upon which similar fact evidence is admitted: it has probative value and is not merely prejudicial.

The principle that the probative value of the evidence must outweigh its prejudicial effect is paramount in similar fact cases, even civil ones; answer D is therefore incorrect. In *O'Brien* v *Chief Constable of South Wales, The Times*, 22 August 2003, it was held that where a claimant's murder conviction was quashed and he wished to bring a claim for police malpractice, it was on occasion permissible to adduce similar fact evidence of similar malpractice by the same officers. This allows evidence of similar facts to be used in civil cases against those who were witnesses in the criminal case; answers A and B are therefore incorrect.

Evidence and Procedure, para. 2.12.4.1

Answer 7.23

Answer **C** — The Criminal Justice Act 2003, s. 100 states:

(1) In criminal proceedings evidence of the bad character of a person other than the defendant is admissible if and only if —
  (a) it is important explanatory evidence,
  (b) it has substantial probative value in relation to a matter which —
    (i) is a matter in issue in the proceedings, and
    (ii) is of substantial importance in the context of the case as a whole, or
  (c) all parties to the proceedings agree to the evidence being admissible.

Section 100 covers evidence of the bad character of any person (not just convictions; answer D is therefore incorrect), whether or not called as a witness, and whether the evidence is to be adduced or elicited by or on behalf of the prosecution, the accused or any co-accused; there are however threshold conditions for admissibility of such evidence governed by subsection (2):

(2) For the purposes of subsection (1)(a) evidence is important explanatory evidence if —
  (a) without it, the court or jury would find it impossible or difficult properly to understand other evidence in the case, and
  (b) its value for understanding the case as a whole is substantial.

Section 100(2) covers evidence of, or a disposition towards, misconduct on the part of someone other than the accused without which the account before the court or jury would be incomplete or incoherent. Therefore if the matter to which the evidence relates is largely comprehensible without the explanatory evidence, the evidence will be inadmissible. Explanatory evidence, to be admissible, must also satisfy s. 100(1)(b), i.e. its value for understanding the case as a whole must be 'substantial', as opposed to minor or trivial. Under the Criminal Justice Act 2003, s. 100(1)(b), the probative value in relation to a matter in issue in the proceedings must be 'substantial' — evidence of only minor probative force should not be admitted. A 'matter in issue in the proceedings' covers both issues of disputed fact and issues of credibility. In order to be admissible, the evidence must also be of substantial importance in the context of the case as a whole — evidence which goes only to some minor or trivial issue should not be admitted. In what way does the value of this drugs caution assist in understanding whether the accused committed the assault or not? In *R* v *Antony Albert Weir & 5 Ors* [2005] EWCA Crim 2866 the Court of Appeal held that the judge had erred in concluding that the evidence of a caution had substantial probative value in relation to a witness's credibility and the evidence of a caution (for possession of cocaine) was inadmissible under s. 100; answers A and B are therefore incorrect. Indeed the Court of Appeal's view was that the judge erred for a number of reasons, including those which were put forward by the judge himself when directing the jury to ignore the evidence of the caution, in fact the trial judge stated the caution 'has got about as much to do with this case as the price of tomatoes'.

Evidence and Procedure, para. 2.10.18.1

Answer 7.24

Answer **D** — An accused may lay claim to a good character not only where they can adduce positive evidence to that effect, but also where they can truthfully assert that they have no previous convictions (*R* v *Aziz* [1996] AC 41).

However, the jury must not be misled by any claim made by the accused, so where, for example, he/she has recently been cautioned for an offence this cannot simply be ignored (*R* v *Martin* [2000] 2 Cr App R 42), nor can the fact that he/she has been found guilty by a foreign court (*R* v *El Delbi* [2003] EWCA Crim 1767). Answers A, B and C are therefore incorrect.

Evidence and Procedure, para. 2.10.18.3

8 | Exclusion of Admissible Evidence

STUDY PREPARATION

There are few more frustrating experiences for police officers than to have brought a person before the court and presented the evidence against them, only to have some of that evidence excluded.

This area of law has grown up partly through the common law decisions of the higher courts and partly through statute. And now there is the additional force of the Human Rights Act 1998, which has focused attention on the defendant's inalienable right to a fair trial and the attendant safeguards under Article 6 of the European Convention on Human Rights.

Many of the occasions where admissible evidence is later excluded by the courts arise in suspect interviews, or on other occasions whereby the police officer(s) concerned say or do something that renders any response by the defendant unreliable or its introduction in evidence unfair. Therefore, areas of confessions and oppression are key features in this chapter, as are the practical consequences of an exclusion ruling being made.

QUESTIONS

Question 8.1

DAILLY was interviewed by police officers in relation to a murder. During the interview, when asked if he had strangled the woman, he nodded his head and said he was sorry. He did not, however, verbally state that he had committed the murder. The following day, he took police to the scene of the murder and gave a running commentary on camera of what he had done, and demonstrated on a female officer how he had strangled the victim.

In relation to 'confession', which of the following statements is true?

A The reconstruction on camera would not be a 'confession' as it is not a PACE interview.

B The fact that he only nodded and said he was sorry is not enough to be a 'confession'.

C Both the actions in the interview and the reconstruction could be a 'confession'.

D A 'confession' could only have been made by a verbal admission that he had committed the murder.

Question 8.2

Section 76(8) of the Police and Criminal Evidence Act 1984 is the section that deals with oppression and gives assistance as to its meaning, and where a confession may be unreliable due to oppression

In relation to what would, or would not be 'oppression' which of the following is correct?

A A court can never conclude that treatment had been 'oppressive' under all the circumstances where the relevant Codes of Practice had been followed.

B Any failure to follow the relevant Codes of Practice will be in itself an automatic reason for excluding evidence.

C Oppression can include where a person other than the person making the confession has been treated in a harsh or wrongful manner.

D It might be possible for the defence to use evidence against officers involved in the case who have allegedly 'mistreated' suspects in other cases.

Question 8.3

Section 82(1) of the Police and Criminal Evidence Act 1984 retained the courts' common law power to exclude evidence at its discretion.

For evidence to be excluded at common law which of the following will the court concern itself with?

A The court will consider how the evidence is obtained and its likely prejudicial effect.

B The court will consider how the evidence is obtained and its likely probative value.

C The court will consider only its likely prejudicial effect.

D The court will consider only its likely probative value.

Question 8.4

BLAKEMORE was arrested for murder. On being told that if he confessed he would be charged with manslaughter only, BLAKEMORE stated he had shot the victim in self-defence. BLAKEMORE then told the officers where to find the gun, which he had hidden in a hedge. The gun was found, and at a second interview BLAKEMORE identified it as the one he had used, again because he believed he would be charged with manslaughter only. Ballistic evidence shows it was the weapon used. BLAKEMORE was charged with murder. At BLAKEMORE's trial, the judge ruled that the confession obtained at the first interview would be excluded as it was 'unreliable'.

In relation to evidence the police can now give, which of the following statements is true?

A The police can state that BLAKEMORE identified the gun, as this was during the second interview, which should be allowed.

B The police can state that they found a gun where BLAKEMORE told them to look, and that it was the gun used in the shooting.

C The police may not be able to make a connection between BLAKEMORE and the gun.

D The police will be able to state that BLAKEMORE said he had used the gun, as this was during the second interview, which should be allowed.

Question 8.5

TAYLOR is standing trial for an offence of burglary. During the burglary, where TAYLOR pretended to be a meter reader, witnesses noted that the offender spoke with a pronounced stammer, and used the term 'pal' significantly. Whilst being interviewed on audio by police officers, TAYLOR stammered and used the word 'pal' 25 times during a 20-minute interview. TAYLOR also confessed to the burglary. At the *voir dire* the judge excluded the confession when the defence submitted it had been obtained unfairly. The prosecution seek to have the evidence of the stammer, and the use of the term 'pal', admitted to show the connection between TAYLOR and the description obtained from witnesses.

Is it likely that this evidence will be allowed during the trial?

A Yes, as it is evidence properly obtained and admissible for a specific purpose.

B Yes, as it is similar fact evidence and admissible to connect TAYLOR to the crime charged.

C No, if the confession is excluded then the entire interview will be excluded.

D No, as it is not one of the 'facts in issue', it will not be admissible.

Question 8.6

Constable PRYCE is involved in an undercover operation relating to the supply of controlled drugs. The officer has been making test purchases from GLOVER, compiling evidence that GLOVER is a drug supplier. Intelligence has recently been obtained that GLOVER may also be involved in the supply of illegal firearms.

Which of the following is true in relation to the attempt to gain evidence of the supply of illegal firearms by GLOVER?

A Constable PRYCE could encourage GLOVER to supply firearms the next time a drug purchase is made.

B A covert human intelligence source (CHIS) could encourage GLOVER to supply firearms while making a drug purchase.

C Any attempt to ask GLOVER to supply firearms may well be seen as entrapment and any evidence obtained would be excluded.

D Any attempt to get GLOVER to supply firearms would not necessarily be entrapment, but safeguards would have to be observed.

Question 8.7

STREETER was suspected of being a child sex offender, and was arrested and interviewed several times. During the first interview he made no comment; however, the officers were dynamic in their interview and STREETER confessed. During later interviews, he voluntarily gave detailed accounts of sexually abusing children over many years. At trial the defence made submission that the first interview was oppressive and that the confession evidence was gained by this oppression and should be excluded. The defence accept that the other interviews were properly conducted with no oppression.

In relation to what will happen if the first interview is excluded under s. 76 of the Police and Criminal Evidence Act 1984, which of the following is true?

A The later interviews will always be admissible as the defence accept they were properly conducted.

B The later interviews will be admissible as the confessions were volunteered by the accused.

C The later interviews *will* be excluded if the first interview is excluded.

D The later interviews *may* be excluded if the first interview is excluded.

Question 8.8

MUMFORD wished to arrange a contract killing of her husband. In the two years preceding his death, she repeatedly stated that she wanted him killed and asked various witnesses whether they would help her kill him. She associated with SHERD who was a customer of her sandwich shop. SHERD associated with RYRIE. At the trial the prosecution have evidence that SHERD twice sent to RYRIE large amounts of money contained in sandwich bags from MUMFORD's shop.

All three are charged jointly with murder, the main evidence being a confession by RYRIE, made to his girlfriend, that he killed MUMFORD's husband and that SHERD was the 'middleman'. There is only other circumstantial evidence against SHERD.

In relation to this confession by RYRIE which of the following is correct?

A The confession is not admissible as it was made to a friend and not to the police.

B The confession is not admissible against the co-defendants as confession is relevant and admissible only against its maker.

C The jury can only consider the confession in relation to RYRIE's guilt, not whilst considering the co-defendants' guilt.

D The jury are entitled to take RYRIE's confession into account whilst considering the co-defendants' guilt.

ANSWERS

Answer 8.1

Answer **C** — A confession is a positive action by, and adverse to, the person making it. The person must use words or some other method of communication; this can include conduct such as a nod of acceptance of an accusation, or a thumbs-up sign, which may properly be regarded as a 'statement' in sign language, or a filmed reenactment where the suspect gives a running commentary explaining his or her movements during an alleged crime. Answer D is therefore incorrect. Confessions do not include silence by a person. The confession does not have to be a pure statement of guilt and can include the answers to questions asked in interview which are *adverse to the defendant*. Also, a confession may be 'wholly or partly adverse' to the maker, with the result that a so-called 'mixed statement', which is part confession and part exculpatory, is a confession for the purposes of the Police and Criminal Evidence Act 1984, and answer B is therefore incorrect. In *Li Shu-Ling* v *The Queen* [1989] AC 270, the accused agreed to take part in a filmed re-enactment of the crime — the murder of a woman by strangulation. He gave a running commentary explaining his movements, which he demonstrated on a female police officer. It was held that the reenactment was to be regarded as a confession, and answer A is therefore incorrect. In *R* v *Z* [2003] 1 WLR 1489, the Court of Appeal outlined that whether the statement was a confession or not was to be decided when it was sought to give the statement in evidence at court. However, answer C is still correct as it *could* be a 'confession' provided the court agreed.

Evidence and Procedure, para. 2.13.2

Answer 8.2

Answer **B** — In s. 76(8) of the Police and Criminal Evidence Act 1984, 'oppression' includes torture, inhuman or degrading treatment, and the use or threat of violence (whether or not amounting to torture).

In *R* v *Fulling* [1987] QB 426, the Court of Appeal held that oppression is:

[The] exercise of authority or power in a burdensome, harsh or wrongful manner; unjust or cruel treatment of subjects, inferiors etc., the imposition of unreasonable or unjust burdens.

Some legal commentators have suggested that oppression involves some kind of impropriety on the part of the police, which might be suggested by a deliberate failure to follow the PACE Codes of Practice, although a failure to follow the Codes is not of itself an automatic reason for excluding evidence; answer B is therefore incorrect.

Given that the courts have occasionally excluded evidence even where the relevant Code of Practice has been followed, the converse does not appear to be true and it is possible that a court might conclude that treatment had been 'oppressive' under all the circumstances even though the Codes of Practice had been followed; answer A is therefore incorrect.

The oppression must have been against the person who makes the confession, and not some third party; answer C is therefore incorrect.

It is a question of fact on each occasion whether a person's treatment was oppressive and whether there was any link between that person's treatment and his/her decision to make the confession. It might be possible for the defence to use evidence against officers involved in the case who have allegedly 'mistreated' suspects in other cases (*R* v *Twitchell* [2000] 1 Cr App R 373).

Evidence and Procedure, para. 2.13.2.3

Answer 8.3

Answer **A** — Section 82(1) of the Police and Criminal Evidence Act 1984 retained the courts' common law power to exclude evidence at its discretion (as to which, see *R* v *Sang* [1980] AC 402). For evidence to be excluded at common law the court will not so much concern itself with how evidence is obtained, but rather the effect that the evidence will have at trial. The court can exclude evidence at common law where the prejudicial effect of the evidence on the defendant greatly outweighs its probative value; answers A, B and D are therefore incorrect.

In these cases the courts are looking at the trial process itself, as opposed to the investigation, and therefore this power has less impact on how investigations should be conducted.

Evidence and Procedure, para. 2.13.2.3

Answer 8.4

Answer **C** — This question shows what could happen where vital evidence is lost due to police impropriety (i.e. a clear inducement to confess), particularly where a false pretence has been used. The first interview was rightly excluded, and for the same reasons it is more than likely that the second interview would also be excluded. Answers A and D are therefore incorrect. In this case, it will not be possible to show any connection between the suspect and the weapon and, unless there is some other evidence to link the weapon to the suspect, the case may fail. The reason is that it would not be possible to say that the police went to the location where the weapon was hidden without at least implying that the suspect had indicated that it was there when interviewed, and answer B is therefore incorrect. All that can be said is that the weapon was found at the particular location, which could be accessible to any number of people, and that the scientific evidence shows it to be the murder weapon.

Evidence and Procedure, para. 2.13.2.2

Answer 8.5

Answer **A** — Dealing with answer D first, one of the 'facts in issue' in any case is that of identification. Clearly the peculiar voice patterns go towards proving the identification of the offender. They are a physical feature of the defendant and not affected by anything that may have been done or said which rendered the *content* of the interview inadmissible, and as such would be allowed (answer D is therefore incorrect). Even where a confession on audio is excluded, it may still be admissible for other matters, such as the fact that the accused speaks in a certain way, or writes or expresses himself or herself in a particular fashion. In such a case it will only be that part of the confession which is necessary to prove the point that will be admissible, and answer C is therefore incorrect. Similar fact evidence relates to evidence of previous convictions or actions which may suggest that the accused has committed the offence charged. This is not the case here and answer B is therefore incorrect.

Evidence and Procedure, para. 2.13.2.2

Answer 8.6

Answer **D** — In cases where officers are trying to obtain evidence of offences yet to be committed, the key question as to the admissibility of evidence is whether the actions of those involved in the 'trap' amount to those of an *agent provocateur*. This is likely where the undercover officer encourages or invites the accused to commit a crime he or she would not have otherwise committed, and answer A is therefore incorrect. Prosecutions based on evidence obtained by entrapment conducted other than by police officers are also subject to the guidelines laid down in *R v Smurthwaite* [1994] 1 All ER 898. Section 78(1) of the Police and Criminal Evidence Act 1984 cannot be circumvented by the police using, as *agents provocateurs*, covert human intelligence sources who will not be called as witnesses, and answer B is therefore incorrect. The Court of Appeal has made it clear, however, that evidence of under-cover police officers, where it was alleged they had been acting as *agents provocateurs*, would not be excluded in circumstances where they had done no more than 'give the defendant an opportunity to break the law' of which the defendant had freely taken advantage (*Attorney General's Reference (No. 3 of 2000)* [2001] 1 WLR 2060). Thus, provided that the use of undercover agents is restricted and safeguards ob-served to prevent abuse, a person's right to a fair trial will not be infringed (*Teixeira de Castro* v *Portugal* (1998) 28 EHRR 101). The courts have accepted that undercover operations may be the only way in which some people are ever brought to trial (*R* v *Latif* [1996] 1 All ER 353), and evidence might not be excluded — answer C is therefore incorrect.

Evidence and Procedure, para. 2.13.3.4

Answer 8.7

Answer **D** — Where a confession made in the course of an interview is excluded on grounds of oppression, it may be necessary to consider whether the effect on the accused was such that the repetition by him of the same information at a later, properly conducted interview ought also to be excluded (*R* v *Ismail* [1990] Crim LR 109). In this case it was held that to accede to the prosecution's submission that misconduct in earlier interviews could be 'cured' by a properly conducted inter-view would be contrary to the spirit of s. 76, which was designed to protect against false confessions. Even if the defence accept that there was no oppression in the later interviews, and that the further confessions were volunteered, they could still seek to have them excluded purely on the grounds the first interview was oppress-ive; answers A and B are therefore incorrect. The other confessions may not be excluded — this, as always, is a matter for the trial judge — answer C is therefore incorrect.

Evidence and Procedure, para. 2.13.2.1

Answer 8.8

Answer **D** — Section 82(1) of the Police and Criminal Evidence Act 1984 makes it clear that the law is no longer concerned with whether a confession was made to a person in authority, such as a police or customs officer, and that the statutory test for admissibility is equally applicable to, for example, an informal admission to a friend or colleague. Answer A is therefore incorrect.

When the case against a defendant in a joint trial depended on the prosecution proving the guilt of a co-defendant, and the evidence against the co-defendant consisted solely of their own out-of-court confession, then that confession would be admissible against the defendant but only insofar as it went to proving the co-defendant's guilt. At the end of the prosecution case the defendant would have a case to answer, because the jury could properly find, first, that the co-defendant was guilty on the basis of their own confession, and then go on to find that the fact of the co-defendant's guilt coupled with any other evidence incriminating the defendant was sufficient to prove the latter's guilt.

This was the finding by a 3:2 majority judgment in the House of Lords in *R v Hayter* [2005] UKHL 6, despite the general principle that confession is relevant and admissible only against its maker. Therefore answers B and C are incorrect.

Evidence and Procedure, para. 2.13.2

9 Disclosure of Evidence

STUDY PREPARATION

Once again, this is an area that began life as a common law development through the courts, being later encapsulated in statute — the Criminal Procedure and Investigations Act 1996 (as amended by the Criminal Justice Act 2003).

Although most of the specific responsibilities under the Act fall on the disclosure officer, the general duties of the disclosure system are important to all police officers and others involved in the gathering of evidence.

As well as understanding the main principles of the Criminal Procedure and Investigations Act — and the code that accompanies it — you should also understand the practical aspects of disclosure schedules, defence statements and retention of materials.

QUESTIONS

Question 9.1

There is a statutory duty imposed by the Criminal Procedure and Investigations Act 1996 to disclose material to the defence.

Upon which of the following is that duty imposed?

A The Crown Prosecution Service.
B A police disclosure officer.
C A police investigating officer.
D A police officer in charge of the case (OIC).

Question 9.2

The Criminal Procedure and Investigations Act 1996 defines what is termed 'a criminal investigation' in relation to recording and retaining material.

At which point in the following examples would the officers involved be deemed to be involved in 'a criminal investigation'?

A Officers are planning surveillance on premises but no suspect has been identified.

B Officers are keeping premises under observation with a view to identifying a suspect.

C Officers are keeping premises under observation and are observing a particular suspect.

D Officers are observing a particular suspect with a view to trying to discover whether a crime has been committed.

Question 9.3

Police officers have been keeping observations on a petrol station, suspecting that an armed robbery will take place. Part of this operation involves videotaping the petrol station and the area surrounding it, and keeping a surveillance log. While engaged on the petrol station observations, the officers witness KHAN commit a series of thefts from unattended motor vehicles. They make original notes in their pocket notebooks of what they saw KHAN do, and they check the videotape, which does not show anything of the thefts from the vehicles.

In relation to the case against KHAN, what do the prosecution have to disclose in order to comply with the Criminal Procedure and Investigations Act 1996?

A Everything they have, as they are engaged on a criminal investigation.

B Only the surveillance log, as the tape does not show the thefts.

C The videotape must be disclosed or the case could be halted.

D Only the officers' pocket notebooks, with the original notes, need be disclosed.

Question 9.4

LEE has been charged with murder, and is awaiting committal to the Crown Court.

In relation to the unused evidential material held by the prosecution, how much, if any, needs to be disclosed prior to committal to ensure LEE's right to a fair trial?

A All of the unused material must be disclosed, or the case may be halted as an abuse of process.

B Some of the material should be disclosed at an early stage (e.g. information to assist a bail application).

C None of the material, as the Criminal Procedure and Investigations Act 1996 requires disclosure after committal only.

D Most of the material should be disclosed, except that material which has been deemed to be 'sensitive'.

Question 9.5

There is a statutory duty on the defence to provide a defence statement to the court and the prosecutor in connection with an indictable offence.

Within what time limit must the defence statement be provided?

A 14 days prior to the trial commencing.

B 14 days after the committal proceedings.

C 14 days after receiving primary initial disclosure.

D 14 days after receiving secondary disclosure.

Question 9.6

By virtue of s. 5 of the Criminal Procedure and Investigations Act 1996, when a case is committed to the Crown Court, the accused must give a defence statement to the prosecutor.

What information should be contained in that statement?

A Only the defence case in general terms.

B The exact nature of the defence case.

C The defence case in general terms and areas where they take issue with the prosecution.

D The defence case in general terms and areas where they take issue with the prosecution, and why.

Question 9.7

DAWLISH is giving evidence at the Crown Court as a prosecution witness. During DAWLISH's evidence-in-chief, she gives evidence which is materially inconsistent with the first statement she made earlier to the police. In her first statement to the police DAWLISH stated that she had seen the accused at the place where the crime was committed about three hours before the crime was committed. This statement was contained in the schedule of unused material, but was not disclosed by the prosecution as it did not undermine their case. It is on her second statement to the police, which was disclosed, that she is now giving evidence.

What should the prosecution now do in relation to the first statement?

A Nothing, as disclosure rules ceased to apply when the trial began.

B Nothing, as the statement only supports the prosecution case; it does not undermine it.

C The prosecution should ensure it is retained in case of any future appeal.

D The prosecution should disclose it immediately so that the defence can use it in cross-examination to discredit the testimony of the witness.

Question 9.8

Detective Sergeant MEREDITH was the disclosure officer on a particular complex fraud case; unfortunately he broke his leg playing rugby. The case is nearing the stage where secondary disclosure is to be made.

At this stage who is responsible for assigning a new disclosure officer?

A Detective Sergeant MEREDITH's first line manager.

B Detective Sergeant MEREDITH's first line manager, or the police officer in charge of the investigation.

C Detective Sergeant MEREDITH's first line manager, or the police officer in charge of the investigation in consultation with the Crown Prosecution Service.

D The prosecutor from the Crown Prosecution Service who is in direct charge of the investigation.

Question 9.9

During a police investigation into a street robbery, a key eyewitness provides a statement outlining in detail the description of the attacker. When the robber is eventually captured, he admits the offence on audio-recorded interview and there is ample supporting evidence to show he is guilty. The key eyewitness's description, however, is completely different from the actual appearance of the accused.

Which of the following is true in relation to whether this statement should be included on the schedule and disclosed?

A The prosecution should disclose it if the disclosure officer considers it undermines the prosecution case.

B The prosecution should disclose it only if the prosecutor considers it undermines the prosecution case.

C The prosecution should disclose it only if the prosecutor and the disclosure officer agree it undermines the prosecution case.

D The prosecution should disclose it even if no one involved in the process considers it undermines the prosecution case.

Question 9.10

Constable CARPENTER is engaged in enquiries into an allegation of assault against BRODERICK. Constable CARPENTER obtains a statement from a witness that indicates that BRODERICK was not the person responsible for the assault.

What action best outlines Constable CARPENTER's responsibility as an investigator in relation to this witness statement as required by the Code of Practice under the Criminal Procedure and Investigations Act 1996?

A He should retain the statement and include it on the relevant sensitive material schedule.

B He should retain the statement and disclose it himself as it undermines the prosecution case.

C He should carry out further investigation to gather further evidence that would assist the defence.

D He should inform the prosecutor and seek guidance as to the correct procedure to follow.

Question 9.11

Constable SONG received anonymous information that stolen vehicles were being hidden in a garage. She attended the area one evening with Detective Constable GRANT in an unmarked police vehicle, which they used to keep observation on the garage. They saw NEWMAN pull up in a Range Rover and they approached him to question him about the car. On seeing them, he sped off and was lost. NEWMAN was traced two days later and was lawfully arrested. This was witnessed by MARTIN. Constable SONG became the disclosure officer, and subsequently discovered that Detective Constable GRANT was under investigation by the complaints department for giving false evidence in court in a recent case.

In relation to material that needs to be disclosed to the defence, which of the following is correct?

A A statement would have to be obtained from MARTIN and disclosed to the defence.

B The investigation against Detective Constable GRANT may have to be disclosed, even though he has not been convicted.

C The details of the police vehicle used for the observation would not need to be disclosed.

D As the anonymous information is inadmissible as evidence, the fact of its existence does not need to be conveyed to the prosecutor.

Question 9.12

SAVILLE was sentenced at court to a term of imprisonment of 18 months. However, owing to the length of time he had spent on remand and other factors, he was released after 5 months from the date of his conviction.

In relation to the retention of material as outlined by the Criminal Procedure and Investigations Act 1996, which of the following statements is true?

A The material no longer needs to be retained as SAVILLE has been released.

B The material will need to be retained for a further month.

C The material will need to be retained for a further 13 months.

D The material will need to be retained for a further 6 months.

Question 9.13

Section 3 of the Criminal Procedure and Investigations Act 1996 requires the prosecution to make primary initial disclosure, where applicable, before the defendant is due to face trial.

When must the primary initial disclosure be made by the prosecution?

A At least 7 days before the trial.

B At least 2 days before the trial.

C As soon as practicable after the duty to disclose material arises.

D At least 7 days from when the duty to disclose material arises.

Question 9.14

EAST appeared in Crown Court as a defendant for an offence of robbery. Before the trial, EAST's solicitor served a defence statement on the prosecution, outlining an alibi for the offence, which the police were able to negate. EAST elected to give evidence on his own behalf during the trial and, under cross-examination, he put forward a different alibi to the offence. As a result, the prosecuting barrister sought permission from the court to examine EAST about the contents of his defence statement.

Could the prosecution's request be granted in these circumstances?

A No, under no circumstances may a defendant be cross-examined in relation to a defence statement.

B Yes, the request may be granted in these circumstances.

C No, a defendant may be cross-examined in relation to a defence statement only when he or she is accused of an offence of perjury.

D Yes, a defendant may be cross-examined in relation to a defence statement on every occasion.

Question 9.15

BOURIMECH has been charged with attempted rape and has been committed for trial. The disclosure officer, Detective Constable JOHNSON has discovered a previous allegation of crime made against the complainant in the attempted rape case, which indicated that she was a prostitute and that she had stolen from the male who had made this complaint. Detective Constable JOHNSON discovered that the male who made this previous allegation had given false details and could not be traced, this crime had in fact been 'no crimed'.

Should this previous unsubstantiated crime complaint be disclosed under the Criminal Procedure and Investigations Act 1996?

A This should be disclosed as it is relevant material.

B This should be disclosed as it undermines the prosecution case.

C This should not be disclosed as it was a false allegation.

D This should not be disclosed as it was not recorded as a crime and is not therefore relevant material.

Question 9.16

WHALEN and AGRID were jointly charged with fraud relating to counterfeit computer software from a major software company. The prosecutor was aware that there was material in the hands of the major software company that may be prejudicial to the prosecution case; however, as the company is American they cannot get hold of the material, and the company is refusing to supply it.

What is their liability in relation to disclosure of this material to the defence?

A The prosecutor must obtain the material, or risk the prosecution being stayed.

B The prosecutor must disclose to the defence why they think the material may be prejudicial.

C The prosecutor is under no duty to disclose material that has not come into their hands.

D The prosecutor can apply to have a witness summons served against the company, but the defence cannot do so.

ANSWERS

Answer 9.1

Answer **A** — The duty imposed by the Criminal Procedure and Investigations Act 1996 falls upon the prosecutor. In cases involving the police, the prosecutor is the Crown Prosecution Service (CPS). Although this could not be achieved without the assistance of the police, the duty is upon the prosecutor, and answers B, C and D are therefore incorrect. While the duty of disclosure is placed on the prosecutor, the police have a responsibility to assist in this process. The Home Secretary's Consultation Document recognised the critical role of the police in an effective and fair disclosure process:

> There will be a heavy reliance on the investigator (the police) to identify material which ought to be disclosed, given the material itself will not necessarily be scrutinised by the prosecutor.... The investigator will also need to assist the prosecutor by telling him what he thinks are the issues of the case: the system demands a significant degree of liaison between the prosecutor and the investigator as a case develops and the issues in the case change.

All three of the roles performed by police officers outlined in the question bear the responsibility of this role.

Evidence and Procedure, para. 2.14.3

Answer 9.2

Answer **A** — The Criminal Procedure and Investigations Act 1996 Code of Practice under Part II of the Act outlines the definitions. Code 2.1 defines criminal investigations as:

> ... investigations which begin in the belief that a crime may be committed, for example when the police keep premises or individuals under observation for a period of time, with a view to the possible institution of criminal proceedings.

In these cases the investigation may well have started some time before the defendant became a suspect, and answers C and D are therefore incorrect. In order to satisfy the disclosure requirements, police officers should consider recording and retaining material in the early stages of an investigation. This would be the earliest stage, even before an actual operation had begun, and answer B is therefore incorrect.

Evidence and Procedure, para. 2.14.3.3, App.2.2

Answer 9.3

Answer **C** — Clearly the officers' eyewitness account of the thefts would have to be disclosed, but what of the details of the surveillance which in effect were not part of the case in question? There is case law in relation to this. The prosecution only have to disclose material relevant to the prosecution in question; for instance, surveillance logs concerning another matter would not need to be disclosed (*R v Dennis*, 13 April 2000, unreported) and answers A and B are therefore incorrect. The videotape, however, is a different matter. In *DPP v Chipping*, 11 January 1999, unreported, the prosecution failed to disclose that there was a closed circuit television at the site where the offences were alleged to have taken place. The police officers viewed the tape but felt that it had no use, and it was destroyed. The court held that this information should have been disclosed. The result of this failure to disclose the evidence led to the case being dismissed as an abuse of process — answer D is therefore incorrect.

Evidence and Procedure, para. 2.14.4.2

Answer 9.4

Answer **B** — There has always been an ethical dimension to the duty to disclose, and the decision in *R v DPP, ex parte Lee* [1999] 1 WLR 1950 is an indication that it survives the introduction of the Criminal Procedure and Investigations Act 1996. In *Lee*, the Divisional Court considered whether the prosecution had a duty to disclose unused material in indictable-only offences prior to committal. The statutory framework for disclosure set out in the 1996 Act is silent as to any such duty until after committal. But there may well be reasons why it would be helpful to the defence to know of unused material at an earlier stage. For example, the following circumstances were considered by the court:

- the previous convictions of the alleged victim when they might be expected to help the defence in a bail application;
- material to help an application to stay proceedings as an abuse of process;
- material to help the defendant's arguments at committal;
- material to help the defendant prepare for trial, e.g. eyewitnesses whom the prosecution did not intend to use.

Kennedy LJ said that a responsible prosecutor might recognise that fairness required that some of this material might be disclosed. Therefore, only some of the material should be disclosed, and answers A, C and D are therefore incorrect.

Evidence and Procedure, para. 2.14.4.3

Answer 9.5

Answer **C** — By s. 5 of the Criminal Procedure and Investigations Act 1996, once primary prosecution disclosure has taken place and the case is committed to the Crown Court, the accused must give a defence statement to the prosecutor. The defence statement must be served within 14 days of the prosecution's compliance with the duty of primary initial disclosure. The court, however, may grant an extension entirely at its discretion, and may order further extensions on the same basis. As the time limit is from primary initial disclosure only, no other time is applicable and answers A, B and D are therefore incorrect.

Evidence and Procedure, para. 2.14.4.5

Answer 9.6

Answer **D** — The defence statement should outline the defence case in general terms. In addition, those issues, relevant to the case, which the accused disputes with the prosecution must be set out with reasons. This requirement to give reasons is intended to stop the defence going on a 'fishing expedition' to look speculatively at material in order to find some kind of defence. Because the defence statement must outline more than just a case in general terms, answer A is incorrect. The defence statement need not go so far as to set out the exact nature of the defence case (e.g. its oral cross-examination), and answer B is therefore incorrect. Note that the defence must outline where they are in dispute with the prosecution *and* state the reasons why, and answer C is therefore incorrect.

Evidence and Procedure, para. 2.14.4.5

Answer 9.7

Answer **D** — The duty is on the prosecution to continue to review the disclosure of prosecution material right up until the case is completed (acquittal, conviction or discontinuance of the case), and answer A is therefore incorrect. Material must be disclosed if the prosecutor forms the opinion that there is material which might undermine the prosecution case, or might reasonably be expected to assist the accused's defence. Even if the information did not undermine the prosecution case, the material might have to be disclosed, and answer B is therefore incorrect. It is worth asking a number of pertinent questions: Would the previous statement bring the witnesses' credibility into question? Would this then assist the accused's defence? If the answer to both these questions is 'yes', the prosecutor would have to do more than just retain the information: it would have to be disclosed immediately to allow the defence an opportunity effectively to cross-examine the witness, and answer C is therefore incorrect.

Evidence and Procedure, para. 2.14.4.9

Answer 9.8

Answer **B** — In all cases there must be an OIC and a disclosure officer.

In the Criminal Procedure and Investigations Act 1996 Code of Practice at para. 3.7 it is outlined that if, during a criminal investigation, the officer in charge of an investigation or disclosure officer for any reason no longer has responsibility for the functions falling to him, either his supervisor or the police officer in charge of criminal investigations for the police force concerned must assign someone else to assume that responsibility. That person's identity must be recorded, as with those initially responsible for these functions in each investigation.

So it can be either the supervisor **or** the police officer in charge of criminal investigations for the police force concerned that has responsibility for reassigning the role, and there is no need to consult the CPS on this matter; answers A, C and D are therefore incorrect.

Evidence and Procedure, para. 2.14.5.11

Answer 9.9

Answer **D** — Where disclosure is required, the first task is to create a schedule of all *non-sensitive material* which may be relevant to the investigation, and which has been retained by the police but which does not form part of the prosecution case. Once the schedules have been completed, the disclosure officer must decide what material, if any (whether listed on the schedules or not), might undermine the prosecution case. The disclosure officer must draw this information to the attention of the prosecutor and the reasons why he or she believes that the material undermines the prosecution case. In addition to the schedules and copies of material which undermine the prosecution case, the Codes of Practice to the 1996 Act require the disclosure officer to provide a copy of any material, whether or not he or she considers it to undermine the prosecution case. One example of this would be a record of the first description of a suspect given to the police by a potential witness, whether or not the description differs from that of the alleged offender. Irrespective of any person's opinion, this material would have to be disclosed, and answers A, B and C are incorrect.

Evidence and Procedure, para. 2.14.5.4

Answer 9.10

Answer **C** — Paragraph 3.4 of the Code of Practice to the Criminal Procedure and Investigations Act 1996, requires investigators to pursue all reasonable lines of inquiry, *whether these point towards or away from the suspect*. Although the officer must retain the statement, it would not fit the definition of sensitive material (i.e. material which the investigator believes it is not in the public interest to disclose). Thus, sensitive material does not mean evidence which might harm the prosecution case, and answer A is therefore incorrect. It is the prosecutors' job to disclose the statement, not the police officers', and answer B is therefore incorrect. Answer D is avoiding the clear responsibility outlined in the Code of Practice and is therefore incorrect.

Evidence and Procedure, para. 2.14.5.4

Answer 9.11

Answer **B** — What is relevant to the offence, and needs to be disclosed, is a question of fact. In *DPP* v *Metten*, 22 January 1999, unreported, the court held that the actual arrest for an offence was not relevant to the case as it did not fall within the definition of an investigation in s. 2(1) of the Criminal Procedure and Investigations Act 1996, and answer A is therefore incorrect.

Material obtained during an investigation does not have to be admissible in court for it to undermine the prosecution case (*R* v *Preston* (1994) 98 Cr App R 405), and therefore the anonymous information should form part of the schedule sent to the prosecutor and answer D is incorrect. Where officers have used an unmarked police vehicle for observation, information relating to the surveillance and the colour, make and model of the vehicle should not be withheld (*R* v *Brown and Daley* (1987) 87 Cr App R 52), and answer C is therefore incorrect. Disclosure of previous convictions and other matters which affect the credibility of the witness, might undermine the prosecution case. Some guidance is given by the case of *R* v *Guney* (1998) 2 Cr App R 242. In *Guney*, the court said that the defence are not entitled to be informed of every occasion when any officer has given evidence 'unsuccessfully', or whenever allegations are made against him or her. However, in this case the court felt that disclosure should have been made. It will therefore be a question of fact in each case, and consultation with the Crown Prosecution Service is advisable if there is any doubt.

Evidence and Procedure, para. 2.14.6.1

Answer 9.12

Answer **B** — Paragraphs 5.6 to 5.10 of the Code of Practice to the Criminal Procedure and Investigations Act 1996 set out the retention periods where a person has been convicted. All material which may be relevant must be retained at least:

- until the person is released from custody or discharged from hospital in cases where the court imposes a custodial sentence or hospital order;
- in all other cases, for 6 months from the date of conviction.

If the person is released from the custodial sentence or discharged from hospital earlier than 6 months from the date of conviction, the material must be retained for at least 6 months from the date of conviction. So, in the circumstances of the scenario, the material needs to be kept for a further month to comply with the Code and answers A, C and D are incorrect.

Evidence and Procedure, para. 2.14.6.3

Answer 9.13

Answer **C** — There are no specific time periods by which primary initial disclosure must be made under s. 3 of the Criminal Procedure and Investigations Act 1996. Answers A and B are therefore incorrect. There are provisions to set such time limits, but at this time disclosure must be made as soon as practicable after the duty arises (and not within 7 days — therefore answer D is incorrect).

It was held in *R* v *Bourimech* [2002] EWCA Crim 2089 that when disclosure is not made within a reasonable period, the case may be lost. In this case, the prosecution disclosed the contents of a crime report to the defence a day before the trial was due to commence. This amounted to unfairness in the proceedings.

Evidence and Procedure, para. 2.14.4.3

Answer 9.14

Answer **B** — This issue was examined in the case of *R* v *Lowe* [2003] EWCA Crim 3182. It was held in this case that there may be occasions where the defence statement is allowed to be used in cross-examination, namely when it is alleged that the defendant has changed his or her defence, or in re-examination to rebut a suggestion of recent invention. Answer A is therefore incorrect.

Such a request will not be granted on every occasion, therefore answer D is incorrect. There is no requirement for the defendant to be facing a charge of perjury, therefore answer C is incorrect.

Evidence and Procedure, para. 2.14.4.4

Answer 9.15

Answer **A** — The Criminal Procedure and Investigations Act 1996 is concerned with the disclosure of material which is obtained during the course of a criminal investigation and which may be relevant to the investigation. Material can be in any form and should be widely interpreted. This applies to any material coming to the knowledge of officers involved in the case at any stage of the investigation or even after a suspect has been charged. This is material which the investigator, OIC or disclosure officer consider has some bearing on any offence being investigated or any people being investigated for those offences or any of the surrounding circumstances.

The material will be relevant whether it is beneficial to the prosecution case, weakens the prosecution case or assists the defence case. It is not only material that will become 'evidence' in the case that should be considered; any information, record or thing which may have a bearing on the case can be material for the purposes of disclosure. The way in which evidence has been obtained in itself may be relevant.

The unsubstantiated crime may not undermine directly the prosecution case, but it is relevant material and ought to be disclosed; answer B is therefore incorrect.

In *R v Bourimech* [2002] EWCA Crim 2089 the Court of Appeal held that material concerning false allegations in the past may be relevant material. Indeed in *Bourimech*, where a similar crime complaint was disclosed in a large clip of other documentation (albeit two days before trial) to the defence, and the defence failed to notice it the appellant's conviction was quashed. The Court held that failure to previously disclose the material did amount to an unfairness in the proceedings; answers C and D are therefore incorrect.

Evidence and Procedure, para. 2.14.6.1

Answer 9.16

Answer **C** — There may be occasions in an investigation where a third party refuses to hand over material in their possession and/or allow it to be examined. Where access to the material is declined or refused by the third party and it is believed that it is reasonable to seek production of the material before a suspect is charged, the investigator should consider making an application under sch. 1 to the Police and Criminal Evidence Act 1984 (special procedure material). Where the suspect has been charged and the third party refuses to produce the material, application will have to be made to the court for a witness summons (such an application can also be made by the defence). Answer D is therefore incorrect. The third party can then argue at court that it is not material, or that it should not be disclosed on grounds of public interest immunity.

In *R v Alibhai and others* [2004] EWCA Crim 681, the Court of Appeal held that the obligation to disclose third party material only arises if and when that material has come into the possession of the prosecutor and, at this early stage, when, in the opinion of the prosecutor, it might undermine the prosecution's case. However, the Attorney General requires the prosecutor to take steps to secure such material. The prosecutor enjoys a margin of consideration in relation to what are reasonable steps.

Clearly the court cannot issue summonses outside its jurisdiction and the prosecution cannot be asked to 'guess' what material the third party had or why he felt it may be prejudicial. Answers A and B are therefore incorrect.

Evidence and Procedure, para. 2.14.6.9

10 | Custody Officers' Duties

STUDY PREPARATION

The duties imposed by the Police and Criminal Evidence Act 1984 on custody officers are many and various, and, once again, there is no substitute for knowing them in detail. This is a big area, both in terms of its volume and its importance. The need to have custody officers at certain police stations, along with the exceptional circumstances when they will not be needed, are key areas; so too are the basic entitlements of anyone when arrested and brought to a police station.

You will need to know the occasions and grounds on which some of a suspect's entitlements can be delayed and, of course, you will have to know the highly examinable areas of clocks, relevant times and time limits. A complex scenario containing different times, days and locations can often induce panic! However, once you have got the formula for working out the relevant times clear in your mind, detention periods and reviews are very straightforward and questions on them should represent 'easy marks'.

Reviews both before and after charge should be known, as should the areas of searching prisoners, seizing property and the treatment of people in police detention.

QUESTIONS

Question 10.1

Inspector FERNQUEST is on duty at a designated police station. There are no sergeants in the custody unit and no sergeant who has no other role to perform in the police station.

In relation to who can perform custody duties in these circumstances which of the following is correct?

A Only an officer of the rank of sergeant may perform the role of custody officer.

B Only an officer of the rank of sergeant may perform the role of custody officer or a constable if a sergeant is not readily available to perform them.

C Inspector FERNQUEST can always perform the role of custody officer.

D Inspector FERNQUEST can perform the role of custody officer if a sergeant is not readily available to perform them.

Question 10.2

PARSONS has been arrested for an offence of theft and placed before the custody officer. Her details are obtained and items of property are taken from her, she is shown a copy of the property taken from her and asked to sign to indicate that this is a true record. She refuses to sign.

What does the Police and Criminal Evidence Act 1984 Codes of Practice state the custody officer should record?

A The fact she refused to sign should be recorded.

B The fact she refused to sign and the time she refused should be recorded.

C The fact she refused to sign should be recorded, also any reason, if given, for the refusal.

D The fact she refused to sign and the time she refused should be recorded, also any reason, if given, for the refusal.

Question 10.3

Constable BEER has arrested HICK for criminal damage at the enquiry office of a non-designated police station, where she works alone. Constable BEER intends dealing with HICK at her own station, as he is likely to be in custody only for an hour. Constable BEER has called for assistance from Constable FRY, who works in a neighbouring station.

Would it be appropriate for Constable BEER to act as custody officer for HICK in these circumstances?

A Yes, provided she informs an on-duty inspector of her intention.

B No, she is the officer in the case and must await the arrival of Constable FRY, who should act as custody officer.

C Yes, provided she informs an Inspector at a designated station of her intention.

D No, HICK may not be dealt with at a non-designated station.

Question 10.4

In certain situations a person will be subject to the Codes of Practice Code C of the Police and Criminal Evidence Act 1984 in relation to police detention.

In which of the following cases will the person be subject to being detained under Code C?

A PARSONS has been removed to a police station for his own safety under s. 135 of the Mental Health Act 1983.

B McVEY is being detained in a custody office in Birmingham, having been arrested on behalf of officers in Scotland, for a warrant for failing to appear in court in Scotland.

C GREEN has been convicted of an offence at court and has been returned to the nearest police station awaiting transport to prison.

D VERON is being detained after being arrested under s. 142(3) of the Immigration and Asylum Act 1999 to have his fingerprints taken.

Question 10.5

McDOUGAL was detained for robbery, and on his arrival at the police station his girlfriend was informed of his arrest. McDOUGAL was wanted for another offence of robbery in another police area, and the custody officer intended to transfer him there when the enquiries were complete in relation to the first offence.

What does Code C say about McDOUGAL's entitlement to have someone informed of his detention, as he will be transferred to another station?

A His girlfriend must be informed of his transfer before he is moved to another station.

B He will be entitled to have someone informed of his detention on arrival at the second station.

C His girlfriend must be informed of his transfer after he has been moved to another station.

D He has no further entitlement to have someone informed of his detention as his girlfriend has been informed.

Question 10.6

HALL has been arrested for the theft of a radio from a motor vehicle. HALL was arrested near the vehicle and he was accompanied by another person, who escaped the police. On his arrival at the custody office, HALL asked the custody officer,

Sergeant HOSKINS, if he could make a telephone call. The arresting officer asked for this right to be delayed, as he believed HALL might try to alert his accomplice of his arrest.

> Who would be able to authorise a delay of HALL's right to a telephone call in these circumstances?

A An inspector may authorise such a delay.

B Only a superintendent may authorise such a delay.

C Nobody, HALL has an absolute entitlement to make a phone call.

D The custody officer may authorise such a delay.

Question 10.7

HANSEN has been detained under the Terrorism Act 2000 for instigating terrorist activities. HANSEN has asked for a nominated person to be informed of her arrest; however, authorisation has been given to delay this right.

> What is the maximum period HANSEN may be detained in these circumstances before she must be allowed to exercise her right to have someone informed of her arrest?

A 24 hours.

B 36 hours.

C 48 hours.

D 96 hours.

Question 10.8

CONNOR has been arrested for armed robbery of a building society, where £50,000 was stolen. The officer in the case has proposed that CONNOR be denied his right to have someone informed of his arrest, as it may alert his accomplice, who has not yet been arrested. The duty Inspector is engaged at a firearms incident, but she can be contacted by mobile phone.

> Would it be lawful for the Inspector to authorise a delay to CONNOR's rights over the telephone in these circumstances?

A Yes, but the decision must be recorded in writing within 24 hours.

B No, the authorisation must be given by an officer not below the rank of super-intendent.

C Yes, but the decision must be recorded in writing as soon as practicable.

D No, the authorisation must be made in person.

Question 10.9

MARTIN was arrested for the kidnap and murder of a young girl. On his way to the police station, MARTIN made an unsolicited comment to Detective Constable BROCK that he had kidnapped another girl that day and that she was being held at a friend's house. On arrival at the station, MARTIN asked for a solicitor. Detective Constable BROCK requested an interview to be authorised immediately, in order to discover the whereabouts of the child.

If Detective Constable BROCK's request were granted, what should the custody officer do if MARTIN's solicitor were to arrive during the interview?

A The solicitor may be allowed access, unless this would cause a risk to the kidnapped girl.

B The authorisation will mean that the solicitor will automatically be excluded from the interview.

C The solicitor must be allowed access to MARTIN as soon as he or she arrives.

D An interview may not be authorised without a solicitor being present in these circumstances.

Question 10.10

KING was arrested at 10 am in Reading for an offence of theft. KING arrived at the police station at 10.15 am, when it was discovered that she was wanted for an offence of theft in Bristol. KING was interviewed and charged with theft, and at 3 pm the same day she was taken to Bristol to be interviewed, arriving at the custody office at 4.30 pm.

What would KING's 'relevant time' be, in relation to her detention in Bristol?

A 10 am.

B 3 pm.

C 10.15 am.

D 4.30 pm.

Question 10.11

Constable JUROVICH has arrested a person under s. 5 of the Prevention of Terrorism Act 2005 in order that a control order can be served against him; this control order imposes obligations on him for purposes connected with protecting members of the public from a risk of terrorism. Constable JUROVICH takes the person to the designated place.

How long can this person be kept at the designated place?

A Initially for 48 hours, which can be extended by a further 48 hours.

B Initially for 36 hours, which can be extended by a further 48 hours.

C Initially for 48 hours, which can be extended by a further 36 hours.

D Initially for 36 hours, which can be extended by a further 36 hours.

Question 10.12

PACE Code C gives guidance as to what a custody officer must record on a custody record when detaining a person with or without charge.

What details should be recorded on the custody record in these circumstances?

A The grounds for detention in the person's presence, unless it is apparent that he or she would not understand what was being said.

B The grounds for detention in the person's presence, regardless of his or her condition.

C The grounds for the person's detention which can be recorded at any time.

D The grounds for detention in the person's presence if it is practicable to do so.

Question 10.13

WEST, HILL and SANTOS have been arrested for criminal damage to a shop window. A witness saw one person from the group throwing a stone through the window, but was not able to identify the exact person who caused the damage. WEST has been interviewed by Constable KEANE, and the officer has asked the custody officer for him to be detained until the other two suspects are interviewed.

Under what circumstances may the custody officer detain WEST further in these circumstances?

A WEST may be detained if the custody officer has reasonable grounds to believe it is necessary to preserve evidence.

B WEST should be released as there is insufficient evidence against him to secure a conviction.

C WEST may be detained if the custody officer has reasonable cause to suspect it is necessary to preserve evidence.

D WEST may be detained until the investigation is complete against all three defendants.

Question 10.14

DENT was arrested for an offence of theft and taken to a nearby police station, arriving there at 2 pm. DENT's detention was authorised by the custody officer at 2.15 pm, and he was interviewed about the offence shortly after. DENT was released on bail at 4 pm, for further enquiries. DENT arrived at the station a week later at 2 pm, and his detention was authorised by the custody officer at 2.15 pm.

> What is the latest time that DENT's detention should be reviewed on the day when he returned to the station to answer his bail?
>
> **A** 6 pm.
> **B** 6.30 pm.
> **C** 6.15 pm.
> **D** 8.15 pm.

Question 10.15

BOWYER has been arrested for a summary offence. At 10 pm, Detective Constable HASSAN approached the custody officer, stating that he was not in a position to charge BOWYER and that a vital witness had been identified who would not be available until 9 am the following day. Detective Constable HASSAN asked if a superintendent could authorise BOWYER's continued detention beyond 24 hours in order to speak to the witness. BOWYER has been in custody for 14 hours.

> Could a superintendent authorise such a request at this stage of BOWYER's detention?
>
> **A** Yes, but only after he has been in custody for at least 15 hours.
> **B** No, not until he has been in custody for 24 hours.
> **C** Yes, but only after an inspector has conducted a second review.
> **D** No, as BOWYER has not been arrested for an indictable offence.

Question 10.16

Under ss. 43 and 44 of the Police and Criminal Evidence Act 1984, where a person has been in custody for 36 hours without being charged, the police must apply to a magistrate to extend that person's detention beyond that time.

> What is the total amount of detention time that can be authorised by magistrates beyond the original 36 hours, before a person must be charged or released (do *not* consider offences under the Terrorism Act 2000)?
>
> **A** 3 days.

B 72 hours.
C 36 hours.
D 60 hours.

Question 10.17

BRIARS has been in custody for 26 hours, having been detained under the Terrorism Act 2000. A warrant of further detention has been applied for and granted by a magistrate, and BRIARS has returned to the custody office.

At what intervals should BRIARS now be reviewed in relation to his detention, and who should conduct the reviews?
A There is no requirement to conduct further reviews.
B Reviews should be conducted at least every 12 hours by an inspector.
C Reviews should be conducted at least every 9 hours by an inspector.
D Reviews should be conducted at least every 12 hours by a superintendent.

Question 10.18

GRECHIN was charged and acquitted of a charge of murder by the Crown Court. Following further enquiries he was arrested under the Criminal Justice Act 2003 for that same murder and is in custody at the police station; GRECHIN is not precluded from further prosecution by virtue of s. 75(3) of that Act

Who is responsible for determining whether there is sufficient evidence to charge GRECHIN with murder again?
A The custody officer.
B An officer of at least the rank of superintendent.
C An officer of at least the rank of assistant chief constable (commander in Met Police).
D The Director of Public Prosecutions (DPP).

Question 10.19

CURSON has been arrested for harassment of her former boyfriend. She has been interviewed and the officer in the case, Constable HUQ, has asked the custody officer to release CURSON on bail to allow further statements to be taken before a decision is made whether or not to charge her. There are several witnesses in the case and not all are available at this time. Constable HUQ has expressed concern that CURSON may commit further offences against her ex-boyfriend and witnesses, and has asked that conditions be attached to her bail to prevent her from doing so.

If the custody officer determines that there is insufficient evidence to charge CURSON because of the evidence that may be provided by witnesses, under what circumstances may he/she attach conditions as requested by Constable HUQ?

A   That there was a genuine risk of CURSON re-offending.
B   That CURSON might interfere with witnesses in the case.
C   That CURSON might interfere with witnesses or the administration of justice.
D   Bail conditions may not be imposed in these circumstances.

Question 10.20

JANSEN has been arrested and charged with an offence of robbery. The custody officer has denied JANSEN bail, and he is being kept in custody for the next available court.

In relation to JANSEN's continued detention, when should reviews be conducted, and by whom?

A   By an inspector, at least every 9 hours.
B   By a custody officer, within 6 hours of the last review.
C   By a custody officer, within 9 hours of the last review.
D   By an inspector within 6 hours of the last review.

Question 10.21

LOCKE was arrested for affray, and on his arrival at the custody suite he was violent towards the custody officer. LOCKE was taken to a cell because of his behaviour and, because he had not been searched, the custody officer ordered him to be searched in the cell. The arresting officer, who was female, was present in the cell when LOCKE was searched by the male custody staff.

Have the provisions of s. 54 of the Police and Criminal Evidence Act 1984 (searching of detained persons) been complied with in these circumstances?

A   Yes, a female officer may search a male prisoner, provided it is not an intimate search.
B   Yes, provided the female officer did not conduct the search.
C   No, the female officer should not have been present at the search.
D   Yes, a female officer may search a male prisoner, provided it is not a strip search.

Question 10.22

PACE Code C, Annex A, allows for a person in police detention to be 'strip searched' in certain circumstances.

Who may authorise such a search for a prisoner in custody?
A   An inspector only.
B   A superintendent only.
C   An inspector before charge, and a custody officer after charge.
D   A custody officer.

Question 10.23

CRAWFORD was arrested and taken to the custody office of a designated police station. The arresting officer told the custody officer that CRAWFORD had a warning signal on Police National Computer (PNC) that, while in custody previously, she had concealed razor blades in her mouth and had used them to cause injury to herself. The custody officer decided that CRAWFORD's mouth should be searched for objects which she might use to harm herself.

Which of the following is true in relation to the search?
A   The custody officer can authorise this search at the custody office.
B   Only a superintendent can authorise this search at the custody office.
C   An inspector can authorise this search at medical premises.
D   Only a superintendent can authorise this search at medical premises.

Question 10.24

EVANS was arrested for deception and was accompanied at the time by her boyfriend BOLTON. When he was interviewed at the station, BOLTON admitted that EVANS was in possession of a stolen credit card, which she had concealed in her vagina. EVANS admitted possession of the credit card, but refused to submit to a search.

Could EVANS be subjected to an 'intimate search' in these circumstances?
A   Yes, but this could not be done by force.
B   Yes, she is in possession of stolen property.
C   Yes, and this may be done, if necessary, by force.
D   No, an intimate search may not be authorised in these circumstances.

Question 10.25

WILSON attends at the police station voluntarily, but after a short while is lawfully arrested for the offence he attended to be questioned about. PACE Code C, para. 12.2 provides a requirement for WILSON to have a continuous 8-hour 'rest period' while he is in detention.

When considering the 24 hours of detention, at what time does the calculation for a 'rest period' commence?

A 24 hours from his time of arrival at the station.
B 24 hours from the time of his last interview.
C 24 hours from the time of his arrest.
D 24 hours from the time his detention was first authorised.

Question 10.26

In relation to the treatment and welfare of a detained person, the PACE Codes of Practice, Code C, paragraph 8.6 describes how many meals a detainee should be offered whilst in custody.

How many meals should be offered to a detained person in any period of 24 hours?

A At least one light meal and at least two main meals.
B At least one light meal and at least one main meal.
C At least two light meals and at least one main meal.
D At least two light meals and at least two main meals.

Question 10.27

GARFIELD is employed as a civilian detention officer by his local police authority.

In relation to duties that he can perform, which of the following is correct?

A He may take a non-intimate sample, but he may not use force to do so.
B He may take a non-intimate sample and may use force to do so where necessary.
C He may take fingerprints and photographs, but may not take non-intimate samples.
D He may take photographs, but may not take fingerprints or non-intimate samples.

Question 10.28

BRIAR, aged 21, was arrested for theft and taken to the custody office, where she asked for her father to be informed of her detention. When the custody officer spoke to BRIAR's father, he informed her that BRIAR was suffering from a mental disorder, which would make it difficult for her to understand questions being put to her about the offence. BRIAR's condition was not apparent to either the custody officer or the arresting officer.

In relation to BRIAR's detention, what action should the custody officer now take?

A The custody officer must contact an appropriate adult, based on the information received from BRIAR's father.

B The custody officer must contact a medical practitioner to seek advice on BRIAR's condition before she is interviewed.

C The custody officer may decide whether or not an appropriate adult should be called, based on her own observations.

D The custody officer must contact a medical practitioner or a social worker to seek advice on BRIAR's condition before she is interviewed.

Question 10.29

CURTIS has been arrested for an offence of assault and has been given his rights under PACE. He has opted to speak with his solicitor on the phone, but wants it done privately.

In relation to this request, which of the following statements is correct?

A He should be allowed to speak to his solicitor, but in private only if this is practicable.

B He should be allowed to speak to his solicitor privately, and such a facility should normally be provided.

C He is allowed to consult with his solicitor privately only if this is done in person.

D He should be allowed to consult with his solicitor, but this must be done whilst the custody officer can hear the conversation.

Question 10.30

RODEN was arrested for an offence of theft, but will not be charged as there was insufficient evidence. Police wish to take RODEN's photograph for future use whilst she is still in police detention.

In relation to taking the photograph, which of the following is correct?

A The photograph can be taken without RODEN's consent and used for identification procedures.

B The photograph can be taken, but only if RODEN gives her permission.

C The photograph can be taken without RODEN's consent, but cannot be used for identification procedures.

D The photograph cannot be taken, as RODEN has not been charged/reported for a recordable offence.

Question 10.31

DEVLIN was stopped while driving his vehicle on a Saturday morning in Margate. The officer who stopped him, Constable GRADY, conducted a Police National Computer (PNC) check and discovered that DEVLIN was wanted for an offence of burglary in the Newcastle area. Constable GRADY arrested DEVLIN at 10 am and took him to the nearest designated station in Margate, where they arrived at 10.30 am. Constable GRADY contacted the police in Newcastle; however, they had no officers available to attend until later that day. The escorting officers finally arrived in the early hours of the next morning, and left with DEVLIN at 4 am on the Sunday. They transported DEVLIN to Newcastle, arriving in that force area at 11.10 am; they eventually arrived at Newcastle Police Station at 11.30 am on the Sunday.

What would DEVLIN's 'relevant time' be, in relation to his detention in Newcastle, if he was not interviewed for the offence in Margate?

A 10.30 am on the Saturday.

B 10 am on the Sunday.

C 11.10 am on the Sunday.

D 11.30 am on the Sunday.

Question 10.32

Constable CHAVEZ arrested CONNELLY at 3 pm on a Saturday for an offence of theft. Constable CHAVEZ radioed through to her station, but discovered that the custody office could not accept her prisoner at that time, as they were too busy. She decided to utilise her powers under s. 30A of the Police and Criminal Evidence Act 1984, to bail CONNELLY to the police station the next day. CONNELLY was released on bail by the officer at 3.30 pm on the Saturday. CONNELLY was due to answer bail at 2 pm on the Sunday, but he was late and arrived there at 2.30 pm. His detention was authorised by the custody officer at 2.50 pm.

From which time on the Sunday would CONNELLY's 'relevant time' be calculated, under s. 41 of the Police and Criminal Evidence Act 1984?

A 2.50 pm, the time he appeared before the custody officer on the Sunday.

B 2.20 pm, taking into account the time he was detained by the officer the previous day.

C 2.30 pm, the time he arrived at the police station on the Sunday.

D 2 pm, the time he was due to answer bail on the Sunday.

Question 10.33

Authorisation to search detainees and examine them to ascertain their identity under s. 54A of the Police and Criminal Evidence Act 1984 must be obtained by the custody officer.

Who, out of the following, can correctly give such authorisation?

A A superintendent only, either orally or in writing, provided it is confirmed in writing as soon as practicable.

B An inspector before charge, or a custody officer after charge, either orally or in writing, provided it is confirmed in writing as soon as practicable.

C An inspector only, either orally or in writing, provided it is confirmed in writing as soon as practicable.

D An inspector only, and permission may only be given in writing.

Question 10.34

BAILEY is 14 years of age and has been arrested on suspicion of raping a girl his own age. The witness has described a distinguishable tattoo that the attacker had on his chest, and BAILEY has agreed to have a photograph of a tattoo on his chest taken for identification purposes. BAILEY was photographed by a male police officer in the medical room and no other people were present. BAILEY was made to remove only his shirt, and the tattoo on his chest was photographed. This was done without the presence of an appropriate adult, as BAILEY had signified that he did not want one present.

Did the search and photographing of the tattoo comply with the Codes of Practice, in respect of dealing with juvenile detainees?

A Yes, as BAILEY had signified that he did not want an appropriate adult present.

B No, there must *always* be at least one other person present, even if an appropriate adult does not have to be present.

C Yes, because the officer was not photographing intimate parts of the body, the presence of an appropriate adult was not necessary.

D No, because an appropriate adult should have been present in the above circumstances.

Question 10.35

BELL was arrested for being found drunk in a public place. He was so intoxicated that, when he arrived at the station, he was placed in a cell after being searched and fell asleep immediately. BELL had nothing in his property which would have assisted in identifying him, therefore the arresting officer asked the custody officer whether BELL could be examined without his consent, while he was asleep, to establish if he had any tattoos that might assist in identifying him.

Could an examination be authorised without BELL's consent, under s. 54A of the Police and Criminal Evidence Act 1984, in these circumstances?

A Yes, because it was not practicable to obtain his consent.

B No, an examination may be conducted without a detainee's consent only where that person has refused to give consent.

C No, an examination may be conducted without consent only in cases of urgency.

D No, because the officer was not attempting to establish whether BELL was a person who had been involved in the commission of an offence.

Question 10.36

REDPATH was arrested for shoplifting and taken to the custody office. On REDPATH's arrival, the custody officer noticed that he was intoxicated. REDPATH was detained for interview and placed in a cell to allow him time to sober up. While he was asleep, REDPATH's sister contacted the custody officer to advise that REDPATH was an alcoholic and might get the shakes while in custody. When he was sober, REDPATH was interviewed and returned to his cell pending preparation of charges. He displayed no symptoms of the shakes, and did not complain of an illness. Unfortunately, while he was in his cell, REDPATH died from asphyxiation. REDPATH was not medically examined while in custody.

Would the police have any liability in relation to the custody officer's failure to act on the information given by REDPATH's sister, and not arranging for him to be medically examined?

A No, as REDPATH's sister is not a registered health care professional or doctor.

B Yes, a custody officer should act on any information relating to a detainee's health care, no matter what the source.

C No, since REDPATH displayed no symptoms of his illness and did not ask to see a doctor.

D Yes, but only if REDPATH's sister informed the custody officer that he was taking medication or seeking medical help for his condition.

Question 10.37

Code C, paragraph 2.1A of the PACE Codes of Practice defines when a detained person will be deemed to be 'at a police station' for the purposes of detention.

Which of the following statements most accurately describes when a detained person will be 'at a police station' according to this code of practice?

A When the person first arrives within the confines of the custody office, whether or not the custody officer is ready to receive them.

B When the person is first brought before the custody officer, within the confines of the custody office.

C When the person first arrives inside a police station, whether this is the custody office or another part of the building.

D When the person first arrives within the confines of the police station, whether this is inside the building or in an enclosed yard which is part of the police station.

Question 10.38

SNOOKS is 13 years of age and was arrested for an offence of aggravated vehicle taking. On his arrival at the custody office, SNOOKS declined legal advice and stated that neither of his parents would attend the police station to act as an appropriate adult. GRIFFITHS works for the local Youth Offending Team (YOT) and attended to act as appropriate adult. On arrival at the custody office, GRIFFITHS told the custody officer that it was their policy that all juveniles represented by the YOT must also be represented by a solicitor. GRIFFITHS insisted on a solicitor being called.

Would GRIFFITHS be able to overrule SNOOKS' decision, and ensure that he seeks legal advice?

A Yes, as GRIFFITHS was acting in SNOOKS' best interests.

B No, GRIFFITHS had no right to ask for a solicitor to attend once SNOOKS had declined legal advice.

C Yes, because SNOOKS is under 14 and it is in his best interests.

~~D~~ No, the decision remains with SNOOKS, who does not have to speak to the solicitor.

Question 10.39

Code C, paragraph 3.4 of the PACE Codes of Practice requires the custody officer to note on the custody record any comment the detainee makes in relation to the arresting officer's account.

According to this code of practice, which of the following statements is correct in relation to who may give the account of the arrest?

A The account may only be given by the arresting officer, but this may be done from a remote location.

B The account may be given from a remote location by the arresting officer, or through another officer accompanying the detainee.

C The arresting officer must be present to give the account in order for any comments to be admissible.

~~D~~ The officer giving the account must be at the custody office, whether it is the arresting officer or another officer.

Question 10.40

A person may be detained without charge when they are suspected of having committed an offence under the Terrorism Act 2000.

What is the maximum period they may be detained for?

A 96 hours.

B 7 days.

~~C~~ 14 days.

D 21 days.

ANSWERS

Answer 10.1

Answer **D** — Section 36 of the Police and Criminal Evidence Act 1984 requires that one or more custody officers must be appointed for each designated police station. However, in *Vince* v *Chief Constable of Dorset* [1993] 1 WLR 415 it was held that a chief constable was under a duty to appoint one custody officer for each designated police station and had a discretionary power to appoint more than one but this duty did not go so far as to require a sufficient number to ensure that the functions of custody officer were always performed by them.

The provision of the facility of a custody officer must be reasonable. Section 36(3) states that a custody officer must be an officer of at least the rank of sergeant. However, s. 36(4) allows officers of **any** rank to perform the functions of custody officer at a designated police station if a sergeant is not readily available to perform; answer A is therefore incorrect. This means that, as unlikely as it seems, officers higher in rank than a sergeant can perform custody duties and not just constables; answer B is therefore incorrect. However this is only where a sergeant is not readily available to perform them; answer C is therefore incorrect.

The effect of s. 36(3) and (4) is that the practice of allowing officers of any other rank to perform the role of custody officer where a sergeant (who has no other role to perform) is in the police station must therefore be unlawful.

Evidence and Procedure, para. 2.15.5

Answer 10.2

Answer **B** — If a person is requested to sign an entry on a custody record in accordance with the Police and Criminal Evidence Act 1984 Codes of Practice and refuses, this too should be recorded, as should the time the detained person refused (Code C, para. 2.7); answer A is therefore incorrect. There is no requirement for the person to give reasons for their refusal, nor for this reason to be recorded; answers C and D are therefore incorrect.

Evidence and Procedure, para. 2.15.5

Answer 10.3

Answer **C** — Section 30 of the Police and Criminal Evidence Act 1984 states that an arrested person should be taken to a designated station as soon as practicable after arrest, unless he or she has been bailed prior to arrival at the police station. Section 30A of the Police and Criminal Evidence Act 1984 allows a constable to release on bail a person who is under arrest. However, an arrested person may be dealt with at a non-designated station, provided the person is not likely to be detained for longer than six hours. Answer D is therefore incorrect.

Where a person is taken to a non-designated station, s. 36(7) states that an officer of any rank not involved in the investigation should perform the role of custody officer. However, if no such person is at the station, the arresting officer (or any other officer involved in the investigation) may act as custody officer. Answer B is therefore incorrect.

Where a person is dealt with in a non-designated station in the circumstances described, an officer of at least the rank of Inspector at a *designated station* must be informed. Answer A is therefore incorrect.

Evidence and Procedure, para. 2.15.5

Answer 10.4

Answer **A** — The Police and Criminal Evidence Act Codes of Practice, Code C, para. 1.10 outlines that the code applies to those persons who have been removed to a police station for their own safety under s. 135 of the Mental Health Act 1983 — therefore the person detained in answer A *will* be subject to the Codes of Practice.

People arrested on warrants issued in Scotland by officers under the Criminal Justice and Public Order Act 1994, s. 136(2), or arrested or detained without warrant by officers from a police force in Scotland under s. 137(2) will not be subject to the Codes (Code C, para. 1.12(i)); therefore answer B is incorrect.

Those who are convicted or remanded prisoners held in police cells on behalf of the prison service under the Imprisonment (Temporary Provisions) Act 1980 will also not be subject of the Codes of Practice (Code C, para. 1.12(iv)). Answer C is therefore incorrect.

Code C, para. 1.12(ii) outlines that the codes do not apply to those detained after being arrested under s. 142(3) of the Immigration and Asylum Act 1999 to have their fingerprints taken. Answer D is therefore incorrect.

Please note that Code C, para. 1.12 also states that although the code does not apply, the provisions on conditions of detention and treatment in paras 8 and 9 of Code C are the *minimum* standards of treatment for such detainees.

Evidence and Procedure, para. 2.15.6.1

Answer 10.5

Answer **B** — A person in police detention is entitled to have one friend or relative or person known to him/her or who is likely to take an interest in his/her welfare informed of his or her whereabouts as soon as practicable (PACE Code C, para. 5.1).

Code C, paras 3.1 and 5.3 outline that this is a continuing right that applies every time a person is brought to a police station under arrest. This means that a person may have another person (or the same person) informed of his or her detention at the second station. Answer D is therefore incorrect. Note it is the detained person's right; no one has the right to be told of detention without the detained person's permission.

There is no specific requirement for the custody officer to re-contact the person who was originally informed of the detention, either before or after the prisoner has been moved. Answers A and C are therefore incorrect.

Evidence and Procedure, para. 2.15.6.2

Answer 10.6

Answer **A** — Detained people are entitled to speak to a person on the telephone for a reasonable time, or send letters. The right can be denied or delayed when a person has been arrested for an indictable offence. Answer C is incorrect for this reason.

PACE Code C, para. 5.6 states that an officer of the rank of *inspector* or above may authorise the delay if he or she has reasonable grounds for believing, amongst other things, that by allowing the person to exercise his or her right, it will alert other people suspected of having committed such an offence but not yet arrested for it. A superintendent may authorise the delay as well as an inspector, and therefore answer B is incorrect. A custody officer may not authorise such a delay (unless of course the custody officer is an inspector). Answer D is therefore incorrect.

Evidence and Procedure, para. 2.15.6.2

Answer 10.7

Answer **C** — The maximum delay of a person's right not to be held 'incommunicado', in a non-terrorist case, is 36 hours. *However*, in terrorist cases, it is 48 hours (Section 41(3) of the Terrorism Act 2000). Consequently, answers A, B and D are incorrect.

Evidence and Procedure, para. 2.15.6.2

Answer 10.8

Answer **C** — First, the inspector must be satisfied that CONNOR is in custody for an indictable offence (which is the case in the scenario). Also, the Inspector must have reasonable grounds for believing that if CONNOR were to exercise his right to have someone informed of his arrest, it might alert other people suspected of the offence but not yet arrested.

PACE Code C, Annex B states that the grounds for action under this Annex shall be recorded and the person informed of them as soon as practicable. The authorisation can initially be made orally, either in person or by telephone, but must be recorded in writing as soon as practicable. Answer D is therefore incorrect.

The decision must be recorded in writing *as soon as practicable*; therefore, answer A is incorrect.

The authorising officer for delaying rights under Code C, para. 5 was reduced from superintendent to inspector by virtue of s. 74 of the Criminal Justice and Police Act 2001; therefore answer B is incorrect.

Evidence and Procedure, para. 2.15.6.2

Answer 10.9

Answer **A** — A superintendent must be satisfied that MARTIN is in custody for an indictable offence (which is the case in the scenario). Also, the superintendent must have reasonable grounds for believing that to delay an interview will involve an *immediate* risk of harm to people (PACE Code C, para. 6.6(b)(i)). Again, given the circumstances in the question, this is a reasonable assumption, and answer D is incorrect for this reason.

If an interview is authorised in these circumstances (sometimes this is called an 'urgent interview'), it does not mean that the solicitor will be automatically excluded on his or her arrival, and answer B is therefore incorrect.

When an interview has been started without the solicitor being present, he or she must be allowed to be present when he or she arrives, *unless* para. 6.6(b)(i) applies (i.e. the delay will involve an immediate risk of harm to people). Answer C is incorrect because of this exception.

Evidence and Procedure, para. 2.15.6.6

Answer 10.10

Answer **D** — Under s. 41(2) of the Police and Criminal Evidence Act 1984, a person's 'relevant time' is calculated from the time he or she arrives at the police station, or 24 hours after he or she was arrested, whichever is earlier. Since most detainees arrive at the station well within 24 hours, their relevant time is generally when they first arrive at the station.

There are several variations contained within s. 41 of the 1984 Act, and the circumstances covered in the question are to be found in s. 41(5). Section 41 states:

(5) If —
    (a) a person is in police detention in a police area in England and Wales ('the first area'); and
    (b) his arrest for an offence is sought in some other police area in England and Wales ('the second area'); and
    (c) he is taken to the second area for the purposes of investigating that offence, without being questioned in the first area in order to obtain evidence in relation to it,
the relevant time shall be —
    (i) the time 24 hours after he leaves the place where he is detained in the first area; or
    (ii) the time at which he arrives at the first police station to which he is taken in the second area,
whichever is the earlier.

Note that under s. 41(5), the detainee has, in effect, two detention clocks running. It is important to note that the second clock will start earlier if the detained person is questioned about the offence under investigation in the other police area. However, in the scenario KING was *not* questioned about the offence in the first station, and she arrived at the second station *less than 24 hours* after her departure from the first station. Her relevant time is, therefore, her time of arrival at the second station (i.e. 4.30 pm). Answers A, B and C are therefore incorrect.

Evidence and Procedure, para. 2.15.6.8

Answer 10.11

Answer **A** — The Prevention of Terrorism Act 2005 allows a control order to be served against an individual that imposes obligations on him/her for purposes connected with protecting members of the public from a risk of terrorism.

Section 5 of the 2005 Act allows a constable to arrest a person to ensure that the order can be served on that person. Section 5(2) requires the constable who has arrested an individual to take him/her to the designated place (which is the same as the Terrorism Act 2000) that the constable considers most appropriate as soon as practicable after the arrest.

An individual taken to a designated place under this section may be detained there until the end of 48 hours from the time of his arrest unless:

- he/she has become bound by a derogating control order made against him/her on the Secretary of State's application; or
- the court has dismissed the application

If the court considers that it is necessary to do so to ensure that the individual in question is available to be given notice of any derogating control order that is made against him, it may, during the 48 hours following his arrest, extend the period for which the individual may be detained under this section by a period of no more than 48 hours (Prevention of Terrorism Act 2005, s. 5).

So this is initially 48 hours, which can be extended by a further 48 hours which is answer A; therefore answers B, C and D are incorrect.

Evidence and Procedure, para. 2.15.7.7

Answer 10.12

Answer **D** — Under PACE Code C, para. 3.23, a custody officer should record the grounds for detention in the person's presence if it is practicable to do so. Therefore, in cases such as when a person is drunk or violent, it may not be practicable to record the grounds in his or her presence. Answer B is therefore incorrect. This recording of the grounds must, by virtue of Code C, para. 3.4, be before that person is questioned about any offence; answer C is therefore incorrect.

Answer A is incorrect. If a person cannot understand what is being said, it may be 'impracticable' to record the grounds for detention in his or her presence; however, it is not written as such in the Codes of Practice.

Evidence and Procedure, para. 2.15.6.9

Answer 10.13

Answer **A** — If the custody officer has determined there is insufficient evidence to charge, the person must be released unless the custody officer has *reasonable grounds for believing* that the person's detention is necessary to preserve or to obtain evidence by questioning the person (s. 37 of the Police and Criminal Evidence Act 1984). Answer C is incorrect as 'reasonable grounds for believing' requires a greater amount of evidence than 'reasonable cause to suspect'.

Although the person may ultimately be detained until all the suspects are interviewed in these circumstances, each case must be considered on its own merit, against the above criteria. Answer D is therefore incorrect.

Where the suspicion rests with several suspects, it may be appropriate to hold all suspects until they are all interviewed before deciding whether there is sufficient evidence to warrant a charge against any or all of them. This continues provided suspicion on that individual has not been dispelled in the interim and the questioning is not unnecessarily delayed (*Clarke* v *Chief Constable of North Wales, Independent,* 22 May 2000); answer B is therefore incorrect.

Evidence and Procedure, para. 2.15.6.12

Answer 10.14

Answer **B** — An officer of at least the rank of inspector must review a person's detention *at least once in the first six hours* of his or her detention. The person's 'review clock' will be calculated from the time that the custody officer first authorised detention. Where a person is released on bail, the 'review clock' will stop until he or she returns to answer bail. It will recommence when the custody officer authorises detention on the second occasion.

In relation to the scenario, DENT's detention was authorised at 2.15 pm, which means that the first review should be conducted within six hours from that time. The time of his arrival, 2 pm, is irrelevant in terms of the 'review clock' (although it is significant in relation to his relevant time and overall period of detention). DENT was released on bail at 4 pm, so that on his return, he has 1 hour and 45 minutes on his 'review clock'.

DENT returned to the station at 2 pm, but again this time is irrelevant in terms of reviews, as his time in custody resumed at 2.15 pm. His review is due in 4 hours and 15 minutes (subtracting the original 1 hour and 45 minutes from 6 hours), at 6.30 pm. Answers A, C and D are therefore incorrect.

Evidence and Procedure, para. 2.15.7.6

Answer 10.15

Answer **D** — An officer of at least the rank of superintendent can authorise a person's continued detention, beyond 24 hours, up to a maximum of 36 hours. The period can be shorter, but if a shorter period is granted, this can be extended up to the 36-hour limit.

The superintendent must be satisfied that an offence being investigated is an 'indictable offence' and that there is not sufficient evidence to charge, *and* the investigation is being conducted diligently and expeditiously, *and* that the person's detention is necessary to secure and preserve evidence or obtain evidence by questioning (s. 42 of the Police and Criminal Evidence Act 1984).

The extension of a person's detention must be made *within 24 hours* of the relevant time. Also, the extension cannot be granted before *at least two reviews* have been carried out by the reviewing inspector.

Although reviews are normally carried out after six and nine hours, they can be conducted earlier. Section 42(4) is deliberately worded, so that the focus is not on the length of time a person has been in custody, but on how many reviews have been conducted.

A superintendent could authorise an extension in these circumstances, but would have to wait until a second review had been conducted.

As BOWYER was arrested for a summary offence no extension beyond the 24-hour period of initial detention can be made; answers A, B and C are therefore incorrect.

Evidence and Procedure, para. 2.15.7.4

Answer 10.16

Answer **D** — A superintendent may authorise a person's detention without charge to a maximum of 36 hours (s. 42 of the Police and Criminal Evidence Act 1984). Any further periods of detention must be authorised by a magistrate.

A magistrate may initially authorise detention for 36 hours (s. 43). However, this period may be extended by 24 hours upon further application (s. 44), which means that a magistrate may authorise a maximum detention period of 60 hours. A person may not be detained for longer than 96 hours in total without being charged or released. Answers A, B and C are therefore incorrect.

Evidence and Procedure, para. 2.15.7.5

Answer 10.17

Answer **A** — Where a person is in custody for an offence under the Terrorism Act 2000, the first review should be conducted as soon as reasonably practicable after his or her arrest and then at least every 12 hours; after 24 hours it must be conducted by an officer of the rank of superintendent or above. Once a warrant of further detention has been obtained there is no requirement to conduct further reviews.

Answer D would be correct only if the person was in custody prior to going to court for the warrant of further detention hearing. Answer B would be incorrect in any circumstances; once a person has been in custody for longer than 24 hours, having been arrested under the 2000 Act, his or her detention must be reviewed by a superintendent. Answer C is incorrect as reviews of people detained under the 2000 Act must be conducted every 12 hours, following the first review.

Evidence and Procedure, para. 2.15.7.7

Answer 10.18

Answer **B** — When a person is arrested under the provisions of the Criminal Justice Act 2003, which allow a person to be re-tried after being acquitted of a serious offence which is a qualifying offence specified in sch. 5 to that Act and not precluded from further prosecution by virtue of s. 75(3) of that Act, the detention provisions of PACE are modified and make an officer of the rank of superintendent or above who has not been directly involved in the investigation responsible for determining whether the evidence is sufficient to charge; answers A, C and D are therefore incorrect.

Evidence and Procedure, para. 2.15.9.1

Answer 10.19

Answer **D** — Section 37(7) of PACE states that:

If the custody officer determines that he has before him sufficient evidence to charge the person arrested with the offence for which he was arrested, the person arrested —
(a) shall be released without charge and on bail for the purpose of enabling the Director of Public Prosecutions to make a decision under s. 37B below,
(b) shall be released without charge and on bail but not for that purpose,
(c) shall be released without charge and without bail, or
(d) shall be charged.

Under s. 37B, where a person is released under s. 37(7)(a) above, the investigating officer must send information to the DPP as soon as possible to consider the evidence against the suspect. Under s. 47(1A) of the Act, a custody officer may attach bail conditions to a suspect who falls within the category described in s. 37(7)(a) above. *However*, in the case described in this particular question, the custody officer has determined that there is *insufficient* evidence to charge the suspect, because of the requirement to speak to witnesses. In this case, s. 47(1A) does not apply and conditions may not be attached to the suspect's bail in these circumstances. Answers A, B and C are incorrect for this reason. Practically speaking, s. 47(1A) above applies to suspects where the custody officer has determined that there is sufficient evidence to charge a suspect, and advice is being sought from the CPS as to the appropriate charge. In those cases, bail conditions may be appropriate.

Evidence and Procedure, para. 2.15.9.1

Answer 10.20

Answer **C** — Where bail has been refused, the decision must be reviewed by the custody officer within 9 hours of the last review (the first being the post-charge review). These reviews must continue. Note the 9-hour, and not the 6-hour, interval; thus answer B is incorrect.

The reviewing officer when a person has been charged is the custody officer and not the inspector. Answers A and D are therefore incorrect.

Evidence and Procedure, para. 2.15.10

Answer 10.21

Answer **B** — Under s. 54(9) of the Police and Criminal Evidence Act 1984, the constable carrying out a search must be of the same sex as the person searched. Section 54 does not prohibit a constable of the opposite sex from being present at a search, provided it is not a strip search or an intimate search. Answer C is therefore incorrect.

Because of the prohibition referred to above, under s. 54(9), a constable may *not* search a person of the opposite sex, whether during an ordinary search, a strip search or an intimate search. Answers A and D are therefore incorrect.

Evidence and Procedure, para. 2.15.11.8

Answer 10.22

Answer **D** — Code C, Annex A, para. 10 outlines the need for strip searches to be carried out. The Police and Criminal Evidence Act 1984, however, outlines who may authorise such a search. Although not specifically mentioning strip searches, s. 54 of the 1984 Act clearly outlines that it is the custody officer who authorises the searching of persons in police detention. Section 54(7) outlines the only exception to this, that is, intimate searches. This is the case before or after charge. As the authority of either an inspector or superintendent is not required, answers A, B and C are therefore incorrect.

Evidence and Procedure, para. 2.15.11.11

Answer 10.23

Answer **A** — An intimate search may be authorised by an inspector and consists of the physical examination of a person's bodily orifices *other than the mouth*. The physical examination of a person's mouth is *not* classed as an intimate search, and may be authorised by a custody officer for the same reasons as a strip search. Answers B and C are incorrect as the search in the scenario does not amount to an intimate search.

An *intimate search* may be conducted only by a medical practitioner (or registered nurse) at medical premises, where the purpose of the search is to discover a Class A drug. Other *intimate searches* may be conducted at the custody office by police officers (provided all the criteria are met). Answer D is therefore incorrect for this reason.

Evidence and Procedure, para. 2.15.11.12

Answer 10.24

Answer **D** — An intimate search may be authorised by an inspector and consists of the physical examination of a person's bodily orifices other than the mouth. The search may be authorised *only* when the authorising officer has reasonable grounds for believing that the person has concealed an article which could be used to cause physical injury, or has concealed a Class A drug which he or she intended to supply to another or export.

Since the search may be authorised only for the above purposes, answers A, B and C are incorrect. Where an intimate search is authorised correctly, reasonable force may be used (s. 117 of the Police and Criminal Evidence Act 1984). However, in these circumstances, the use of force is not permitted.

Evidence and Procedure, para. 2.15.11.12

Answer 10.25

Answer **C** — PACE Code C, para. 12.2 provides that a detained person must have a continuous eight-hour 'rest period' while he or she is in detention; this period should normally be at night. The period should be free from questioning, travel or any interruption by police officers in connection with the case. Under para. 12.2, the period of rest may not be interrupted or delayed, except at the request of the person, his or her appropriate adult, or his or her legal representative, unless there are reasonable grounds for believing that it would:

- involve a risk of harm to persons or serious loss of, or damage to, property; *or*
- delay unnecessarily the person's release from custody; *or*
- otherwise prejudice the outcome of the investigation.

If a detainee is arrested at a police station after going there voluntarily, the period of 24 hours is calculated from the time *the person was arrested*, and not from the time of arrival at the police station or when detention was first authorised. Answers A and D are therefore incorrect.

Answer B is incorrect as, on occasion, a person may spend 24 hours in custody without being interviewed. Although this may be rare, logic would suggest that the person must be allowed to rest during that period!

Evidence and Procedure, para. 2.15.11.17

Answer 10.26

Answer **C** — At least *two light meals* and *one main meal* shall be offered in any period of 24 hours. Answers A, B and D are therefore incorrect. Drinks should be provided at meal times and upon reasonable request between meal times (PACE Code C, para. 8.6). Meals should so far as practicable be offered at recognised meal times (Code C, note 8B).

Evidence and Procedure, para. 2.15.11.17

Answer 10.27

Answer **B** — Sections 38 and 39 of the Police Reform Act 2002 provide certain police powers for police authority employees. This recognises that many of the functions that were traditionally carried out by police officers are now performed by accredited (and trained) staff, and gives statutory footing to their actions. Part of this group are detention officers, and they are given power to carry most of the functions that were previously given only to police officers. It includes taking non-intimate samples; answers C and D are therefore incorrect. By virtue of s. 38(8) of the Police Reform Act 2002, detention officers have the same power to use *reasonable* force that is given to police officers in the execution of the same duties; answer A is therefore incorrect.

Evidence and Procedure, para. 2.15.3.2

Answer 10.28

Answer **A** — PACE Code C, para. 1.4 states categorically that if an officer has *any suspicion* or *is told in good faith* that a person of any age is suffering from a mental disorder or is otherwise mentally vulnerable, in the absence of clear evidence to dispel that suspicion, the person shall be treated as such for the purposes of the Codes. There is no room for interpretation, and the custody officer must contact an appropriate adult in these circumstances. Answer C is therefore incorrect.

Although a custody officer may contact a medical practitioner or a social worker for advice as to how to deal with a person suffering from a mental disorder, Code C, para. 1.4 makes it clear that the information given by BRIAR's father is sufficient to ensure that a person is treated as such in these circumstances. Answers B and D are therefore incorrect.

Evidence and Procedure, para. 2.15.13

Answer 10.29

Answer **B** — Code C, note 6J clearly outlines that whenever a detainee exercises his or her right to legal advice by consulting with or communicating with a solicitor, he or she must be allowed to do so in private; therefore, answer D is incorrect. This means both personal consultations and those done via the telephone; answer C is therefore incorrect. Although this may well present practical difficulties in a busy custody unit, note 6J makes it clear that the normal expectation is that such a facility *will* be available, and a private consultation should be allowed; answer A is therefore incorrect.

Evidence and Procedure, para. 2.15.6.6

Answer 10.30

Answer **A** — Section 64A of the Police and Criminal Evidence Act 1984 has been amended by the Serious and Organised Crime and Police Act 2005. This means that a person who is detained at police station or elsewhere than at a police station may be photographed with his/her consent; or if it is withheld or it is not practicable to obtain it, without his/her consent (guidance is provided in Code D, paras 5.12 to 5.18). This applies to all persons who are in police detention, and not just those charged or reported for an offence; therefore answer D is incorrect.

Code D para. 5.12 sets out the circumstances where a person who is not detained at a police station may be photographed.

Photographs can be taken with or without consent (although consent should be asked for). Code D, paras 5.12 to 5.18 outline these requirements. As photographs can be taken without consent, answer B is incorrect. A photograph taken under s. 64A may be used by, or disclosed to, any person for any purpose related to the prevention or detection of crime, the investigation of an offence or the conduct of a prosecution or the enforcement of a sentence. Code D, Note 5B gives examples where such photographs may be of use. The use of the photograph is for any conduct which constitutes a criminal offence (whether under UK law or in another country). This therefore allows the photograph to be used in the preparation of any identification procedure that is being arranged involving the suspect (Code D, para. 3.30); answer C is therefore incorrect.

Evidence and Procedure, para. 2.15.12

Answer 10.31

Answer **B** — Question relating to relevant times can appear daunting, but they can be solved using fairly constructed formulas. In the scenario, DEVLIN has not been arrested for a 'local offence' so the last part of the table 4 at para. 2.15.7.3 applies, therefore the relevant time is the time he arrived at a police station in the police area where he was wanted (not just the time he arrived in that force's area; therefore answer C is incorrect) *or* 24 hours after arrest, whichever is the earliest. He was arrested at 10 am on Saturday, and arrived at the station at 11.30 am on the Sunday, therefore the relevant time is 10 am on the Sunday (by applying the formula, and noting that 10 am is in fact earlier than 11.30 am!). Answer D is therefore incorrect. Had DEVLIN been questioned by Margate police about the burglary, the relevant time would have been 10.30 am on the Saturday (time of arrival at local station); but as he was not questioned, answer A is incorrect.

Evidence and Procedure, para. 2.15.6.8

Answer 10.32

Answer **C** — Section 41(2)(ca) of the Police and Criminal Evidence Act 1984 takes into account police officers' powers to bail people from the scene of their arrest.

Where a person has been bailed under s. 30A of the Act, his or her relevant time will be the time that he or she arrives at the station (2.30 pm in the scenario). Answers A, B and D are incorrect for this reason.

Evidence and Procedure, para. 2.15.6.8.

Answer 10.33

Answer **C** — The authority to search detainees and examine them to ascertain their identity is contained in s. 54A of the Police and Criminal Evidence Act 1984. An officer of at least the rank of Inspector may authorise a person to be searched or examined in order to ascertain if the person has any mark that would tend to identify him or her as a person involved in the commission of an offence, or any mark that would assist to identify him or her (including showing that he or she is not a particular person). Answers A and B are therefore incorrect. Authority may be given either orally or in writing, provided it is confirmed in writing as soon as practicable (see Code D, para. 5.2). Answer D is therefore incorrect.

Evidence and Procedure, para. 2.15.12.1

Answer 10.34

Answer **D** — The authority to search detainees and examine them to ascertain their identity is contained in s. 54A of the Police and Criminal Evidence Act 1984 and governed by Code D, paras 5.1 to 5.11. Note that this power can be authorised by an Inspector where consent is absent, although where consent is given it must be proper consent. For a juvenile aged 14 or over this must be his or her consent, and that of the appropriate adult. The search, if it involves the removal of more than the person's outer clothing, will be conducted in accordance with Code C, annex A, para. 11 (strip searches). Paragraph 11(c) states that except in cases of urgency, where there is a risk of serious harm to the detainee or others (which is not the case in the scenario), a search of a juvenile may take place in the absence of an appropriate adult only if the juvenile signifies in the presence of the appropriate adult that he or she does not want the adult to be present during the search, and the appropriate adult agrees; therefore answer A is incorrect. Thus, even though the officer was not photographing intimate parts of the body, because this case involved a juvenile, the consent of both the detainee and the appropriate adult must be obtained; answer C is therefore incorrect. If an appropriate adult is not present without appropriate consent, there need to be at least two people present during the search only where intimate parts of the body may be exposed; answer B is therefore incorrect.

Evidence and Procedure, para. 2.15.12.1

Answer 10.35

Answer **D** — The authority to search detainees and examine them to ascertain their identity is contained in s. 54A of the Police and Criminal Evidence Act 1984 and Code D, para. 5. An officer of at least the rank of inspector may authorise a person to be searched or examined for two general purposes, namely, in order to ascertain if the person:

- has any mark that would tend to identify him or her as a person involved in the commission of an offence, (para. 5(1)(a)); *or*
- has any mark that would assist to identify him or her (including showing that he or she is not a particular person), (para. 5(1)(b)).

The detainee in the scenario would fall within para. 5(1)(b) above. Searches and examinations may be conducted without the person's consent in order to identify him or her for either of the above reasons. However, the requirements are different, depending on the paragraph concerned. A search or examination under para. 5(1)(a) above may be carried out without the person's consent only when consent is withheld, or it is not practicable to obtain consent. A search or examination under para. 5(1)(b) above (which is applicable to the scenario) may be carried out without the person's consent only when the detainee has refused to identify himself or herself, or the authorising officer has reasonable grounds for suspecting that the person is not who he or she claims to be.

Returning to the scenario, the detainee had not been given the opportunity to refuse to identify himself, therefore a search under this section could not take place at this time. As can be seen above, the search could not be authorised because it was not practicable to obtain his consent, because this requirement only applies to detainees who fall within para. 5(1)(a) above. Answer A is therefore incorrect.

Answer B is incorrect because, as can be seen above, an examination may be conducted without a detainee's consent for reasons other than where a person has simply refused to give consent.

Lastly, an examination without a detainee's consent may be authorised for any of the reasons listed above. There is no mention in the Codes of Practice of 'urgent' cases. Answer C is therefore incorrect.

(Note that reasonable force may be used, if necessary, to carry out a search or examination under this section.)

Evidence and Procedure, para. 2.15.12.1, App.2.5

Answer 10.36

Answer **B** — Any information that is available about the detained person should be considered in deciding whether to request a medical examination. In *R v HM Coroner for Coventry, ex parte Chief Constable of Staffordshire Police* (2000) 164 JP 665 the detained person had been drunk on arrest and was detained to be interviewed. The detained person made no complaint of his condition but his sister called the police to advise them that he would get the shakes. It was clear at interview and the following morning that he did have the shakes but no complaint was made and no doctor was called. A verdict of accidental death aggravated by neglect was an option in the case, as the deceased had died whilst in police custody. The court considered the facts, such as the deceased's withdrawal and the warning as to his condition, from which a properly directed jury could have concluded that had certain steps been taken it was at least possible that the deceased would not have died. In this case a verdict of accidental death aggravated by neglect was left open to the jury, even though a doctor at the inquest gave evidence that he doubted whether calling a doctor would have made any difference to the eventual outcome.

The clear message from this case is that the custody officer must take into account *any* information about a person's health, whether it comes from the detainee, the arresting officer or any other source. Answer A is therefore incorrect. Whether or not the detainee displayed symptoms of illness is immaterial and therefore answer C is incorrect. Also, the fact that the detainee's sister failed to mention whether or not the person was taking medication or seeking medical help is also immaterial and answer D is therefore incorrect.

Evidence and Procedure, para. 2.15.11.18

Answer 10.37

Answer **D** — According to the PACE Codes of Practice, Code C, paragraph 2.1A:

> A person is deemed to be 'at a police station' for these purposes if they are within the boundary of any building or enclosed yard which forms part of that police station.

This definition is far wider than merely inside a police station (and answer C is incorrect) or within the confines of a custody office (and answer B is incorrect). It is important to note this addition to the Codes of Practice, because the time the person arrives at the police station forms the basis of a detainee's relevant time and could have an effect later in the person's detention when investigating officers are seeking extensions. It should also be noted that since many custody offices have CCTV cameras fitted, the accuracy of such information is crucial in case of challenges. Answer A is completely wrong, as a person may be waiting in a police vehicle in a yard outside a busy custody office for some time and this will count towards their overall detention time.

Evidence and Procedure, para. 2.15.5

Answer 10.38

Answer **D** — The situation in this question is covered by Code C, paragraph 6.5A of the PACE Codes of Practice, which states:

> In the case of a juvenile, an appropriate adult should consider whether legal advice from a solicitor is required. If the juvenile indicates that they do not want legal advice, the appropriate adult has the right to ask for a solicitor to attend if this would be in the best interests of the person. However, the detained person cannot be forced to see the solicitor if he is adamant that he does not wish to do so.

As can be seen from this paragraph, a juvenile cannot be made to speak with a legal representative, even if this is in his/her best interests, regardless of his/her age or the local YOT's policy. Answers A and C are therefore incorrect. The appropriate adult *does* have the right to ask for a solicitor to attend if it is in the best interests of the detainee (and answer B is incorrect); however, this right does not extend to forcing the juvenile to speak to the solicitor once he/she has arrived at the custody office.

Evidence and Procedure, para. 2.15.6.6

Answer 10.39

Answer **B** — The PACE Codes of Practice, Code C, paragraph 3.4 states that the custody officer shall:

> note on the custody record any comment the detainee makes in relation to the arresting officer's account but shall not invite comment. If the arresting officer is not physically present when the detainee is brought to a police station, the arresting officer's account must be made available to the custody officer remotely or by a third party on the arresting officer's behalf. If the custody officer authorises a person's detention the detainee must be informed of the grounds as soon as practicable and before they are questioned about any offence.

Answer A is correct in the sense that the information regarding a person's arrest may be given from a remote location; however, it is incorrect as the information may also be given by another officer accompanying the detainee. Answer C is incorrect, as the arresting officer need not be present when giving the information, and answer D is incorrect as para. 3.4 above clearly states that the information may be given from a remote location.

Evidence and Procedure, para. 2.15.6.9

Answer 10.40

Answer **C** — The maximum period a person may be detained without charge under PACE is 96 hours, following the granting of an extension by the magistrates' court. However, when a person is in police detention and is suspected of having committed an offence under the Terrorism Act 2000, the *maximum* period is 28 days (Terrorism Act 2000, sch. 8, para. 36(3A). Answers A, B and D are therefore incorrect.

Evidence and Procedure, paras 2.15.7, 2.15.7.5

11 | Identification

STUDY PREPARATION

The area of identification was regulated by the Police and Criminal Evidence Act 1984 and principally Code D of the Codes of Practice. This is the starting point. However, identification is a very fertile area for defence lawyers and, not surprisingly, case law in this area has extended or restricted the legislation — depending on your viewpoint. One thing is certain — the case law has complicated the subject for those who are trying to study it.

The law regulating the various methods of identification (e.g. witness testimony, ID parades, DNA samples and fingerprints) should be known, and you should be able to recognise the relevant circumstances and authorisation levels that must exist.

QUESTIONS

Question 11.1

The definition of a suspect being 'known', is given in the PACE Codes of Practice, Code D.

In which of the following cases would the suspect be 'known'?

A Where there is ample information known to the police to justify the arrest of a person for suspected involvement in the offence.

B Where there is ample information known to the police to give reasonable grounds to arrest a person for suspected involvement in the offence.

C Where there is ample information known to the police to give reasonable suspicion to arrest a person for involvement in the offence.

D Where there is ample information known to the police to justify the arrest of a person for actual involvement in the offence.

Question 11.2

Constable BRANNIGEN was off duty when she witnessed a robbery; she tried to tackle the robbers but was knocked unconscious. Constable BRANNIGEN regained consciousness six hours later, and two hours after this she was interviewed by detectives. She gave a description of one of the suspects, but named the other as MACKONICY, a well-known local criminal.

Which of the following statements is true?

A Constable BRANNIGEN's description of the suspects is not 'a first description' as it was given several hours after the incident.

B Constable BRANNIGEN may be shown photographs to help identify both the suspects.

C Constable BRANNIGEN may *not* be shown photographs to help identify the suspects, as she is a police officer.

D Constable BRANNIGEN's description of the suspects would be 'a first description' even though it was given several hours after the incident.

Question 11.3

STEVENS was involved in a fight, and Constable WRIGHT tried to arrest him. STEVENS escaped and Constable WRIGHT circulated his description. Constable WRIGHT resumed driving the police van. A short time later Constable WRIGHT was called to transport a prisoner. The prisoner was placed in the van and Constable WRIGHT was asked to identify the suspect as STEVENS, who had escaped earlier. This was because the arresting officer recognised STEVENS from the description circulated by Constable WRIGHT. Constable WRIGHT identified STEVENS as the person who had escaped, which STEVENS strongly denied.

Is this identification of STEVENS procedurally correct?

A Yes, provided Constable WRIGHT recorded the first description he gave.

B Yes, as the confrontation was unavoidable.

C No, STEVENS should have been kept away from Constable WRIGHT and an identification parade arranged.

D No, as Constable WRIGHT should not have been asked if he recognised STEVENS.

Question 11.4

Police officers investigating a robbery have obtained some forensic evidence and some video evidence that implicates four people. The officers have also obtained witness statements that state that the witnesses may well be able to recognise the suspects. One witness is certain that he will be able to identify the suspect. The officers are convinced that the evidence they have is unequivocal and a conviction is likely.

In relation to identification parades, which of the following statements is true?

A The officers should hold a parade *only* if the suspects dispute the identification during interview.

B The officers should arrange an identification parade as a matter of course, as they have witnesses.

C The officers need not hold an identification parade as there is other evidence implicating the suspects.

D The officers need not hold an identification parade as there is video evidence implicating the suspects.

Question 11.5

SADDIQUE has been arrested on suspicion of robbery, and there are eye-witnesses available. SADDIQUE denies involvement and disputes the identification. He demands an identification parade. The local area has a very low-percentage Asian population and the identification officer states that he will not run an identification parade, as it is unlikely that sufficient volunteers will be found. SADDIQUE's solicitor offers to find volunteers to assist.

In relation to these circumstances, which of the following is true?

A The identification officer can proceed to other methods as he feels there is little chance of obtaining sufficient volunteers.

B The solicitor's offer cannot be accepted; the courts have held that such an agreement is outside PACE Code D.

C The identification officer must at least take reasonable steps to obtain sufficient volunteers.

D The identification officer can proceed to other methods, as he has reasonable grounds to suspect that it will not be possible to obtain sufficient volunteers.

Question 11.6

STEWART has been accused of rape and disputes identification. The investigating officer considers that a video identification would, *in the circumstances*, be the most satisfactory course of action to take as an identification parade is not practical. The identification officer *may* show a witness a video film of a suspect.

In conducting the video identification, the identification officer should ensure that, in addition to the suspect, at least how many other people are on the film?

A 8 people.

B 10 people.

C 11 people.

D 12 people.

Question 11.7

FOLAN has been arrested for an offence of murder. This crime relates to the body of his wife that was discovered buried in the foundations of a building; it is estimated that it had been there for 20 years, about the time FOLAN's wife was reported as missing by her family. Police have evidence that FOLAN worked on this building as a bricklayer 20 years ago, and would have had legitimate access to it. The police have also located five other workers from that time and intend showing them a picture of FOLAN they obtained from 20 years ago to say whether they remembered seeing him at the building site at the time his wife disappeared.

A The suspect is known and an identification procedure must be held in any eventuality.

B An identification procedure will have to be held only if FOLAN disputes ever having been to the building site.

C An identification procedure will have to be held if FOLAN disputes that he murdered his wife.

D An identification parade need not be held as this is a recognition case and not an identification case.

Question 11.8

An armed robbery had taken place at a post office by a suspect wearing a mask to hide his features. The suspect demanded money, and this was recorded on video, which had a voice track. The post office worker who received the verbal threat, thought he recognised the voice as belonging to ROBB, a well-known local person.

In relation to voice identification, which of the following is true?

A The witness can give identification evidence of the voice, based on what he heard at the time.

B Only an expert witness can give voice identification evidence, based on the voice recording on the video.

C The jury should be allowed to hear the recording and compare it to the suspect's voice in court.

D Voice identification is not part of PACE Code D and is therefore inadmissible.

Question 11.9

BALLINGER was arrested on suspicion of burglary, as fingerprint identification from the scene of the crime was available. BALLINGER initially denied the offence, and the taking of his fingerprints was authorised to prove or disprove his involvement in the offence and taken for that purpose. Following further comparison and further interviews, BALLINGER admits the offence. BALLINGER has been charged and the officer in charge of the case wishes to take his fingerprints and photograph. BALLINGER refuses this request.

Which of the following statements is true?

A As BALLINGER has been charged, his fingerprints can be taken without his consent.

B As BALLINGER has been charged, his fingerprints can be taken only *with* his consent.

C As BALLINGER has refused, an inspector's authority, in writing, is required.

D As BALLINGER has refused, an inspector's authority, which can be oral or written, is required.

Question 11.10

DYSERT was charged with an assault and had her fingerprints taken. At court, she was found not guilty of the offence, and she has no previous convictions.

What should now happen to DYSERT's fingerprints held on file?

A The fingerprints must be destroyed as soon as practicable.

B The fingerprints must be destroyed upon application by DYSERT.

C The fingerprints can be retained and may be used in future police investigations.

D The fingerprints can be retained, but may not be used for future evidential purposes.

Question 11.11

HOWE has been charged with driving whilst disqualified, and when interviewed he made no comment at all. The police have on record a person with the same name who was also disqualified in the same year that HOWE is suspected of being, and identification of HOWE as the actual disqualified driver has not been made. The Crown Prosecution Service (CPS) propose to call HOWE's solicitor; in addition to currently representing HOWE she was present in court when the male known as HOWE was disqualified. The CPS only intend asking questions for the purpose of solely identifying the person disqualified from driving at the original court hearing.

Can the solicitor be called to identify HOWE as the disqualified driver?

A The solicitor cannot be called, as this would breach legal professional privilege.

B The solicitor cannot be called, as this would breach HOWE's right to be represented by a lawyer of his choice.

C The solicitor can be called, as she was a person present when HOWE was originally disqualified.

D The solicitor should not ordinarily be called, but can be called and this should only be entertained as a last resort.

Question 11.12

DOHENY is standing trial for rape, and DNA evidence will be an issue for the jury.

In relation to DNA evidence against DOHENY, which of the following is true?

A The DNA evidence will be sufficient to prove DOHENY was the assailant.

B The DNA evidence must be supported by other direct evidence.

C The DNA evidence can be supported only by other identification evidence.

D The DNA evidence can be supported by mere circumstantial evidence.

Question 11.13

Section 62 of the Police and Criminal Evidence Act 1984 allows for the taking from a suspect of intimate and non-intimate samples. Police officers wish to take a penile swab from a suspect in custody.

Is this penile swab an intimate sample?

A Yes, this is an intimate sample even though it is not a body orifice.

B Yes, as the legislation states that the penis is in effect a body orifice.

C No, as intimate samples are samples of blood, semen, or any other tissue fluid, urine or pubic hair.

D No, as a non-intimate sample is described as a swab taken from any part of a person's body including the mouth but not any other body orifice.

Question 11.14

The analysis of intimate samples may provide essential evidence in showing or refuting a person's involvement in an offence.

In relation to who may take intimate samples, which of the following statements is true?

A A registered medical practitioner must take all intimate samples, except for samples of urine or dental impressions.

B A registered nurse may only take an intimate sample if it is a sample of urine.

C A registered paramedic may take an intimate sample.

D Dental impressions may only be taken by a registered dentist or a registered medical practitioner.

Question 11.15

EARNSHAW was charged with an offence of theft and a non-intimate sample (mouth swab) was obtained on 21 March. EARNSHAW pleaded guilty and was convicted on 28 March. On 2 April the laboratory informed the officer in the case that the sample obtained after charge was 'insufficient' for analysis.

In relation to obtaining another sample, which of the following is true?

A Another sample can be obtained only with the consent of EARNSHAW.

B Another sample can be required, but must be before 2 May.

C Another sample can be required, but must be before 28 April.

D Another sample can be required, but must be before 21 April.

Question 11.16

In relation to intimate samples, they may be taken from persons in police detention or, in certain circumstances, from persons who are not in police detention.

In relation to the authority needed for the taking of such samples, which of the following is true?

A Inspector's authority in detention; superintendent's authority not in detention.

B Inspector's authority irrespective of whether the person is in detention or not.

C Superintendent's authority irrespective of whether the person is in detention or not.

D Superintendent's authority in detention; inspector's authority not in detention.

Question 11.17

COPE was arrested for an assault by DC WARNER. He was released on bail for an identification procedure and his fingerprints were taken prior to his release. On the day that he was due to answer bail, COPE's brother, who was similar in appearance, attended the station instead of COPE, in an attempt to confuse witnesses. However, after the brother had been booked in by the custody officer, DC WARNER suspected that he was not the person who had been released on bail. DC WARNER contacted the duty inspector by telephone and asked for permission to obtain fingerprints from COPE's brother because of his suspicions.

Would the duty inspector be able to authorise such a request in these circumstances?

A No, this power is only given to a court, when a person has been charged with an offence.

B No, this power is only given to an Inspector where a person has been charged with an offence.

C Yes, but the fingerprints may be taken only when the Inspector has provided written authority.

D Yes, and the fingerprints may be taken immediately.

Question 11.18

DAWSON is aged 14 and is in police detention, having been given a reprimand for an offence of theft. She is accompanied at this time by her parent. The officer in the case now intends taking DAWSON's fingerprints.

From whom should the officer in the case seek consent, prior to taking the fingerprints?

A From DAWSON or the parent.

B From DAWSON only.

C From the parent only.

D From DAWSON **and** the parent.

Question 11.19

Samples can be defined as 'intimate' or 'non-intimate.'.

Which of the following will be classed as 'non-intimate' within the definition outlined in Code D, para. 6.1 of the PACE Codes of Practice?

A A skin impression other than a fingerprint.

B   A sample of urine.
C   A blood sample.
D   A dental impression.

Question 11.20

A person who has been detained under the Terrorism Act 2000 may have his or her fingerprints taken without his or her consent, in order to ascertain their identity. This may take place when the person has refused to identify himself or herself, or where there are reasonable grounds for suspecting that the person is not who he or she claims to be.

Who may authorise fingerprints to be taken in these circumstances?
A   An officer of at least the rank of inspector.
B   An officer of at least the rank of superintendent.
C   An officer of at least the rank of assistant chief constable/commissioner.
D   An officer of at least the rank of superintendent, or, in cases of urgency, an inspector.

Question 11.21

O'BRIEN is 16 years of age and in police detention, having been arrested on suspicion of rape. Authorisation has been given to take samples of O'BRIEN's pubic hair, which will involve the removal of his clothing. O'BRIEN has agreed to the provision of the samples and has signed the custody record accordingly. O'BRIEN's mother was at the custody office earlier for the interviews, but has now gone to work. She will not be available to return to the custody office for another three hours.

Would the police need to consult with O'BRIEN's mother before taking the sample of pubic hairs in these circumstances?
A   No, he does not want his mother there and has signed the custody record; this is sufficient.
B   Yes, because O'BRIEN's mother was not present when he made the decision.
C   No, because O'BRIEN's mother has left the station and is not readily available.
D   No, because O'BRIEN is over 14, he may make such a decision for himself.

Question 11.22

GARCIA is in custody for an assault. During interview, the investigating officer outlined the description of the suspect, given by a witness. GARCIA is disputing that he was the person responsible, citing a case of mistaken identity. The investigating officer now believes that an identification procedure should take place. GARCIA's solicitor, who was present at the interview, has asked the investigating officer for a copy of the first description given by the witness.

What does Code D, para. 3.1 of the PACE Codes of Practice state about *when* either GARCIA or his solicitor should be given a copy of the first description?

A It must be given when the notice is served on him stating that the police intend holding an identification procedure.

B If practicable, it must be given to GARCIA or his solicitor before the identification procedure takes place.

C It must be given now, as the solicitor has requested to see it.

D It must be given to GARCIA or his solicitor before the identification procedure takes place.

ANSWERS

Answer 11.1

Answer **A** — The rules for identification differ between those cases where the suspect *is known* and those where the suspect is *not known*. PACE Code D, para. 3.4 defines the term 'known' as where 'there is sufficient information known to the police to justify the arrest of a particular person for suspected involvement in the offence'. As soon as the police have information that would give good reason to arrest a suspect, that person becomes 'known'. This good reason does not have to extend as far as reasonable grounds (therefore answer B is incorrect), nor reasonable suspicion (therefore answer C is incorrect), and is there to provide protection for the suspect. As soon as there are grounds to justify arresting the suspect, he or she should be arrested and afforded the rights to formal identification processes. Code D also states that it involves a suspect's *suspected* involvement in the offence, not his or her actual involvement, and answer D is therefore incorrect.

Evidence and Procedure, para. 2.16.4.1

Answer 11.2

Answer **D** — PACE Code D requires that a first description provided of a person suspected of a crime (regardless of the time it was given) must be recorded (para. 3.1). This was the first description as given by Constable BRANNIGEN and should be recorded in accordance with Code D. How strong the evidence would be, given the circumstances of the officer's head injury, would be a matter for the court, but Code D must be complied with, and answer A is therefore incorrect. As far as showing photographs is concerned, one of the suspects is 'known', and therefore showing the officer photographs to identify both would be a breach of the Codes, and answer B is therefore incorrect. Showing photographs of the accomplice, who is merely described, may be appropriate if the suspect is 'not known'. Code D provides for witnesses (including police officers) to be shown photographs, or be taken to a place where the suspect might be for the purpose of identification (paras 3.2 and 3.3), and answer C is therefore incorrect.

Evidence and Procedure, paras 2.16.4.2, 2.16.4.3

Answer 11.3

Answer **C** — It is essential that once a person becomes a 'known suspect', he or she is afforded the rights and protection provided by PACE Code D. In this case the second officer stated he recognised STEVENS from the description given by Constable WRIGHT and, by Code D, para. 3.4, this makes the suspect 'known'. It is important that any witnesses, *including police officers*, who might be used at an identification process, are kept apart from the suspect. As this was not the case, the Codes were breached, and therefore answers A and B are incorrect. As *any* contact could jeopardise a conviction, it is imperative that the witness officer should not see the suspect. This risk is not reduced simply by not asking the officer if he recognised the suspect, and answer D is therefore incorrect. In *R* v *Lennon*, 28 June 1999, unreported, a suspect was arrested for public order offences after his description was circulated by the police officers who witnessed the offence. After the suspect was placed in a van, the officers accidentally went in the van and identified the suspect. The court held that the person was a 'known' suspect and the identification evidence should have been excluded. Also of interest here is *K* v *DPP* [2003] EWHC 351 (QBD appeal).

Evidence and Procedure, para. 2.16.4.2

Answer 11.4

Answer **B** — The House of Lords in *R* v *Forbes* [2001] 2 WLR 1 held that if the police are in possession of sufficient evidence to justify the arrest of a suspect, and that suspect's identification depends on eye-witness identification evidence, even in part, then if the identification is disputed, PACE Code D requires that an identification procedure should be held with the suspect's consent, unless one of the exceptions applies. The House of Lords went on to say that this mandatory obligation to hold an identification procedure under Code D, para. 3.4 applies even if there has been a 'fully satisfactory', or 'actual and complete' or 'unequivocal' identification of the suspect, and therefore answers C and D are incorrect. Code D, para. 3.12 ii also states that an identification procedure must be held where:

> there is a witness available, who expresses an ability to identify the suspect, or where there is a reasonable chance of the witness being able to do so, and they have not been given an opportunity to identify the suspect in any of the procedures set out in paragraphs 3.5 to 3.10.

Despite the wording of Code D, it has been held that a suspect's right to have an identification parade is not confined to cases where a dispute over identity has already arisen; that right also applies where such a dispute might reasonably be anticipated (*R* v *Rutherford and Palmer* (1994) 98 Cr App R 191). If, for example, the police have arrested a suspect on the basis of other evidence, and there are witnesses who indicate that they might be able to make an identification, an identification procedure should be arranged. A positive identification would strengthen the case for the prosecution; moreover, defendants should not be deprived of the opportunity to have witnesses to the crime declare that the offender seen by them is not on the procedure. The position may be different if the witness has already stated that he or she would not be able to identify the offender (*R* v *Montgomery* [1996] Crim LR 507), and answer A is therefore incorrect. Note that the order of identification procedures is:

- video identification;
- identification parade;
- group identification.

Evidence and Procedure, para. 2.16.4.3

Answer 11.5

Answer **C** — If the police fail to hold a parade when the suspect requests one, this is clearly a decision they may have to justify at the trial. In *R* v *Gaynor* [1988] Crim LR 242, the trial judge took the view that the police could have made a greater effort to find volunteers of Gaynor's racial group than they did, and he excluded evidence from a group identification that had been held in lieu. Whilst *Gaynor* may have been a perfectly valid decision on its own facts, the Court of Appeal in *R* v *Jamel* [1993] Crim LR 52 appears to have taken a softer line, holding that the defence could not object to the holding of a group identification if the holding of a parade (made up with mixed-race volunteers) might, in the circumstances, have taken weeks to arrange; in other words, 'impracticable' may mean impracticable within a reasonable timescale.

All reasonable steps must be taken to investigate the possibility of one identification option before moving on to an alternative, and an offer from a suspect's solicitor to find volunteers to stand on a parade is such a 'reasonable' step (*R* v *Britton and Richards* [1989] Crim LR 144). So belief on the part of the identification officer, even on reasonable grounds, is unlikely to satisfy the court and answers A and D are therefore incorrect. Clearly a solicitor's offer of help can be taken and answer B is therefore incorrect. Note, however, that it is important to follow the guidance in the PACE Codes regardless of what agreement is obtained from the suspect, or his or her solicitor. In *R v Hutton* [1999] Crim LR 74, the court said it was a mistake, whether it arose out of a request made by the defence solicitor or not, to have all participants on the parade masked.

Evidence and Procedure, para. 2.16.4.3

Answer 11.6

Answer **A** — PACE Code D, para. 3.14 outlines that the identification officer, in consultation with the officer in charge of the investigation, shall determine whether to hold a video identification or hold an identification parade. Video can be used where an identification parade is not practical, although the emphasis is placed on video identification with moving images or if necessary still images.

Code D, Annex A states how a video identification should be run. Point 2 of the Annex states that the set of images must include the suspect and at least 8 other people who so far as possible resemble the suspect in age, height, general appearance and position in life. The answer is therefore '8' and answers B, C and D are incorrect.

Evidence and Procedure, para. 2.16.4.2, App.2.6

Answer 11.7

Answer **D** — Code D, para. 3.12 provides that there is no need to go through any of the identification procedures where it is not practicable or it would serve no useful purpose in proving or disproving whether the suspect was involved in committing the offence: as for example where the suspect is already well known to the witnesses, or where there is no reasonable possibility that a witness would be able to make an identification at all or it would serve no useful purpose in proving or disproving whether the suspect was committing the offence.

The Court of Appeal has held that Code D was not designed to apply also to situations in which the police seek to connect a suspect with events that occurred many years previously, when his appearance was markedly different.

In this scenario the purpose of the identification is not to place FOLAN at the scene of the crime at or about the exact time of either the offence being committed, or the body being buried. FOLAN's co-workers are not being asked to link him directly to the offence, rather do they recognise him as having worked at the building when it was being erected. In *R v Ridley, The Times*, 13 October 1999, the Court of Appeal stated that there has never been a rule that an identification parade had to be held in all recognition cases and that it will be a question of fact in each case whether or not there is a need to do so. The view that an identification procedure is not required in these cases is supported by para. 3.12 (ii) of the codes of practice.

In these circumstances there will be no need, in accordance with Code D, to hold an identification procedure as it would serve no useful purpose, no matter what the defendant disputes; answers A, B and C are therefore incorrect.

Evidence and Procedure, paras 2.16.4.3, 2.16.4.4

Answer 11.8

Answer **A** — At trial, evidence may properly be admitted from people who claim to have recognised the defendant's voice (*R v Robb* (1991) 93 Cr App R 161), and answer D is therefore incorrect. Although expert evidence may be adduced, it is certainly not limited to experts, and answer B is therefore incorrect. If there are taped recordings of the offender's voice, expert evidence may also be admissible on the question of whether this matches the voice of the defendant. The jury should be allowed to hear any such recordings for themselves, so that they may form their own judgement of the opinions expressed (*R v Bentum* (1989) 153 JP 538), but no courtroom comparison is allowed and answer C is therefore incorrect.

Evidence and Procedure, para. 2.16.4.11

Answer 11.9

Answer **B** — Naturally, a person can consent to having his or her fingerprints taken at any time; the law deals with occasions where such consent is missing. Such cases are covered by s. 61 of the Police and Criminal Evidence Act 1984. Under s. 61(3), fingerprints of a person detained at a police station may be taken without that person's consent in the following two circumstances:

- where an officer of at least the rank of inspector authorises them to be taken; *or*
- where the person has been charged or reported for a recordable offence *and* the person's fingerprints have not already been taken in the course of the investigation of the offence by the police.

Under s. 61(4), an inspector may give authority for fingerprints to be taken only if he or she has reasonable grounds:

- for suspecting the person is involved in a criminal offence; *and*
- for believing that the person's fingerprints will tend to confirm or disprove his or her involvement.

Such authority is not suitable *after* charge and answers C and D are therefore incorrect. The inspector's authority may be given orally or in writing, but if given orally, he or she must confirm it in writing as soon as is practicable (s. 61(5)). Note that the power to take fingerprints after charge applies only where the fingerprints have not previously been taken, and answer A is therefore incorrect.

Evidence and Procedure, para. 2.16.5.1

Answer 11.10

Answer **C** — Until recently, under s. 64 of the Police and Criminal Evidence Act 1984, if the person from whom fingerprints were taken was cleared of the original offence, the fingerprints must ordinarily have been destroyed as soon as was practicable. The Criminal Justice and Police Act 2001 has removed the requirement to destroy fingerprints of those persons who are not convicted, and custody officers should no longer inform detained persons of the right to destruction; answers A and B are therefore incorrect. The 2001 Act removes this obligation in relation to fingerprints where the person is cleared of the offence for which the fingerprints were taken, or where a decision is made not to prosecute. The obligation to destroy is replaced by a rule to the effect that any fingerprints or samples retained can be used only for the purposes related to the prevention and detection of crime, the investigation of any offence or the conduct of any prosecution. This means that if a fingerprint match is established at a subsequent crime scene regarding an individual who has previously been cleared of an offence, the police are able to use this information in the investigation of the crime, and answer D is therefore incorrect.

Evidence and Procedure, para. 2.16.5.3

Answer 11.11

Answer **D** — In *R (on the application of Howe)* v *South Durham Magistrates' Court* [2004] EWHC 362 (Admin) the claimant was charged with driving whilst disqualified and without insurance. At no time did he admit that he was the Christopher Howe who had been disqualified. As it was necessary for the prosecution to prove that the defendant before the court was the person disqualified from driving, the prosecution applied for a witness summons to be issued to a solicitor, who had been the solicitor acting for the Christopher Howe who was disqualified and who was also acting for the claimant in respect of the present charge. This was opposed citing that the issuing of the summons would involve a breach of legal professional privilege, also that it would violate the claimant's rights under art. 6 of the European

Convention on Human Rights by depriving him of his right to be represented by a lawyer of his choice and that it would conflict with his right not to incriminate himself.

The Administrative Court held that questions solely as to the identity of the person disqualified from driving in the original court hearing and as to the identification of the claimant as being that person did not infringe legal professional privilege; answer A is therefore incorrect. The admissible question would be whether, when the solicitor first saw the claimant in connection with the prosecution, he knew him or remembered him. The solicitor was not being called in his capacity as the claimant's solicitor, but as a person who was present in court at the relevant time. With regard to the argument that the claimant would be deprived of the solicitor of his choice, although that was important it was not an absolute right and there was no risk of injustice to the claimant if he was required to make a fresh choice of solicitor; answer B is therefore incorrect.

The court was 'mystified' by the dilemma supposedly faced by the claimant's solicitor. After all, if this witness could categorically state that their client was not the person disqualified this would have a devastating effect on the prosecution case. However if they knew the person to be disqualified it would be embarrassing to admit they represented them knowing they were indeed guilty.

As a cautionary warning, however, the court did not view this case as any sort of licence to increase the amount of such applications by the CPS, and stated that calling a solicitor in such circumstances must only be a last resort; answer C is therefore incorrect.

Evidence and Procedure, para. 2.16.4.5

Answer 11.12

Answer **D** — DNA extracted from blood or semen stains, or even from body hairs, etc., found at the scene of the crime or on the victim is compared with samples (typically derived from mouth swabs) taken from the suspect. The process has been refined in recent years, but is essentially similar to that described by Lord Taylor CJ in *R v Deen, The Times*, 10 January 1994. A positive match between the two profiles does not necessarily provide comparable proof of guilt, and the courts have made it clear that DNA evidence alone will not be sufficient for a conviction; there needs to be other supporting evidence to link the suspect to the crime, and answer A is therefore incorrect. This may be any supporting evidence linking the suspect to the area or circumstances of the crime, or may come from questions put to the suspect during interview. It would include circumstantial evidence, i.e. being seen in the area. It need not be direct evidence gained by other identification procedures or otherwise, answers B and C are therefore incorrect. In *R v Lashley*, 25 February 2000, unreported, in addition to the DNA evidence, evidence that the suspect had connections in the area was enough for the jury to consider the likelihood that the defendant was the assailant.

Evidence and Procedure, para. 2.16.6.1

Answer 11.13

Answer **A** — The definition of an intimate sample is:

- a sample of blood, semen, or any other tissue fluid, urine or pubic hair;
- a dental impression;
- a swab taken from any part of a person's genitals or from a person's body orifice other than the mouth.

The definition of a non-intimate sample is:

- a sample of hair, other than pubic hair, which includes hair plucked with the root;
- a sample taken from a nail or from under a nail;
- a swab taken from any part of a person's body including the mouth but not any other body orifice other than a part from which a swab taken would be an intimate sample;
- saliva;
- a skin impression which means any record, other than a fingerprint, which is a record, in any form and produced by any method, of a skin pattern and other physical characteristics or features of the whole, or any part of, a person's foot or of any other part of their body.

So a swab from a person's penis would be an intimate sample and the Serious Organised Crime and Police Act 2005 has extended the definition beyond a 'body orifice', although not gone as far as declaring the penis to be a body orifice; answer B is therefore incorrect. Answer D is almost correct, apart from the caveat in the definition that states 'a swab taken from any part of a person's body including the mouth but not any other body orifice other than a part from which a swab taken would be an intimate sample.' Easy eh!; answers C and D are therefore incorrect as a penile swab is an intimate sample.

Evidence and Procedure, para. 2.16.8.1

Answer 11.14

Answer **C** — Code D para. 6.4 of the PACE Codes of Practice outlines who may take intimate samples. Para. 6.4 states:

> Dental impressions may only be taken by a registered dentist. Other intimate samples, except for samples of urine, may only be taken by a registered medical practitioner or registered nurse or registered paramedic.

The taking of an intimate sample need not be done by a registered medical practitioner; it can also be taken by a registered nurse or registered paramedic, therefore answers A and B are incorrect. Dental impressions may only be taken by a registered dentist, and may not be taken by a registered medical practitioner, therefore answer D is incorrect.

It would appear that although a sample of urine is an intimate sample, it may be taken by any other person who is not in the above list.

Evidence and Procedure, para. 2.16.8.7

Answer 11.15

Answer **B** — By s. 63A of the Police and Criminal Evidence Act 1984, a constable may require a person to attend at a police station to have a non-intimate sample obtained:

- where a person has been charged with a recordable offence or informed that he or she will be reported; *or*
- where the person has been convicted of a recordable offence;

and, in either case, the person has not had a sample taken in the course of the investigation into the offence, or he or she has had a sample taken but it proved either unsuitable for the same means of analysis or insufficient.

The requirement to attend a police station must be made:

- within one month of the date of charge or of conviction; *or*
- within one month of the appropriate officer being informed that the sample is not suitable or has proved insufficient for analysis.

As it is 'or', the requirement runs to the latest date in the scenario — 2 May — and answers C and D are therefore incorrect.

Answer A is incorrect because it is unnecessary to obtain the consent of a person convicted of an offence, and a person can be arrested for failing to comply with the requirement.

Evidence and Procedure, para. 2.16.10.2

Answer 11.16

Answer **B** — Section 62 of PACE sets out police powers in relation to intimate samples, and the circumstances under which they may be obtained. They are subject to the consent of the person, as well as authorisation by the appropriate police officer. The Criminal Justice and Police Act 2001, s. 80(1) lowered the level of authority from superintendent to inspector; therefore answer C is incorrect. This authority remains at the same level irrespective of whether the person is in police detention or not, as outlined in Code D, para. 6.2; therefore, answers A and D are incorrect.

Evidence and Procedure, para. 2.16.8.1

Answer 11.17

Answer **D** — An officer of at least the rank of inspector (or the court) may authorise taking the fingerprints of a person who has answered bail at a court or police station, if the person answering bail has done so on behalf of a person whose fingerprints were taken on a previous occasion and there are reasonable grounds for believing that he or she is not the same person, or the person claims to be a different person from a person whose fingerprints were taken previously (s. 61(4A) and (4B) of the Police and Criminal Evidence Act 1984).

Since this power relates to a person answering bail at a police station as well as a court, answer A is incorrect. Answers A and B are also incorrect because the power may be utilised before a person has been charged with an offence. The authority to take fingerprints in these circumstances may be given orally or in writing; but if given orally, it must be confirmed in writing as soon as is practicable. Answer C is therefore incorrect.

Evidence and Procedure, para. 2.16.5.1

Answer 11.18

Answer **D** — For the purposes of taking fingerprints, appropriate consent means:

- in relation to a person who is 17 years or over, his or her own consent;
- in relation to a person who is aged between 14 and 17 years, his/her own consent **and** the consent of his or her appropriate adult;
- in relation to a person under the age of 14, the consent of his or her appropriate adult only.

DAWSON was between the ages of 14 and 17 years, therefore consent could have been obtained from her, and from her appropriate adult. Answers A and C are incorrect for this reason.

Evidence and Procedure, para. 2.16.5.2

Answer 11.19

Answer **A** — The PACE Codes of Practice, Code D, para. 6.1 provides the following definition of intimate and non-intimate samples:

(a) an 'intimate sample' means:
    (a) a sample of blood, semen, or any other tissue fluid, urine or pubic hair;
    (b) a dental impression;
    (c) a swab taken from any part of a person's genitals or from a person's body orifice other than the mouth.
(b) a 'non-intimate sample' means:
    (i) a sample of hair, other than pubic hair, which includes hair plucked with the root;
    (ii) a sample taken from a nail or from under a nail;
    (iii) a swab taken from any part of a person's body including the mouth but not any other body orifice other than a part from which a swab taken would be an intimate sample;
    (iv) saliva;
    (v) a skin impression which means any record, other than a fingerprint, which is a record, in any form and produced by any method, of the skin pattern and other physical characteristics or features of the whole, or any part of, a person's foot or of any other part of their body.

Answers B, C and D are *all* intimate samples; the question asked you to identify samples which were *not* classed as intimate samples, therefore if you selected any of these, the answer was incorrect. A skin impression which is not a fingerprint is a non-intimate sample.

Evidence and Procedure, para. 2.16.7.1

Answer 11.20

Answer **B** — A person who has been detained under the Terrorism Act 2000 may have his or her fingerprints taken without his or her consent in these circumstances only when authorisation has been given by an officer of at least the rank of superintendent. Answers A and C are therefore incorrect. There are no provisions for this power to be delegated to an inspector in any circumstances, therefore answer D is incorrect.

Evidence and Procedure, para. 2.16.12.1

Answer 11.21

Answer **B** — Code D, para. 6.9 of the PACE Codes of Practice outlines the provisions for taking an intimate sample, where clothing needs to be removed in circumstances likely to cause embarrassment. Para. 6.9 states:

> When clothing needs to be removed in circumstances likely to cause embarrassment to the person, no person of the opposite sex who is not a registered medical practitioner or registered health care professional shall be present (unless in the case of a juvenile, mentally disordered or mentally vulnerable person, that person specifically requests the presence of an appropriate adult of the opposite sex who is readily available) nor shall anyone whose presence is unnecessary.
> However, in the case of a juvenile, this is subject to the overriding proviso that such a removal of clothing may take place in the absence of the appropriate adult only if the juvenile signifies, in their presence that they prefer the adult's absence and they agree.

Answer A is incorrect; the decision was made by O'BRIEN when his mother was not present and she should have been consulted in respect of that decision. The fact that O'BRIEN's mother was not readily available is immaterial — this issue is only relevant when a juvenile, mentally disordered or mentally vulnerable person specifically requests the *presence* of an appropriate adult of the opposite sex who is readily available, therefore answer C is incorrect. Para. 6.9 above applies to *all* juveniles under 17, therefore answer D is incorrect.

Evidence and Procedure, para. 2.16.8.7

Answer 11.22

Answer **B** — The PACE Codes of Practice, Code D, para. 3.1 states that a record shall be made of the suspect's description as first given by a potential witness. A copy of the record shall *where practicable*, be given to the suspect or their solicitor before any identification procedures are carried out. Since this paragraph does not say it *must* be given before the identification procedure, answer D is incorrect. There is nothing in the Codes stating that the description must be given straight away. Answer C is therefore incorrect.

Lastly, while it is general practice for the identification officer to serve a copy of the first description with the Notice to Suspect outlining the identification procedure, it is not laid down that the description *must* be served at this point, only that it is done so (if practicable) before the procedure takes place. Answer A is therefore incorrect.

Evidence and Procedure, para. 2.16.4.1

12 | Interviews

STUDY PREPARATION

Another area of direct practical relevance to all police officers is that of interviews of suspects. This area is heavily regulated by the Police and Criminal Evidence Act 1984 and the Codes of Practice.

Key aspects of this area are:

- cautioning;
- interview procedure at police stations and elsewhere;
- access to legal advisers;
- interviews with vulnerable people, the use of interpreters and emergency.

QUESTIONS

Question 12.1

MILLER was under police surveillance suspected of being involved in unlawful drug supply. MILLER was observed meeting another man, and a large packet was placed in the boot of MILLER's vehicle. MILLER then drove on to a motorway and was followed by the surveillance officers. While on the motorway, officers from the Road Policing Unit, not knowing of the surveillance operation, stopped MILLER for speeding. The traffic officers lawfully searched the boot of MILLER's vehicle and found the package. One of the officers said, 'What's in the package?'

Would the question asked by the officer be an interview as defined by Code C of the Police and Criminal Evidence Act 1984?

A Yes, as the question criminally implicated MILLER.

B Yes, as other police officers were investigating MILLER for an offence.

C No, as the officers did not suspect MILLER of an offence at this stage.

D No, but MILLER would have to be informed that he was not under arrest and free to leave.

Question 12.2

An unsolicited comment made by a suspect and recorded in a police officer's pocket notebook may be admissible in evidence against that suspect, provided the PACE Codes of Practice have been complied with.

In relation to the admissibility of such an unsolicited comment, which of the following is true?

A The comment is admissible only if signed by the suspect at the time.

B The comment is inadmissible if the suspect refuses to sign the note.

C The comment may be endorsed by the suspect two days later and still be admissible.

D The comment need only be signed by the suspect, not necessarily the maker of the note, to be admissible.

Question 12.3

Police officers have been called by the principal of a high school to interview a juvenile who has caused damage to school property. The principal did not witness the incident, but wishes the juvenile to be interviewed on the school premises as the youth is due to sit a GCSE in two hours. The parents of the juvenile have been contacted, but are unavailable for some time.

Can the principal be the 'appropriate adult'?

A In these circumstances, only the principal can be the appropriate adult.

B The principal can be the appropriate adult as the parents are not readily available.

C The principal can be the appropriate adult provided the parents agree.

D The principal will not be able to be the appropriate adult in these circumstances.

Question 12.4

MILLIGAN has been arrested on suspicion of a burglary that occurred one month ago, and is being transported in the back of a police vehicle. On the journey MILLIGAN calls out to a passer-by, 'tell Jonesy the coppers have got me'. The officers are aware that there is another suspect outstanding, and ask MILLIGAN to explain who

'Jonesy' is and where he is. MILLIGAN tells them. The officers then ask MILLIGAN where the outstanding property is, and if 'Jonesy' is guilty of the burglary.

Is this 'interview with a person who is under arrest' lawful?

A No, such an interview can be conducted only at a police station.

B No, as they did not stop the interview after they identified the location of 'Jonesy'.

C Yes, as it was to clarify a voluntary statement made by MILLIGAN.

D Yes, as there was property still to be recovered, and to facilitate the arrest of 'Jonesy'.

Question 12.5

A suspect has been arrested for possession of controlled drugs, and police officers have taken him to his home address to carry out a search. During the search some cannabis is found along with items of drug paraphernalia. A large sum of money has also been found.

In relation to the questions the officers can ask of the suspect at the scene, which of the following is true?

A Questions can be asked only relating to ownership of the items found.

B No direct questions can be asked, but any comments made should be recorded contemporaneously.

C The suspect could be asked where the money had come from.

D The suspect could be asked the location of other premises where drugs could be found.

Question 12.6

SCHIFFO has been arrested on suspicion of kidnapping and the victim is still missing. On legal advice, SCHIFFO exercised his right to silence throughout the interview. There is sufficient other evidence available and SCHIFFO is charged. After caution he says, 'Try as hard as you like, you won't find her where I have hidden her'.

In relation to the options open to the investigating officer, which of the following is correct?

A No action can be taken as SCHIFFO has been charged with an offence and cannot be further interviewed.

B The officer can re-interview, but must caution the suspect as in PACE Code C, para. 16.5 caution (old caution).

C The officer can re-interview and there is no need to re-caution SCHIFFO, but he should be reminded that he is under caution.

D The officer can re-interview and must further caution SCHIFFO, as in PACE Code C, para. 10.5 caution.

Question 12.7

McGUIGAN has been arrested and is about to be interviewed on audio. The custody officer tells McGUIGAN that his nominated solicitor refuses to attend, and asks if he wishes to nominate another solicitor or the duty solicitor. However, McGUIGAN declines to ask for the duty solicitor or another solicitor.

In the circumstances outlined above, can the audio-recorded interview proceed?

A Yes, provided an officer of the rank of inspector or above has given agreement for the interview to proceed in these circumstances.

B Yes, provided an officer of the rank of inspector has given agreement and the suspect agrees in writing.

C No, as McGUIGAN has not stated that he has changed his mind over legal advice the duty solicitor must be called.

D Not unless delay will involve an immediate risk of harm to people or serious loss of, or damage to, property.

Question 12.8

POPOV is a Ukrainian national who is in police custody, and is being interviewed in relation to the offence for which he is under arrest. POPOV has his solicitor with him, as well as an interpreter, and he is being interviewed by Constable BRYANT.

Which of the following is correct?

A The interviewing officer is responsible for ensuring that POPOV can understand and be understood.

B The solicitor is responsible for ensuring that POPOV can understand and be understood.

C The custody officer is responsible for ensuring that POPOV can understand and be understood.

D The interpreter is responsible for ensuring that POPOV can understand and be understood.

Question 12.9

DWYER has been arrested and is in custody at the police station suspected of a series of rapes; this followed a description obtained from his various victims. The suspect has, in accordance with his rights, asked for his solicitor to be called. Prior to the arrival of his solicitor DWYER is examined by the police surgeon and samples obtained. Officers also attend at DWYER's home address and carry out a search in compliance with s. 18 of the Police and Criminal Evidence Act 1984 and various items are seized as being of evidential value. Prior to the first interview the inter-view co-ordinator is considering what will be disclosed to DWYER's solicitor

In relation to the various items obtained what should be disclosed to the solicitor at this stage of the investigation?

A There is no specific provision within the Police and Criminal Evidence Act 1984 for the disclosure of any information by the police at the police station, with the exception of the custody record and, in identification cases, the initial description given by the witnesses.

B There is no specific provision within the Police and Criminal Evidence Act 1984 for the disclosure of any information by the police at the police station, with the exception of the custody record and any records in relation to samples obtained.

C There is no specific provision within the Police and Criminal Evidence Act 1984 for the disclosure of any information by the police at the police station, with the exception of the custody record and any items seized as being of evidential value

D There are specific provisions within the Police and Criminal Evidence Act 1984 for the disclosure of any information held by the police that would assist the defence in preparing their case.

Question 12.10

Detective Sergeant LANTZOS is carrying out an audio-recorded interview with a suspect for murder, and it is now a recognised meal time. The interview is almost complete, two hours after it started, and the suspect will be released on police bail at its conclusion.

In relation to the correct procedure, which of the following is true?

A The officer must terminate the interview to allow the suspect to eat.

B The officer must take a short break of 15 minutes to allow the suspect to get refreshments.

C The officer can carry on with the interview, recording the grounds for continuing the interview on the audio record, and then release the prisoner.

D The officer can carry on with the interview, recording the grounds for continuing the interview on the custody record, and then release the prisoner.

Question 12.11

HOUSE is being interviewed by detectives in relation to an allegation of fraud. During the audio-recorded interview, HOUSE alleges that his rights under PACE Code C were breached and that he wishes to make a formal complaint.

Which of the following is correct?

A The audio recording should be stopped and an inspector summoned to deal with the complaint.

B The custody officer is responsible for deciding whether the interview should continue or not in these circumstances.

C The interviewing officer should make a note in his or her pocket notebook, and later, on the custody record, of the complaint.

D The custody officer should be summoned immediately, and the audio recording left running until he or she arrives.

Question 12.12

BATES is in custody for an offence. She requested legal advice and was allowed to consult on the telephone with the duty solicitor. Shortly afterwards, another solicitor, FRIEND, summoned by BATES's father, attended at the police station.

In relation to FRIEND, which of the following is correct?

A FRIEND must be allowed private consultation with BATES.

B BATES does not need to be told about FRIEND as she has already received legal advice.

C BATES must be told that FRIEND is present and should be allowed a consultation.

D BATES does not need to be told about FRIEND as she did not request advice from him.

Question 12.13

WALLACE, who is from Glasgow, has voluntarily attended a police station in London knowing he is wanted for questioning in Glasgow. When contacted, Strathclyde Police state that they cannot send an officer, and request that officers of the

Metropolitan Police interview him and establish an address to allow service of a citation (summons). Strathclyde Police provide details of the incident to their colleagues.

In these circumstances which of the following is true?

A The Metropolitan Police officers cannot interview, as only officers in forces bordering Scotland may conduct such an interview.

B When the Metropolitan Police officers conduct the interview, a PACE caution should be used.

C Where a Scottish caution is given by a Metropolitan Police officer, that officer should ensure WALLACE understands it.

D As under Scots law WALLACE is not entitled to legal representation, the interview can proceed without a solicitor, even if requested.

Question 12.14

Constable HSIAO arrested a male for throwing a brick at a passing train from an overhead bridge at 11 pm. At 7 am an officer from the British Transport Police (BTP), Constable GREENHAUGH attended at the custody unit to deal with the prisoner. Whilst speaking to the custody sergeant she noticed that Constable GREENHAUGH's breath smelt of alcohol, the custody officer asked Constable GREENHAUGH 'how did you get here?' he replied 'job car'. The custody officer called the duty inspector, as she suspected the BTP officer had driven with excess alcohol; the duty inspector also smelt alcohol on the BTP officer's breath. The Inspector then asked Constable GREENHAUGH 'have you been drinking?' and 'did you drive to the police station?'. Both questions were answered 'yes'. A preliminary breath test was conducted, and following a positive test an evidential sample was obtained that exceeded the prescribed limit.

At what point in these circumstances should a caution have been given?

A Prior to the custody officer asking how Constable GREENHAUGH had got to the police station.

B Prior to the duty inspector asking any questions of Constable GREENHAUGH given the custody officer's suspicion.

C Following the positive preliminary breath test.

D Following the evidential breath test that exceeded the prescribed limit.

Question 12.15

YOUDE was arrested for an indictable offence and, when his detention was first authorised, he asked to consult with a solicitor. However, there has now been a delay of over an hour in his solicitor arriving at the police station. The superintendent in charge of the station has now authorised an interview to take place with YOUDE, without the solicitor being present, because there are urgent questions that need to be asked of him, and awaiting the solicitor's arrival will cause an unreasonable delay to the process of the investigation.

If YOUDE were to make no comment during the interview, without his solicitor being present, would a court be able to draw adverse inferences from his silence?

A Yes, provided it can be shown that the superintendent has correctly applied the Codes of Practice with her decision.

B No, as YOUDE has not been allowed to consult with a solicitor.

C Yes, unless the defence can show that there has been an intentional breach of the Codes of Practice by the police.

D No, if the defence can show that YOUDE indicated at the start of the interview that he did not wish to be interviewed without his solicitor being present.

Question 12.16

Constable BECKER was interviewing VINNEY, who had been arrested the previous evening for an assault. The interview was being conducted on audio, in an interview room at the police station. During the interview, VINNEY disclosed to Constable BECKER that he was assaulted by the arresting officer the previous evening, and stated that he wished to make a formal complaint.

What action should Constable BECKER now take, in respect of the complaint made to her?

A She should stop the audio recording immediately and ask the custody officer to attend the interview, where the complaint may be repeated in his or her presence.

B She may carry on the interview, provided she informs the custody officer that a complaint has been made at the conclusion of the interview.

C She should stop the audio recording immediately and inform the custody officer that a complaint has been made.

D She may carry on the interview, provided she informs the duty Inspector that a complaint has been made at the conclusion of the interview.

Question 12.17

The Police and Criminal Evidence Act 1984, Code C, para. 13.4 gives guidance in relation to written statements under caution from suspects, when the statement is made in a language other than English, and an interpreter is present.

What does this Code of Practice state in relation to who should write the statement under caution?

A The interpreter should write the statement in the language in which it is made, and translate it there and then.
B The interviewee should write it in his or her own language, and the interpreter should translate it there and then.
C The interpreter should write the statement in the language in which it is made, and translate it in due course.
D The interviewee should write it in his or her own language, and the interpreter should translate it in due course.

Question 12.18

PERKINS was in detention, having been arrested for burglary. Two people escaped from the police at the scene with the stolen property. When PERKINS' detention was first authorised, he declined legal advice. PC GOODE, the investigating officer wished to interview PERKINS straight away because of the outstanding property and to establish who had been with PERKINS. However, it was discovered that PER-KINS had injured his leg and the custody officer determined he had to go to hospital after detention was authorised. The custody officer agreed that PC GOODE could accompany PERKINS to hospital and interview him there. It transpired that PERKINS was cooperative and the officer asked him some questions in the ambulance and further questions at the hospital with permission from a doctor.

Assuming that PC GOODE followed the Codes of Practice relating to cautioning suspects and legal advice prior to the interviews, how much time will count towards PERKINS' overall detention time when he returns to the custody office?

A The whole time spent away from the custody office.
B The whole time spent at the hospital.
C Only the time spent during the interview at the hospital.
D Only the time spent questioning him.

Question 12.19

Detective Constables PENHALE and ALI were interviewing PARKES for an offence of murder. The interview was being visually recorded. About an hour into the interview, the officers decided to have a short break and Detective Constable PARKES left the interview room to obtain refreshments, leaving Detective Constable ALI alone in the room with PARKES.

What advice is contained in the PACE Codes of Practice, Code F, paras 4.12 and 4.13, as to whether or not the video recording equipment should be turned off in these circumstances?

A It *must* not be turned off, because PARKES and another police officer have remained in the interview room.

B It *may* be turned off, because one of the interviewing officers has left the interview room.

C It *must* be turned off, because one of the interviewing officers has left the interview room.

D It *must* be turned off and the recording media removed, because one of the interviewing officers has left the interview room.

Question 12.20

In certain circumstances, Code C, para. 6.9 of the PACE Codes of Practice allows the removal of a legal representative from an interview because of their behaviour.

Which of the following statements is correct in relation to the authorisation required to implement para. 6.9?

A A superintendent may make such an authorisation, but if one is not available, it may be done by an inspector.

B Only an inspector or above may make such an authorisation.

C Either a superintendent or an inspector or above may make an authorisation, but only if they witness the behaviour.

D Only a superintendent or above may make such an authorisation.

Question 12.21

Constable MABETT was interviewing PERRETT for a domestic-related assault. PERRETT was represented by SUMMERS, a fully-qualified solicitor. During the interview, Constable MABETT observed SUMMERS passing handwritten notes to PERRETT. As a result, the officer believed that PERRETT was answering questions based on advice contained in the notes.

Considering Code C, para. 6.9 of the PACE Codes of Practice, would this amount to 'unacceptable' behaviour and be sufficient evidence to merit SUMMERS' removal from the interview?

A No, this would only be possible if SUMMERS were continually interrupting the officer and affecting the flow of the interview.

B No, because SUMMERS is a fully-qualified solicitor and not an accredited or probationary representative.

C No, this would only be possible if SUMMERS were continually answering questions on PERRETT's behalf.

D Yes, this behaviour would be sufficient for the officer to stop the interview and seek to have SUMMERS removed.

Question 12.22

TUCKER works for a firm of solicitors as an accredited representative and attended the custody police station one day on behalf of a firm of solicitors he had recently joined. The custody officer, PS BRADBURY met TUCKER in the foyer. Unfortunately for TUCKER, PS BRADBURY had just been promoted from a different force area and recognised TUCKER as a person who had been recently arrested and convicted in that area for an offence of burglary, under a different name. When challenged, TUCKER admitted that this was true, and the custody officer contacted the duty inspector.

In these circumstances, could the inspector prevent TUCKER from entering the custody office?

A No, the decision must be made by a superintendent, who must inform the Law Society if entry is refused.

B Yes, and the inspector should inform other custody staff in the area, to ensure that TUCKER is not allowed entry to those either.

C Yes, and the inspector must inform a superintendent, who must inform the Law Society if entry is refused.

D Yes, and the inspector may inform a superintendent, who may inform the Law Society if entry is refused.

ANSWERS

Answer 12.1

Answer **C** — 'Interview' is defined by PACE Code C, para. 11.1A, as follows:

> An interview is the questioning of a person regarding his involvement or suspected involvement in a criminal offence or offences which...is required to be carried out under caution.

The vital question is then, 'do the traffic officers suspect Miller's involvement in an offence?'. Code C, para. 10.1 outlines when a caution need not be given when questions are asked for other necessary purposes, and para. 10.1(c) states:

> In furtherance of the proper and effective conduct of a search...

This was confirmed in *R v McGuiness* [1999] Crim LR 318, where the court held that only when a person is suspected of an offence need a caution be given; answer B is therefore incorrect.

The wording of the question asked, however, is vital. In *R v Miller* [1998] Crim LR 209, the court held that asking a person the single question, 'Are these ecstasy tablets?', criminally implicated the person and therefore the conversation was an interview. In this example, there is no such criminal implication; answer A is therefore incorrect. In cases where the person is not under arrest, certain information must be given to him or her. This is covered by Code C, para. 10.2, which states:

> Whenever a person who is not under arrest is initially cautioned or is reminded that he is under caution he must at the same time be told that he is not under arrest and is not obliged to remain with the officer...

As this is *after* caution, answer D is also incorrect.

Evidence and Procedure, para. 2.17.2

Answer 12.2

Answer **C** — There will be occasions where suspects make 'unsolicited comments' implicating them in an offence before they are suspected of any involvement and therefore before they are cautioned (or further cautioned if already suspected). Such statements are likely to be admissible provided they comply with PACE Codes of Practice. To comply with PACE Code C, para. 11.13, the suspect must be given the opportunity either 'to read that record and to sign it as correct', or to 'indicate the respects in which he considers it inaccurate'; answer A is therefore incorrect. Any refusal to sign the notes shall be recorded by the maker; but provided the note has been shown, such refusal would not exclude the comment and answer B is therefore incorrect. Code C, para. 11.13 goes on to say that 'any such record must be timed and signed by the maker', and answer D is therefore incorrect. If the endorsement cannot be achieved straightaway, the prosecution may not be able to argue that it was not practicable. This is demonstrated by *Batley* v *DPP*, *The Times*, 5 March 1998, where it was held that as Code C did not require an *immediate* endorsement and no time factor was laid down, there was nothing to constrain the police from returning the next day to get their endorsement.

Evidence and Procedure, para. 2.17.3

Answer 12.3

Answer **D** — Interviews at educational establishments should take place only in exceptional circumstances and with the agreement of the principal or the principal's nominee (PACE Code C, para. 11.16). This is the mandatory practice; however, it is not mandatory that the principal be the appropriate adult, and therefore answer A is incorrect. If waiting for the parents (or other appropriate adult) to attend would cause unreasonable delay, the principal can be the appropriate adult, and this is not dependent on the parent's consent and therefore answer C is incorrect. The only exception to this is where the juvenile is suspected of an offence against his or her educational establishment, as the youth is in the question. In these circumstances the principal cannot be the appropriate adult and answer B is therefore incorrect (Code C, para. 11.16).

Evidence and Procedure, para. 2.17.5

Answer 12.4

Answer **B** — The general rules for the conduct of interviews are contained in PACE Code C, para. 11.1. The suspect under arrest should be interviewed about an offence only at a police station. However, there are exceptions to this rule based on the necessity for the interview, and answer A is therefore incorrect. Code C, para. 11.1(b) covers one of those exceptions, i.e. where delay would be likely to 'lead to the alerting of other persons suspected of having committed an offence but not yet arrested for it'. However, interviewing in these circumstances should cease once the relevant risk has been averted or the necessary questions have been put (para. 11.1). Code C, para. 11.1(c) outlines that interviewing would be lawful if delay would 'hinder the recovery of property'. One month after the offence would be unlikely to hold credence with the court. This, together with the fact that questions could not be asked regarding 'Jonesy's' guilt, makes answer D incorrect. Clarification over a voluntary statement relates to prisoners being transferred between forces, i.e. no questions may be put to the suspect about the offence while he or she is in transit between the forces except in order to clarify any voluntary statement made by him or her (Code C, para. 14.1), and answer C is therefore incorrect.

Evidence and Procedure, para. 2.17.6

Answer 12.5

Answer **C** — The courts have recognised that there may be times when a person who is under arrest will be asked questions other than at the police station. One such example is where the arrested person is present while officers search his or her home address, and answer B is therefore incorrect. In *R v Hanchard*, 6 December 1999, unreported, the questions which were admissible included whether cannabis at the address belonged to the suspect and where a large quantity of money had come from (answer A is therefore incorrect). Questions going beyond what is needed for the immediate investigation are in breach of the PACE Code of Practice. Asking for evidence of offences unconnected with the search clearly would be such a breach, and therefore answer D is incorrect.

Evidence and Procedure, para. 2.17.6

Answer 12.6

Answer **B** — Once a person has been charged with an offence, generally he or she cannot be interviewed about that offence. However, the rule that questioning must cease after the charge has exceptions, and answer A is therefore incorrect. One of these exceptions is that questions may not be put unless they are necessary for the purpose of preventing or minimising harm or loss to some other person, or to the public. The suspect must first be cautioned before any such questions are put, and therefore answer C is incorrect. This caution is the one outlined in Code C, para. 16.5: 'You do not have to say anything, but anything you do say may be given in evidence.' This caution is what is known as the 'old style' caution, and answer D is therefore incorrect. The reason for this is that no inferences can be drawn from a refusal to answer these questions, as outlined in Code C, Annex C.

Evidence and Procedure, para. 2.17.7

Answer 12.7

Answer **A** — If legal advice has been requested, a legal representative must be present at the interview unless PACE Code C, para. 6.6 applies. This paragraph gives direction where solicitors have been contacted but have declined to attend. In such circumstances, if the person has been advised of the Duty Solicitor Scheme but has declined to ask for the duty solicitor, or the duty solicitor is unavailable, the interview may be started without further delay, provided that an officer of the rank of Inspector or above has given agreement for the interview to proceed in these circumstances, whether audio recorded or otherwise. The suspect does not have to agree to this situation and answer B is therefore incorrect. This authority to interview granted by the inspector is separate from the authority to interview granted by a superintendent. Code C, para. 6.6 also outlines that a superintendent can authorise an interview without a solicitor if delay will involve an immediate risk of harm to people or serious loss of, or damage to, property. However, this does not need to apply in every case and where, as outlined in the scenario, the suspect effectively changes his mind about representation, the interview can go ahead; answer D is therefore incorrect. Although the suspect can change his or her mind about legal advice, even where this is not the case (as outlined above) the interview can proceed, and answer C is therefore incorrect.

Evidence and Procedure, para. 2.17.9.13

Answer 12.8

Answer **A** — It is the interviewing officer who is responsible for ensuring that the detained person can understand and be understood (*R* v *West London Youth Court, ex parte J* [2000] 1 All ER 823), and only the interviewing officer. Answers B, C and D are therefore incorrect.

Evidence and Procedure, para. 2.17.9.15

Answer 12.9

Answer **A** — It is important not to confuse the duty of disclosure to a person once charged with the need to disclose evidence to a suspect before interviewing them. After a person has been charged, and before trial, the rules of disclosure are clear and almost all material must be disclosed to the defence.

However, this is not necessarily the case at the interview stage of the investigation. There is no specific provision within the Police and Criminal Evidence Act

1984 for the disclosure of any information by the police at the police station, with the exception of the custody record and, in identification cases, the initial description given by the witnesses. Further, there is nothing within the Criminal Justice and Public Order Act 1994 that states that information must be disclosed before an inference from silence can be made. Indeed, in *R* v *Imran* [1997] Crim LR 754 the court held that it is totally wrong to submit that a defendant should be prevented from lying by being presented with the whole of the evidence against him/her prior to the interview.

So only the custody record and the initial descriptions need to be disclosed; answers B, C and D are therefore incorrect.

Evidence and Procedure, para. 2.17.9.7

Answer 12.10

Answer **C** — Exceptions exist to the rule that breaks from interviewing must be made. These breaks are to be made at recognised meal times (PACE Code C, para. 12.8). Short breaks for refreshment must also be provided at intervals of approximately two hours. However, subject to the interviewing officer's discretion, a break can be delayed if there are reasonable grounds for believing that it would:

- involve a risk of harm to people, or serious loss of, or damage to, property;
- delay unnecessarily the detainee's release;
- otherwise prejudice the outcome of the investigation.

It is the officer's choice and a break does not have to be taken (answers A and B are therefore incorrect). Any decision to delay a break during an interview must be recorded, with grounds, in the interview record (either on the written record, or on audio) (Code C, para. 12.12), and answer D is therefore incorrect. Note that it would be a good idea to note the delay in the custody record as well, as it is more accessible than the audio recording for all practical purposes.

Evidence and Procedure, para. 2.17.9.11, App.2.5

Answer 12.11

Answer **D** — If the suspect makes a complaint regarding his or her treatment since arrest, the interviewing officer must inform the custody officer and follow PACE Code C, para. 12.9, which states:

If in the course of the interview a complaint is made by the person being questioned or on his behalf concerning the provisions of this code then the interviewing officer shall:

(i) record it in the interview record; and

(ii) inform the custody officer, who is then responsible for dealing with it in accordance with section 9 of this code.

Note that it is recorded on the interview record, and answer C is therefore incorrect. Code C, para. 9.2 states that 'a report must be made as soon as practicable to an officer of the rank of Inspector or above who is not connected with the investigation'. However, it is not necessary to stop the audio recording; indeed, it should be kept running in accordance with Code E, note 4E, and answer A is therefore incorrect. Code E, note 4E also outlines that 'continuation or termination of the interview should be at the discretion of the interviewing officer' and not the custody officer, and therefore answer B is incorrect.

Evidence and Procedure, para. 2.17.9.8, App.2.5

Answer 12.12

Answer **C** — If a solicitor arrives at the station to see a suspect, the suspect must be asked whether he or she would like to see the solicitor *regardless of what legal advice has already been received* and regardless of whether or not the advice was requested by the suspect; answers B and D are therefore incorrect (PACE Code C, para. 6.15). Note that it is the suspect's choice whether to speak to the solicitor, who has no automatic right of consultation even if summoned by a relative, and answer A is therefore incorrect. However, where a solicitor does arrive at the police station to see a suspect, that suspect has to be told of the solicitor's presence and must be allowed to consult with the solicitor should he or she wish to do so.

Evidence and Procedure, para. 2.17.9.13

Answer 12.13

Answer **C** — English and Welsh officers interviewing suspects in England and Wales, when they are aware that the interview is required for a prosecution in Scotland, should comply with the PACE Codes of Practice, save that a Scottish caution should be used, and answer B is therefore incorrect (the use of the English/Welsh caution may render the interview inadmissible in Scotland). Note that this applies to all such officers — not just those on bordering forces — and answer A is incorrect. As the PACE Codes of Practice have to be complied with, the suspect is entitled to legal advice even though under Scots law the suspect is not entitled to legal representation, and therefore answer D is incorrect. In all circumstances, officers should ensure that suspects fully understand the significance of a caution, even if it is not one with which they are familiar.

Evidence and Procedure, para. 2.17.12

Answer 12.14

Answer **C** — The Police and Criminal Evidence Act 1984 Code C, para. 10.1 states:

> A person whom there are grounds to suspect of an offence, see Note 10A, must be cautioned before any questions about an offence, or further questions if the answers provide the grounds for suspicion, are put to them if either the suspect's answers or silence, (i.e. failure or refusal to answer or answer satisfactorily) may be given in evidence to a court in a prosecution...

In *Ridehalgh* v *DPP* [2005] EWHC 1100 (Admin) the appellant was a serving officer of the British Transport Police, and on the date of the alleged offence he went to a police station whilst on duty in order to deal with a detainee. An acting police sergeant noticed the appellant, as he thought, smelling of alcohol, and no doubt since the appellant was a serving police officer, the sergeant decided to seek the services of a senior colleague. A police inspector was called, and together they approached the appellant. A conversation then took place, amounting to questions about whether the officer had been drinking and whether he had driven to the police station. An important issue in the case was whether that conversation constituted an interview for the purposes of the Code of Practice under the Police and Criminal Evidence Act 1984, that would have required a caution in line with Code C para. 10.1.

The Administrative Court held that where police officers question people, in any circumstances, in the course of possible investigations relating to the commission of a criminal offence, there inevitably comes a time when it begins to occur to them that an offence might have been committed. They need to make further enquiries to establish whether there are grounds for suspecting the particular person, the potential defendant, of committing the offence. If the stage comes when there are such grounds, then the duty to caution arises. In *Ridehalgh* all that the officers had prior to the questioning of the appellant was a smell of alcohol on his breath; no indication as to when and how much alcohol had been taken; and no indication as to whether or not he had been driving and that prior to these questions being answered a caution was not necessary; answers A and B are therefore incorrect.

A positive preliminary breath test would give reasonable suspicion that an offence had been committed, where the officer was certain a vehicle had been driven and this should be the point of caution prior to any further questions being asked; answer D is therefore incorrect.

Evidence and Procedure, para. 2.17.3

Answer 12.15

Answer **B** — The case of *Murray* v *United Kingdom* (1996) 22 EHRR 29 changed the situation in respect of adverse inferences being drawn from silences, where the detainee has asked to speak to a solicitor prior to interview and has not been allowed to do so. The ruling in *Murray* also caused a change to the Codes of Practice. There will, of course, be instances where the police can legitimately deny a detainee access to a solicitor prior to interview, and the situation described in the scenario complies with Code C, para. 6.6.(b)(ii), where a superintendent may authorise an interview to take place without a solicitor being present, when the detainee has requested one, when the solicitor has been contacted and awaiting his or her arrival will cause an unreasonable delay to the process of the investigation.

However, when this power is utilised, Code C states that there will be a restriction on the court drawing adverse inferences from any silence; this is regardless of whether the superintendent has correctly applied the Codes of Practice (answer A is therefore incorrect). There will be no requirement for the defence to show that there has been an intentional breach of the Codes of Practice (answer C is therefore incorrect), or that the defendant indicated at the start of the interview that he did not wish to be interviewed without his solicitor being present (answer D is therefore incorrect). The detainee is simply afforded protection by the Codes of Practice because he or she has not been allowed access to a solicitor during interview, when he or she has asked for one.

Evidence and Procedure, para. 2.17.4

Answer 12.16

Answer **B** — Under Code E, Note for Guidance 4F, if a complaint is made during an interview about a matter not connected with conduct of the interview itself, the interviewing officer has the decision whether or not to continue the interview. Therefore, there is no need to stop the interview, and answers A and C are incorrect. When the interviewing officer does carry on with the interview, he or she should inform the detainee that the matter will be brought to the custody officer's attention at the conclusion of the interview. The interviewing officer must then do this as soon as practicable at the conclusion of the interview. Answer D is incorrect, as the interviewing officer has no duty to inform an inspector (although the custody officer will have to do so, when the complaint is brought to his or her attention).

Lastly, even though there is no necessity to call the custody officer to the interview room, Code E, Note for Guidance 4F states that if a custody officer is called to deal with a complaint, the audio recording should be left running until the custody officer has entered the room and spoken to the interviewee. Answer A is incorrect for this reason also.

Evidence and Procedure, para. 2.17.9.8

Answer 12.17

Answer **C** — Code C, para. 13.4 states that where a person makes a statement under caution in a language other than English, the interpreter should record the statement in the language in which it is made; the person must be invited to sign it; and an official English translation must be made in due course. There is no provision in the Codes of Practice for the interviewee to write the statement, therefore answers B and D are incorrect. Also, there is no requirement for the statement to be translated immediately, and answer A is therefore incorrect.

Evidence and Procedure, para. 2.17.10

Answer 12.18

Answer **D** — While the situation in the question is unusual, the actions of the police were perfectly legal. Under the PACE Codes of Practice, Code C, para. 14.2, if a person is in police detention at a hospital they may not be questioned without the agreement of a responsible doctor. Note for guidance 14A continues: *if questioning takes place at a hospital under paragraph 14.2, or on the way to or from a hospital,* **the period of questioning concerned** *counts towards the total period of detention permitted.* Answers A and B are therefore incorrect. Answer C is incorrect, because both the interview on the way to the hospital and the interview at the hospital will count towards the overall detention time.

Note that in circumstances where a person is interviewed away from the custody office, it would be advisable as far as possible to record the interview on a portable tape recorder to demonstrate that the Codes of Practice have been complied with. Also, the situation would have been different if the detainee had requested legal advice when detention was first authorised. In this case, permission to interview without the solicitor being present would have to be granted either by a superintendent (if the matter was urgent — Code C, para. 6.6(b)) or by an inspector (if the detainee changed his/her mind — Code C, para. 6.6(d)).

Evidence and Procedure, para. 2.17.6, App.2.4

Answer 12.19

Answer **B** — The advice concerning visually recorded interviews is contained in Code F of the PACE Codes of Practice. Code F, para. 4.13 states that:

> When a break is to be a short one, and both the suspect and a police officer are to remain in the interview room, the fact that a break is to be taken, the reasons for it and the time shall be recorded on the recording media. The recording equipment may be turned off, but there is no need to remove the recording media. When the interview is recommenced the recording shall continue on the same recording media and the time at which the interview recommences shall be recorded.

Since the officers only intended the break to be a short one, para. 4.13 applies in these circumstances. The above paragraph states that in these circumstances, the officers *may* turn off the recording equipment, as both the suspect and an officer have remained in the room. Since there is a choice, answers A and C are incorrect. There is no requirement to remove the recording media, because one of the officers and the suspect are still in the room, and there is no likelihood of it being interfered with. Answer D is therefore incorrect.

Whether or not the recording equipment is turned off is a matter for the officers to decide in the circumstances. Further advice is contained in Note for Guidance 4E, which states that the officer:

> should bear in mind that it may be necessary to satisfy the court that nothing occurred during a break in an interview or between interviews which influenced the suspect's recorded evidence.

In these circumstances, it may be prudent to leave the recording equipment on, because the detainee's solicitor has left the room.

Note that in extended breaks, where the suspect leaves the interview room, the recording equipment *must* be turned off and the recording media removed (see para. 4.12).

Evidence and Procedure, para. 2.17.9.12, App.2.7

Answer 12.20

Answer **A** — Provision is made under the PACE Codes of Practice, Code C, para. 6.9 to remove a solicitor from an interview, if the interviewer considers a solicitor is acting in such a way that their conduct is such that the interviewer is unable to put questions to the suspect properly. Further guidance is contained in para. 6.10, which states that the interviewing officer must stop the interview and consult an officer not below superintendent rank, if one is readily available, and otherwise an officer not below inspector rank not connected with the investigation. Since either of these officers may take the decision, answers B and D are incorrect. Note for Guidance 6E states:

> An officer who takes the decision to exclude a solicitor must be in a position to satisfy the court the decision was properly made. In order to do this they may need to witness what is happening.

It is not mandatory that the authorising officer witnesses the behaviour (therefore answer C is incorrect); however, it would be advisable to do so in order that an informed decision is reached. In practice, it is advised that the authorising officer listens to the audio recording of the interview to assist in the decision-making process. The solicitor could then be given a warning and the interviewing officer advised to stop the interview if it re-occurs. This way, the solicitor will have been given every opportunity to correct their behaviour.

Evidence and Procedure, para. 2.17.9.13, App.2.4

Answer 12.21

Answer **D** — The PACE Codes of Practice, Code C, para. 6.9 allows for a solicitor to be removed from an interview, if the interviewer considers a solicitor is acting in such a way that their conduct is such that the interviewer is unable to put questions to the suspect properly. Authorisation for the removal of the solicitor must be sought from a superintendent, or if one is not readily available, an inspector not connected with the investigation.

Note for Guidance 6D outlines behaviour which would amount to 'unacceptable' behaviour. It would *not* include behaviour where:

> the solicitor gives advice which has the effect of the client avoiding giving evidence which strengthens a prosecution case, or where the solicitor intervenes in order to seek clarification, challenge an improper question to their client or the manner in which it is put, advise their client not to reply to particular questions, or if they wish to give their client further legal advice.

However it *would* include behaviour where:

> the solicitor's approach or conduct prevents or unreasonably obstructs proper questions being put to the suspect or the suspect's response being recorded. Examples of unacceptable conduct include answering questions on a suspect's behalf or providing written replies for the suspect to quote.

Therefore, the behaviour of the solicitor in the scenario would fall within the meaning of 'unacceptable' and answers A and C are incorrect. Paragraph 6.9 above does not distinguish between solicitors and accredited or probationary representatives — any one of this group could be excluded from an interview under this paragraph. Answer B is therefore incorrect.

Evidence and Procedure, para. 2.17.9.13, App.2.4

Answer 12.22

Answer **D** — An accredited or probationary representative sent to provide advice by, and on behalf of, a solicitor shall be admitted to the police station for this purpose unless an officer of inspector rank or above considers such a visit will hinder the investigation and directs otherwise (PACE Code C, para. 6.12A). Answer A is incorrect.

The inspector should take into account in particular whether the identity and status of an accredited or probationary representative have been satisfactorily established and/or they are of suitable character to provide legal advice, e.g. a person with a criminal record is unlikely to be suitable unless the conviction was for a minor offence and not recent (para. 6.13).

The exclusion of an accredited or probationer solicitor has to be considered in relation to the specific investigation and whether that person is likely to interfere with the investigation, and the decision has to be made in relation to each individual case. It is *not* permissible to have blanket bans on such persons (*R v Chief Constable of the Northumbria Constabulary, ex parte Thompson* [2001] 1 WLR 1342). Answer B is therefore incorrect.

In relation to informing the Law Society, if an inspector considers a particular solicitor or firm of solicitors is persistently sending probationary representatives who are unsuited to provide legal advice, they should inform an officer of at least superintendent rank, who may wish to take the matter up with the Law Society. This is not mandatory in every case and would depend on the company itself. Answer C is therefore incorrect.

Lastly, if the inspector refuses access to an accredited or probationary representative, the inspector must notify the solicitor's company, to give them an opportunity to make alternative arrangements (para. 6.14).

Evidence and Procedure, para. 2.17.9.13, App.2.4

Question Checklist

The checklist below is designed to help you keep track of your progress when answering the multiple-choice questions. If you fill this in after one attempt at each question, you will be able to check how many you have got right and which questions you need to revisit a second time. Also available online, to download visit www.blackstonespolicemanuals.com.

	First attempt Correct (✓)	Second attempt Correct (✓)
1 Sources of Law and the Courts		
1.1		
1.2		
1.3		
1.4		
1.5		
1.6		
1.7		
1.8		
1.9		
1.10		
1.11		
1.12		
1.13		
1.14		
1.15		
2 Summonses and Warrants		
2.1		
2.2		
2.3		
2.4		
2.5		
2.6		

	First attempt Correct (✓)	Second attempt Correct (✓)
2.7		
2.8		
2.9		
2.10		
2.11		
2.12		
3 Bail		
3.1		
3.2		
3.3		
3.4		
3.5		
3.6		
3.7		
3.8		
3.9		
3.10		
3.11		
3.12		
3.13		
3.14		
3.15		
3.16		

	First attempt Correct (✓)	Second attempt Correct (✓)
3.17		
3.18		
3.19		
4 Court Procedure and Witnesses		
4.1		
4.2		
4.3		
4.4		
4.5		
4.6		
4.7		
4.8		
4.9		
4.10		
4.11		
4.12		
4.13		
4.14		
4.15		
4.16		
5 Youth Justice and Youth Crime and Disorder		
5.1		
5.2		
5.3		
5.4		
5.5		
5.6		
5.7		
5.8		
5.9		
5.10		
5.11		
5.12		
5.13		
5.14		
5.15		
5.16		

	First attempt Correct (✓)	Second attempt Correct (✓)
6 Sentencing		
6.1		
6.2		
6.3		
6.4		
6.5		
6.6		
6.7		
6.8		
7 Evidence and Similar Fact Evidence		
7.1		
7.2		
7.3		
7.4		
7.5		
7.6		
7.7		
7.8		
7.9		
7.10		
7.11		
7.12		
7.13		
7.14		
7.15		
7.16		
7.17		
7.18		
7.19		
7.20		
7.21		
7.22		
7.23		
7.24		
8 Exclusion of Admissible Evidence		
8.1		
8.2		

	First attempt Correct (✓)	Second attempt Correct (✓)
8.3		
8.4		
8.5		
8.6		
8.7		
8.8		

9 Disclosure of Evidence

	First attempt Correct (✓)	Second attempt Correct (✓)
9.1		
9.2		
9.3		
9.4		
9.5		
9.6		
9.7		
9.8		
9.9		
9.10		
9.11		
9.12		
9.13		
9.14		
9.15		
9.16		

10 Custody Officers' Duties

	First attempt Correct (✓)	Second attempt Correct (✓)
10.1		
10.2		
10.3		
10.4		
10.5		
10.6		
10.7		
10.8		
10.9		
10.10		
10.11		
10.12		
10.13		
10.14		

	First attempt Correct (✓)	Second attempt Correct (✓)
10.15		
10.16		
10.17		
10.18		
10.19		
10.20		
10.21		
10.22		
10.23		
10.24		
10.25		
10.26		
10.27		
10.28		
10.29		
10.30		
10.31		
10.32		
10.33		
10.34		
10.35		
10.36		
10.37		
10.38		
10.39		
10.40		

11 Identification

	First attempt Correct (✓)	Second attempt Correct (✓)
11.1		
11.2		
11.3		
11.4		
11.5		
11.6		
11.7		
11.8		
11.9		
11.10		
11.11		
11.12		

	First attempt Correct (✓)	Second attempt Correct (✓)
11.13		
11.14		
11.15		
11.16		
11.17		
11.18		
11.19		
11.20		
11.21		
11.22		
12 Interviews		
12.1		
12.2		
12.3		
12.4		
12.5		

	First attempt Correct (✓)	Second attempt Correct (✓)
12.6		
12.7		
12.8		
12.9		
12.10		
12.11		
12.12		
12.13		
12.14		
12.15		
12.16		
12.17		
12.18		
12.19		
12.20		
12.21		
12.22